Phonetic Symbol Guide

Second Edition

Phonetic Symbol Guide

Second Edition

Geoffrey K. Pullum and
William A. Ladusaw

THE UNIVERSITY OF CHICAGO PRESS

Chicago and London

Geoffrey K. Pullum and William A. Ladusaw are both professors of linguistics at the University of California, Santa Cruz.

The University of Chicago Press, Chicago 60637

The University of Chicago Press, Ltd., London

© 1986, 1996 by The University of Chicago
All rights reserved. Published 1996
Printed in the United States of America

05 04 03 02 01 00 99 98   5 4 3 2

ISBN (cloth) : 0-226-68535-7
ISBN (paper) : 0-226-68536-5

Library of Congress Cataloging-in-Publication Data

Pullum, Geoffrey K.
    Phonetic symbol guide/Geoffrey K. Pullum and William A. Ladusaw.
  — 2nd [updated] ed.
       p.   cm.
    Includes bibliographical references (p.).
    ISBN 0-226-68535-7. — ISBN 0-226-68536-5 (pbk.)
    1. Language and languages—Phonetic transcriptions.   I. Ladusaw,
William A., 1952-   .   II. Title.
P226.P85   1996   95-42773
414—dc20   CIP

CONTENTS

PREFACE

This book is a fully updated edition of a work first published in 1986. It is intended as a comprehensive work on both current and historical phonetic transcription practice. It covers the phonetic symbol usages of such major traditions as the early Amerindianist work of the Boas school; the American structuralist phonetics and phonology associated with Bloch, Smith, and Trager; and the internationally known system of phonetic representation traditions and transcription principles associated with the International Phonetic Association (IPA). In addition it covers less well known traditions like those of Romance philologists, Germanicists, Slavicists, Indologists, Sinologists, Africanists, and so on, and includes entries for rare and obsolete symbols that have been suggested for use by respected specialists in phonetics but which will be unfamiliar to most linguists and speech scientists.

This edition has approximately sixty entries more than the first edition. It adds coverage of some symbols that the first edition overlooked, but it also takes account of material that could not possibly have been covered in 1986: the many changes and new proposals that have been introduced into the literature during the past decade of revision and innovation in phonetic transcription practice.

One set of events in the last decade that would on its own have necessitated a new edition of this book was the burst of activity aimed at revising the IPA's phonetic alphabet and transcription principles. The IPA system was very stable for forty years after the publication of *The Principles of the International Phonetic Association* in 1949. Although some minor changes in the list of approved symbols were agreed on by the council of the IPA in 1979, the association generally maintained an extremely conservative policy. When this book was first published, the likelihood of a reference guide to phonetic transcription traditions needing a major overhaul of its treatment of IPA symbols within a decade seemed remote. But as it turned out, the seven years following the appearance of this book saw more changes in the IPA system than any other period in this century.

A discussion about revising the IPA's phonetic alphabet began in various journal articles in 1987. In 1989 a convention was held to recommend specific revisions. The council actions thereafter amounted to a fairly radical set of revisions. The entire symbol set for clicks was eliminated and replaced by the set employed in South African work; an eclectic new set of policies on the representation of tone was introduced; a new series of symbols for voiceless implosives was added; the whole system of diacritics was overhauled; and scores of other changes were made. But discussion continued. Four years later, in 1993, the IPA council announced some further changes, including alterations (after half a century of occasional discussion, [g] and [g] now at last officially have the same meaning in the IPA system), additions (two new vowel symbols were approved), and retractions (the voiceless implosive symbols added in 1989 were withdrawn).

At length the unusual ferment abated, and the 1989 and 1993 decisions appear to have ushered in a new period of stability in the IPA. It is likely to be many years before any further revision of the 1993 system is seriously contemplated. This makes it a suitable time to bring out the present revised edition of *Phonetic Symbol Guide,* which contains complete coverage of the 1989 and 1993 IPA changes.

It remains the case, however, that this book is not just a guide to the IPA's proposals, and does not advocate or endorse any particular choice of symbols for the representation of human speech. All of the first edition's coverage of non-IPA phonetic traditions is retained in this revision, and in some cases it has been expanded. Our general policy has been to lean in the direction of inclusiveness: we are unlikely to omit a symbol we have seen anywhere in print unless we are sure it represents a purely idiosyncratic or nonce usage and will not be found elsewhere in the scientific literature on language and speech. It is our intention that the reader should be able to use this edition of *Phonetic Symbol Guide* to figure out the intended meaning of any phonetic symbol used in a systematic way in the literature on languages and linguistic science over the last hundred years.

In the process of preparing this edition, we have also corrected some errors and inconsistencies in the first edition, acted on some sensible suggestions made in the published reviews, improved the wording of a large number of entries, updated charts where necessary, and provided some additional aids and conveniences for the reader. The latter include an analytical table of entries that shows the symbol shapes as well as the names for all symbols to which we assign major entries, and a full index.

Many people assisted us in the preparation of this book. Kenneth Christopher and Brigitte Ohlig assisted us with research and text handling in the process of preparing the first edition; Dan Wenger was an invaluable resource on computer-related matters; useful information and comments were received from Judith Aissen, Jane Collins, Nora England, Mary Haas, Jorge Hankamer, Peter Ladefoged, Aditi Lahiri, Ian Maddieson, L. K. Richardson, William Shipley, and others; and Karen Landahl read right through the manuscript and gave many helpful suggestions. This new edition benefited from the wise remarks of many expert phoneticians at the Kiel convention and many reviewers in journals and magazines around the world; and we received useful information or assistance from Michael Ashby, Francis Cartier, Sandra Chung, John Esling, R. H. Ives Goddard III, Caroline Henton, Kenneth C. Hill, Thomas Hukari, Alan Kaye, Michael McMahon, Philip Miller, Toby O'Brien, William Poser, John Renner, Barbara Scholz, John Seaman, Laurence Urdang, John Wells, Kenneth Whistler, Philip Whitchelo, and Arnold Zwicky. There are doubtless others too, but sometimes one learns things of interest from people at conferences who aren't wearing their name badges at the time. Apologies to those who know they slipped us a reference or made a suggestion and do not see their names listed here.

We continue to be interested in receiving correspondence (with full bibliographical references, please, and preferably a photocopy of the crucial page) from anyone who spots a phonetic symbol in print that we do not seem to have covered. We can be reached at the addresses given below.

Geoffrey K. Pullum

Stevenson College
University of California,
 Santa Cruz
Santa Cruz, CA 95064
U.S.A.

William A. Ladusaw

Cowell College
University of California,
 Santa Cruz
Santa Cruz, CA 95064
U.S.A.

TABLE OF ENTRIES

xii

INTRODUCTION

This book is primarily intended for use in the way that a dictionary is used. It provides a source in which the user can look up an unfamiliar phonetic or phonological symbol by reference to its form (its shape and graphic relationship to other symbols), and find an entry giving comprehensive guidance concerning its meaning (its recognized interpretation according to various traditions of scholarship in phonetics and phonology).

To some extent, the book can also be used as a guide to how to use phonetic symbols, and we have included a number of charts and other aids to the working linguist or phonetician with this in mind. Nevertheless we have a principally descriptive aim, not a prescriptive one: we explain how the symbols are employed in the literature of phonetics and linguistics, and we do not, for the most part, approve or proscribe specific usages. Likewise, the book is not intended as an introduction to phonetics; we presuppose, rather than supply, a grounding in phonetic theory (though we do supply a glossary of articulatory phonetic terminology which we hope will be useful).

Those who will most immediately and obviously benefit from this book include phoneticians, linguists, anthropologists, speech pathologists, audiologists, language teachers, translators, interpreters, speech engineers, philologists, and students of any of these subjects. But we hope that it will also be of use to those with a more peripheral interest in language who may encounter phonetic transcriptions in material they read.

What we have tried to do in this book, in short, is to collate and systematize information about the definitions for phonetic symbols that have been set down by recognized phonetic authorities, and about the actual usage that will be encountered in linguistic writings of all sorts.

We are general linguists, not primarily researchers in phonetics. However, between us we have taught phonetics and phonology in courses at various levels on a dozen campuses in Britain and the United States, and we have over thirty years of day-to-day acquaintance with the literature of the linguistic sciences. Moreover, we know what it is like to confront traditions conflicting with the ones in which we were trained: one of us was trained in the tradition associated with the International Phonetic Association (IPA) and later learned American transcription practices on the streets, and the other had the converse experience. In addition, we share an interest in typography and related matters that makes us sensitive to some of the minutiae that become relevant when one pays close attention to the interpretation of published phonetic transcriptions.

We believe that it has been an advantage to us to be working as experienced consumers of phonetic practice rather than primary purveyors of it. We are accustomed to reading work in the fields of syntax and semantics where linguists with little interest in phonetics or phonology (or else their editors, publishers, and typesetters) have made errors regarding transcription that clearly indicate the need for a reference work such as the present one. Where a research specialist in phonetics might see no ambiguity in a given usage because detailed knowledge of the subject matter permitted instant disambiguation, we see the ambiguity and the danger of misinterpretation. We have plenty of firsthand experience of encountering materials in phonetic or phonological transcriptions that initially seem obscure or baffling, and this has guided us in deciding what needs clear explanation in a book like this.

In addition, we have no axes to grind: there may be phoneticians with strong opinions about whether '[y]' is properly used for a palatal glide or for a front rounded vowel, but not us. The view of phonetic transcriptional practice presented in this book is not tacitly subordinated to the viewpoint of any school of thought, because we belong to none. We have no aim beyond that of not being unnecessarily puzzled, hindered, or misled by the transcriptional practices we find in the literature that we consult.

THE SCOPE OF THIS BOOK

In making decisions about the content and format of the book it has been necessary to make many difficult decisions about what to include and exclude. We have not attempted to gather together in one volume every symbol ever used to represent a sound in the long history of phonetics and phonology, or, worse, every font variant or transform of all the symbols that have been used since the invention of printing. Our goal is to provide a background of general knowledge for the symbols that linguists, phoneticians, and other students of language are likely to encounter in reading either contemporary books and journals or older works that are important enough to be consulted today.

Transliteration and romanization are activities which are logically distinct from phonetic transcription, but in practice the distinction is sometimes very hard to draw. For example, only a thin line separates the International Phonetic Association's phonetic alphabet from the International African Institute's proposed African orthography, and only minor additional steps need be taken to arrive at such systems as the conventional transliteration of Russian into roman letters or the pinyin romanization for Chinese. Note also that Kenneth Pike's famous *Phonemics* (1947) was subtitled *A Technique for Reducing Languages to Writing.* We have therefore included here some comments about the common use of some symbols in orthographies and romanizations. Such comments are not intended to be comprehensive. Where they have been included, it is either because such uses of the symbol conflict with their phonetic interpretations and a possible misinterpretation of the romanization might result, or because the orthographic use supplied an interpretation which was taken over in the use of the character as a phonetic symbol (e.g., the Old English orthographic characters *ash* and *eth*).

Phonetic transcription practices are often inculcated through a complex history of practical experience rather than through a rigorously codified rulebook. Many people will not be able to say exactly where they picked up a given idea—say, that an umlaut over a vowel symbol indicates a reversal of backness, or that a dot under a consonant indicates a retroflex articulation—but will nonetheless feel that the convention is generally recognized and could be used productively to create new transcriptions where necessary. Moreover, the tacit understanding about transcription that govern some traditions—particularly the American tradition—represent not a firm common ground but one that shifts over time like any other cultural system. We have tried in this book to present explicitly two very clear traditions: that of the IPA, which is the clearest, having a recognized international governing body to sanction its recommendations, and a more tenuous tradition we identify as "American" (we discuss these two traditions further below).

Even the IPA position on many topics has shifted during the hundred years of the association's existence, and in the case of our effort to interpret and codify an American tradition, we are to some extent creating a consensus through judicious selection among variants rather than reporting a consensus that already exists. Much the same is true for our references to other traditions such as those of Slavicists, Indologists, etc. In other words, the reader who expects all phonetic practice to be amenable to rigorous pigeonholing according to the categories mentioned in this book will be somewhat alarmed by the diversity that is actually found.

SCOPE OF THE REFERENCES

Part of what this book aims to do is to permit the user to develop a historical and comparative perspective on the business of phonetic transcription. Such a perspective is often not provided by a linguistics graduate education. In the interest of the rapid acquisition of a fixed set of transcriptional practices that will be regarded pro tem as correct for purposes of the class, a study of the variability found in the literature is (quite rightly) postponed. But the professional linguist or phonetician will find it desirable or even necessary to develop a considerable tacit understanding of the variability of transcription practices in order to become fully comfortable with the whole literature of linguistics through the years. We attempt here to provide some of the basis for such an understanding, and to leave enough of a bibliographical trail through the references we cite to permit the serious researcher to achieve much more than that.

We have not been (nor could we have been) exhaustive in the literature we cite in our references. But we have, we believe, referenced most of the works of major influence in the two traditions that we seek to document. Where we articulate a usage which we believe to be generally true of another group (historical linguists, Indologists, Slavicists, or whatever), we have cited a randomly chosen work in the area. The choice of these works has often been serendipitous or even just arbitrary, so we warn the reader not to consider us to be claiming that all such works are of equal influence in the linguistic community.

In our research for this book we have encountered a number of works which make recommendations regarding transcription systems which we have not included in the texts of our entries. These range from invented alphabets of gentleman scholars and dilettantes to serious works by linguists, missionaries, and anthropologists who were influential but did not ultimately become contributors to the major traditions documented here. (For interesting surveys of some of these, see Albright 1958, Pitman and St. John 1969, and the edition of Lepsius 1863 by J. Alan Kemp, which contains much interesting auxiliary material and a large bibliography.) Among the systems we have had to exclude are some of the well thought-out and elegantly designed sets of symbols in the IPA tradition developed for the click sounds of various Khoisan languages. Some of the symbols proposed by Doke (1926a, 144), for example, are not covered in this book, not having attained currency anywhere.

We have also encountered proposals that might become standard but are recent enough that their currency is not yet established. Among these, we should mention the proposals of Grunwell et al. (1980) for transcribing disordered speech and those of Bush et al. (1973; see Ingram 1976 (p. 93)). Many of these proposals are similar to standard IPA proposals or are rather crude iconic extensions of them. As they are not encountered in general linguistic and phonetic works, we have decided not to include them in our purview.

THE IPA TRADITION

The official names announced for the IPA at its foundation in 1886, namely *Association Phonétique International, Weltlautschriftverein,* and *International Phonetic Association,* make one thing quite clear: the IPA was internationalist from the outset. Although the original shared interest of the members was the application of phonetics to the teaching of languages, particularly English, a more general focus of interest emerged fairly rapidly. As early as 1886, Otto Jespersen suggested that a phonetic alphabet applicable to all languages be devised, and a first version was ready by 1888.

The principles that guided the construction of this alphabet are set out in the classic booklet *The Principles of the International Phonetic Association,* published by the IPA at University College London in 1949 and hereafter cited as *Principles.* These principles are mostly the same ones that guide the council of the IPA in making its decisions down to the present. (One exception is that an early effort to make IPA symbols as similar as possible to their correspondents in ordinary orthographies has been abandoned, clarity and distinctness being considered more important.) They are five in number. We paraphrase them here; for the original formulation, see *Principles* (pp. 1–2).

1. Wherever possible, differently shaped letters (not just diacritically modified letters) should be used for any two sounds that can distinguish one word from another in a single language.
2. Wherever possible, a single letter should be used for two sounds that are so similar that they never distinguish one word from another in a single language.
3. Wherever possible, only letter shapes that harmonize typographically with the letters of the roman alphabet should be used.
4. Wherever possible, use diacritics only in four circumstances: (i) for suprasegmental phenomena like length, stress, and intonation; (ii) for marking allophonic distinctions; (iii) where one diacritic can make it unnecessary to design a whole set of related new characters (e.g., with the tilde diacritic to indicate nasalized vowels); (iv) to represent minute shades of sound for scientific purposes.
5. Wherever possible, development of the alphabet should be along lines that accord with the phonemic principle and the cardinal vowel system.

It is an explicit attempt to follow these rules of thumb through the past century that has given rise to the IPA's current phonetic alphabet as surveyed in this book in the sections headed **IPA Usage.** The principles demand that there be as many distinct symbols as necessary, that there be no more distinct symbols than are necessary, that typographical appearance of symbols be taken seriously, that diacritical marks be kept to a minimum, and that phonetic transcription be grounded in scientific phonetics and phonology. They are sensible and carefully chosen. But as we shall see in the next section, these are not the only possible principles that could guide the development of a system of phonetic transcription.

THE AMERICAN TRADITION

The comments listed under the **American Usage** sections of the entries and some of the charts at the back are meant to document a tradition of transcription which has paralleled the development of the IPA but remained distinct from it on some points. Among the more obvious points of difference are the almost universal use among American linguists of the transcription '[ü]' for a high front rounded vowel in place of the IPA's '[y]' and the use of the wedge diacritic on symbols for palato-alveolar fricatives and affricates. It would be incorrect to suggest that American linguists do not know or use the IPA, but some conventions such as the ones just mentioned are almost universally used by American scholars, and quite generally supplant IPA recommendations. Because of their vitality and also their essential coherence, we believe it is proper to document them as a distinct tradition.

To accomplish this, it was necessary to induce from current and past practice an analog of the IPA's *Principles* manual for the American community. We began by considering the recommendations which have been published over the past 80 years of American linguistics and then sifted through them to find the ones which have caught on. These we have considered to be the basis of American usage, and they are sufficient to indicate points of possible confusion.

The American tradition has its roots in the practices of Americanists—the transcription practices arising from work beginning in the late 19th century on the indigenous languages of North America. After the publication of *The Handbook of American Indian Languages* (Boas 1911), a committee of the American Anthropological Association consisting of Franz Boas, P. E. Goddard, Edward Sapir, and A. L. Kroeber published recommendations for a transcription system to be used in the publication of texts and grammars of American languages (Boas et al. 1916).

These recommendations present a transcription system responsive to principles quite different from those of the IPA. While the IPA sought an alphabet which would provide symbols for "many minute shades of sound," offering "two distinct letters without diacritical marks" for sounds which contrasted in languages (*Principles,* 1), the Americanists sought a "practical" system for publication. It is practical in a number of respects. It explicitly seeks to avoid the creation of special characters which would not be available in standard faces and fonts, in order to expedite the publication of the texts. It sanctions a phonological approach to transcription, consigning phonetic detail to textual discussion in favor of allowing the denotations of the characters to shift in the pursuit of typographical ease. Finally, it is specific to the needs of Americanists rather than intendedly universal, seeking to provide characters for sounds routinely encountered in American languages, rather than to achieve universal coverage.

The American tradition emphasizes "compositionality" in symbolizations much more than the IPA system does. The basic vowel symbols of the system were patterned after Sweet's, but they were supplemented not by new characters but by diacritics which indicated reversal of backness (the umlaut), centrality (the overdot), and so on. Compositionality is also seen in the consonant system, where sounds at cardinal points of articulation are defined and retraction and advancement diacritics (the underdot and subscript arch respectively) are employed to represent nearby articulation points. Notice also the recommendation of Herzog et al. (1943) that the wedge diacritic should be used as an invariant indicator of palato-alveolar articulation. Explanation of these and other points in American and Americanist transcription are documented in the various entries in the guide. We have made brief mention of some relevant points here in order to give those familiar with American phonetic transcription an indication of our selection criteria for "American usage," and to make those unfamiliar with it aware that it is not a random set of variations from the IPA.

TONE TRANSCRIPTION

The organization of this book favors symbols for segmental transcription at the expense of notations for suprasegmental phenomena of tone and intonation. We have dealt with the common use of grave and acute accents, wedges, circumflexes, and breves as indicators of stress and tone in their entries. In doing so, we have presented the recommendations of *Principles* and the published American recommendations, though they leave quite a wide margin for variation. It is interesting, for example, to note the variation in the sample transcriptions of tone languages in *Principles,* nearly all of which alter the interpretations of the recommended symbols to suit the needs of each new language.

The transcription system chosen for tonal and intonational phenomena, either in a given language or for general use, reflects the phonological theory that underlies that system. As general theories of tone and intonation have developed, transcription practices have changed. We have not attempted to generalize across all of this variation, or to anticipate the directions in which currently emerging theories of the domain will lead.

THE MEDIA OF TRANSCRIPTION

Throughout this guide the reader will encounter metacomments about typography. Behind these there is a general point that merits some attention: the effect of medium on transcription. The primary media that are relevant are handwriting, typesetting, typing, and computer word processing.

Many works dealing with phonetic transcription (e.g., *Principles,* 53; Gleason 1955 (p. 8); Smalley 1963 (p. 232)) rightly give attention to how phonetic symbols are to be written clearly and easily by hand. It is easy to see why. Linguistic or anthropological field work is one of the primary situations in which phonetic transcriptions are generated, and virtually all field notes are made in handwriting. The handwritten medium may well influence preferences for notation: the Polish hook may seem faster to write as a nasal vowel diacritic than the superscript tilde; the underdot may be a clearer way of marking a retroflex consonant than the lengthened tail of the IPA symbol, and so on.

In the context of typesetting, entirely different considerations come to the fore. Designing new characters is an expensive business if it means contracting with a typesetter to have new molds made from artists' drawings, and hundreds of new pieces of type cast in lead. The economic pressure to use an easily available diacritic combination, or to substitute a letter from an already available font, may be very strong. At the very least, prior availability of a character (e.g., in the Greek alphabet) or the fact that an easy modification can generate the character (e.g., turning an ⟨e⟩ to get a schwa) may loom as a large consideration in getting a particular transcriptional usage embedded in general practice.

Typing on a typewriter is different again. Turning a letter is very difficult (though perfectionists may recall having tried taking the paper out of the typewriter and re-inserting it upside down to get Schwa and Turned V and the like), but other things, like back-up and overstrike, are very easy, and new conventions become practical: putting a hyphen through a letter to indicate spirantization of a stop or centralization of a vowel, for example.

Finally, the medium of the future: word processing on computing machines. Here standards like the ASCII (American Standard Code for Information Interchange) signal set may have to be reckoned with: the tilde and the circumflex have a place in the ASCII scheme but the wedge and the umlaut do not. However, more and more power to break away from inventories of pre-set symbols and into the creative designing of new characters and fonts is being made available by modern software and hardware. This technology brings greatly enhanced capabilities within reach. The production of this book crucially depended on modern computer systems and software. But the medium also brings new freedom to deviate without limit and in unpredictable ways from every convention and style that has gone before. The freedom that a few influential figures like Sir Isaac Pitman and George Bernard Shaw had to devise and promulgate their own writing systems in printed form is fast becoming available to everyone with a font-editor program and a laser printer. This may in due course introduce new complexities into the task of interpreting published phonetic transcriptions.

HOW TO FIND THINGS

This book has been organized, as far as possible, so that simply from the look of a symbol the user will be able to track it down quickly. If the symbol sought looks anything like a letter of the roman alphabet as used for English, it will be found where the English alphabetical order would suggest. Letters from other alphabets have been interpolated into the ordering either according to the sounds they represent (after roman letters which represent similar sounds, for example) or according to their shape, whichever seemed the most natural. Characters which are modifications of an ordinary letter are placed after that letter but before the next. More radical modifications follow less radical modifications, with turning (rotation through 180°) considered a particularly radical modification, and digraphic combination (as in ⟨æ⟩) even more so. Leafing through the book and glancing down the table of entries should give the user a good idea of the resulting arrangement fairly rapidly: variants of *a* including α and *æ*, then variants of *A,* then variants of *b* and *B,* then β, then variants of *c,* and so on in what we hope is just the order you would have guessed we would use.

We have included cross-referencing guides at those very few points where we felt a tension between ordering by denotation and ordering by form (there are less than two dozen cross-references in the book). Ordering by form (as in a dictionary) penalizes the reader who is working from a preliminary general idea of a symbol's denotation but does not know its form (the problem that a poor speller has with standard dictionaries: you must be able to spell a word before you can look it up); but we have devised this guide primarily for use by someone who has *seen* a symbol and needs to determine what sound it probably was used to denote, so we have been able to organize by form to a very large extent. Ordering entries by denotation (as in a thesaurus) would pose a different problem: where to find a completely alien character you have seen when you have no idea of its denotation.

MAJOR AND MINOR ENTRIES

There are two types of entry: major and minor. Major entries always begin a new page; the large illustrative character is in a double-edged box, and the name is in capital letters. We have given a major entry to every character that was officially approved by the International Phonetic Association as of the last revision of the IPA in 1993, and to no others. Thus the set of entries with double-edged boxes around the symbol illustration constitutes a complete guide to the IPA.

Interspersed among the major entries are the minor entries. These do not necessarily get their own new page; the large illustrative character is in a single-edged box, somewhat smaller than with the major entries, and the name of the character is in lower case. Minor entries cover characters in a variety of different categories. Some are frequently used by linguists but happen to be outside the set currently approved by the IPA. Some have been seriously proposed for use and are in use by some but have not yet gained wide currency. Some are compositions of IPA or other characters with diacritical marks so that at least some of their denotations are compositionally derived and not separately recognized by the IPA. Some are well established in specific subfields (e.g., among Slavicists, Indologists, Germanicists, or Sinologists) but not familiar among other general linguists. Some are less-common symbols from a tradition that is not as well known as it once was (a good example is the Bloch and Trager tradition of the 1940s (Bloch and Trager 1942)).

No value judgment is implied by the fact that a given symbol is treated in a minor entry; the minor-entry symbols are just as useful as they always were. A symbol like [č], for instance, is very widely used among American linguists for the voiceless palato-alveolar affricate (IPA[tʃ]), and will surely continue to be, while [ç] denotes a rarer sound (a voiceless alveolo-palatal fricative) and is seen less often. However, the latter happens still to be IPA approved. Should it be? In general, we simply do not permit ourselves any judgments of this kind (though we sometimes note specific reasons for saying that a certain symbol is not *likely* to be much used in the future, or points of consistency suggesting that a symbol might have been accepted without valid reason). But it is no value judgment to observe that [č] does not belong to the current IPA alphabet.

The distinction between major and minor entries is not carried into the listing of diacritical marks, which follows the listing of letter-sized symbols; all accent marks and other diacritics are given minor entries. However, we assign a double-edged box to any diacritic with a current official IPA value. In addition, a guide to the set of diacritical marks currently approved by the IPA can be found in the charts on pages 305 and 306.

ORGANIZATION OF ENTRIES

At the head of each major entry, beside the large picture of the symbol, is a convenient, though not necessarily official, working name for it. We have sometimes been able to use already current standard names (Greek letters all have well-known names, for example), but in other cases we have invented names according to fairly straightforward conventions. For example, an *h* with a dash or hyphen through the upright near the top is called Crossed H; an *h* with a dash or hyphen through its body would be called Barred H; an *h* with an oblique stroke (solidus or slash) through it would be Slashed H; an *h* with the top bent over rightward like a hook is called Hooktop H; an *h* rotated till it is upside down is called Turned H; and so on.

We have been careful here to distinguish among *turned, inverted,* and *reversed* characters. A turned character is one that has been rotated 180°. An inverted character is one that has been reflected through a horizontal midline (switching top and bottom). A reversed character is one that has been reflected through a vertical midline (switching left and right).

All major entries and all entries for symbols that have a history of use or official approval by the IPA begin with a section headed **IPA Usage,** even if the symbol in question is not used at all under current IPA proposals. This part of the entry explains the officially sanctioned use according to *Principles* and later official revisions. (Both the IPA as an association and the International Phonetic Alphabet are referred to as the IPA; the ambiguity is never pernicious.) We consider this an important feature of the guide, for *Principles,* apart from not being an up-to-date record of the IPA's position, was never designed as a reference guide (there is no index of symbols, for example). We hope to have provided here a more organized form of access to the large amount of information included in pages of *Principles* and elsewhere in the IPA's publications.

The next section in each entry is headed **American Usage.** This section attempts to do two things: first, to summarize a kind of informally standardized American usage that goes back ultimately to Boas and Sapir and is generally adhered to in such journals as *Language* or the *International Journal of American Linguistics;* and second, to mention uses of symbols proposed in the most influential American texts on articulatory phonetics and to explain how these proposals differ from the IPA's recommendations.

If there are further ways in which the symbol is employed, a section headed **Other Uses** follows.

Additional details that need to be pointed out about the symbol or what it stands for will be in a section headed **Comments** after that.

Finally, we provide a section titled **Source** in all the major entries and some minor ones. The information in this section is not meant to be paleographic. It includes two types of information: (a) an indication of the history of the character if that might help in suggesting a mnemonic for its transcriptional use, and (b) significant typographical information about the character.

NOTATIONAL MATTERS

We have distinguished carefully between references to symbols, letters, sounds, and symbols as used to transcribe sounds. When we refer to a symbol in its own right, e.g., to make a point about its shape, we put it in angled brackets thus: "the symbol with the shape ⟨z⟩." When we refer to a letter in a widely known alphabet like the Roman one, we italicize the letter thus: "the letter *z*." When we refer to a sound, we use a transcription of it according to the principles of the IPA, enclosed in square brackets. To forestall possible ambiguity we occasionally prefix the square brackets with the letters *IPA* thus: "the voiced alveolar fricative, IPA [z]." When we refer to a transcription according to a particular set of conventions, for example, the American conventions, we again use square brackets surrounding a symbol, and sometimes add quotation marks if it would make our intent clearer, thus: "The transcription '[z]' means the same under American conventions as it does in the IPA system." The only other thing square brackets are used for is to enclose occasional mentions of phonetic or phonological feature specifications, e.g., [+voice]; it is always clear from the context that these are not phonetic transcriptions, because although the plus sign and the minus sign have both been used as transcription symbols (see entries), they are postfixed to other symbols, and never appear as the first symbol in a transcribed form.

CHARTS

At the end of the book are a number of charts of symbols. The first two show the cardinal vowel system developed by Daniel Jones as a set of reference points for calibrating vowels articulatorily and auditorily. The next two show a fuller set of vowel symbols in the IPA tradition on charts of the same layout as the cardinal vowel charts, one for unrounded vowels and the other for rounded vowels.

Next are three charts of vowel symbols in the American tradition. The first is Bloch and Trager's (1942). The second is a simplification of it that lacks Bloch and Trager's symmetry but has the advantage of roughly corresponding to most American practice today. The third is further simplified and corresponds to the tradition established by Chomsky and Halle (1968).

Next follows a chart of consonant symbols in the American tradition, which, we should stress, we have at many points made maximally distinct from the IPA by deliberately giving possible American usages with the underdot diacritic for retraction (p. 245) and the subscript arch diacritic for fronting (p. 265), rather than their IPA equivalents (though the IPA symbols have also been used by American linguists). Finally we give charts of the official 1993 IPA.

We do not intend to suggest that the non-IPA usages in our American consonant chart *ought* to be used by American linguists. Quite the contrary: we suggest that the IPA prejudice against diacritics is well founded, and that it will generally be good policy to use the IPA's distinctive consonant symbols as fully as media restrictions permit. From this standpoint, our chart represents a standardization of a set of maximal divergences from the IPA system, and not at all a recommendation for such divergence. To guard against confusion arising from the mixing of traditions, we have not used ⟨c⟩ or ⟨j⟩ at all in the American chart. The entries for these symbols make it clear that they have no codifiable place in American transcription.

It is perhaps unavoidable that by supplying such charts we should be seen as having made a set of implicit recommendations. As we have said, this was not our intention in constructing them, but for those who will be looking at least for advice from what we have put into our charts, we would stress the following points.

First, the charts do not include anything like all the symbols in the book; we have deliberately avoided cluttering them with rarities, idiosyncrasies, exotica, digraphs, and representations for finer distinctions than linguists usually make.

Second, they do not include a place for every type of speech sound attested in languages. For an effort to classify the entire range of sounds found in a sample of 317 of the roughly four thousand languages in the world, the reader should consult Maddieson 1984, noting that Maddieson must use combinations of up to six characters and diacritics to represent some sounds (and his segment inventory is not exhaustive; languages with the bilabial click, IPA [ʘ], happen to be absent from his sample).

Third, our charts do not attempt to list all the possibilities derivable by means of diacritic modification. The diacritics section of the book (pp. 230–267) should be consulted in this regard. For example, our IPA consonant chart shows no IPA symbols for dental stops, because, as is well known, the IPA convention is to use symbols like ⟨t⟩ and ⟨d⟩ (which we arbitrarily label as "alveolar"), marking them with the subscript bridge diacritic (p. 234) if it is necessary to distinguish dentals from alveolars.

Fourth, and finally, the charts do not come with a guarantee. It is not necessarily the case that a transcription done by reference to the charts we provide here will be fully acceptable for its purpose. The most we can say is that our IPA charts set out the alphabet sanctioned by the world's most important international authority for phonetics, and that with regard to the American tradition, a transcription done by reference to our charts for American vowel and consonant representation, taking careful note of the information to be found in the entries for the symbols, is likely to be found acceptable for publication in most American linguistics and phonetics journals, and will probably not cause readers unnecessary puzzlement.

Puzzlement can always arise, however, in the difficult business of recording human speech in terms of a uniform, discrete alphabet. We can think of only one way to guard against it completely. It is very simple and obvious. When linguistic transcriptions are presented, they should be accompanied by a note stating clearly which transcription system has been used, with detailed notes on any unusual or potentially ambiguous symbols. If the publishers of books and journals in linguistics and phonetics chose to publish with their style sheets a detailed and carefully typeset chart showing the alphabet that they prefer, that would be even better. In the meantime, failing an industry-wide standard, each phonetician or linguist is an independent authority. We hope this book will be of use as a reference aid to guide those authorities in making their decisions.

CHANGES IN THE SECOND EDITION

The preface gives a brief statement of the ways in which this edition differs from the first edition. We supply a few more details here. The most obvious events motivating the preparation of this new edition have been those taking place within the IPA community between 1987 and 1993. Discussion of a full-scale revision of the IPA's alphabet began in volume 16 of the *Journal of the International Phonetic Association* (*JIPA*). This was the centenary edition of the journal (originally called *Le Maître Phonétique*), dated 1986 but published in September 1987. It contains an article by Peter Ladefoged and Peter Roach (the president and secretary-treasurer of the IPA) under the title "Revising the International Phonetic Alphabet: A plan" (Ladefoged and Roach 1986), in which it was pointed out that for the most part the IPA's alphabet had seen hardly any revision for forty years. The discussion that followed (see the preliminary reports published in *JIPA* 18 (1988)) led to a convention held in the summer of 1989 in Kiel, Germany, to revise the association's phonetic alphabet and transcription principles. The recommendations made by the participants in the convention were subsequently ratified by the council of the association, and promulgated via a report in *JIPA* 19 (1989), 67–80, and the unpaginated centerfold between pages 81 and 82). The wide-ranging revisions that were adopted would on their own have sufficed to necessitate a second edition of this book—though it was perhaps fortunate that one was not produced, for as noted in the preface, there were further revisions to come in 1993 before the IPA settled down to a new period of stability.

The IPA revisions necessitated the writing and rewriting of many new entries for this book. But in general, we have tried to be conservative in our changes unrelated to new developments, except where we were faced with errors of fact in the first edition. For example, we have made an effort not to change too many of the symbol names we introduced, since they have been finding a wide array of uses and applications (for example, in explanatory tables accompanying phonetic symbol fonts for word processing programs, and in macro names for calling up particular phonetic symbols in typesetting programs such as T_EX). A few, however, have been changed to eliminate inconsistencies (for example, it would be hard to find much rationale for the first edition's choice of "Upper-case C" but "Capital D"; we now opt for "Capital" in each case).

We have made some minor changes in general phonetic terminology throughout the book. One example is that when talking about vowel "height" (acoustically, first-formant value) in connection with vowel symbols used in the IPA tradition, we use the open/close (jaw position) terminology favored by IPA phoneticians rather than the high/low (tongue height) terminology normally used in the American tradition. The translation is straightforward, as shown in the following chart. Notice that each terminological system can provide for at least seven distinct vowel heights.

Another case of terminological regularization in this edition is that our occasional uses of the terms *glide* or *semivowel* for nonfricative continuant oral consonants like IPA [w] and [j], and also lateral reso-

high/low (U.S) terminology	close/open (IPA) terminology	front	central	back
high	close	i y	ɨ ʉ	ɯ u
lower high	semi-close	ɪ ʏ		ʊ
upper mid	close mid	e ø	ɘ ɵ	ɤ o
mean mid	mid		ə	
lower mid	open mid	ɛ œ	ɜɞ	ʌ ɔ
higher low	semi-open	æ	ɐ	
low	open	a ɶ		ɒ ɑ

nants like [l], have been systematically replaced by the more standardly used modern term *approximant*. And a third is that the term *median* has been substituted for *central* wherever it refers to the defining property of nonlateral consonants (an obstruction somewhere down the median line separating the left and right halves of the oral tract), leaving *central* to refer unambiguously to the halfway point in the front/back vowel quality dimension; thus *median* applies only to consonants and is a synonym for *nonlateral,* while *central* applies only to vowels and implies a vowel quality midway between "front" and "back."

One change we have made is worth explaining despite the fact that it will not be immediately apparent to the reader from a quick browse. It involves a subtle change in the semantics of our distinction between "major entries" and "minor entries," mentioned above. The first edition assigned major-entry status to every then-current official IPA symbol, and also to certain other symbols that we judged to be standard American practice or in some other way fairly central. But our aim tended to shift in the implementation, and in addition some familiar letters (e.g., several capitals or small capitals) seem to have earned their major-entry status mainly because they looked familiar to us, although they were not in widespread use. In some other cases our policy underwent an unnoticed slide from the goal of codifying an emerging American standard toward simply counting things as American usage simply because they had been proposed by residents of the United States. The upshot was that when we reexamined the motivations of our distinction between major and minor entries we were at some points unable to reconstruct our own rationale for it. Furthermore, the distinction was clearly not doing much useful work. Thus it seemed appropriate to us to make the modest number of changes needed to assign our major-entry format a new meaning that has the virtue of being completely sharp and clear: we now accord major entry status to *all and only those symbols that are officially sanctioned in the 1993 revision of the IPA.*

The symbols that shift into minor-entry format under this new policy are not numerous. Some symbols to which we had already accorded major-entry status (e.g., [ə] and [ʙ]) have now become official IPA symbols, so in those cases there has been no change. A few IPA symbols that were never used much by American phoneticians (e.g., [ɷ] and [ɩ] have lost their IPA recognition, leaving no reason for according them major-entry status. And a few other letters (including [ʌ], [D], [E], [H], [L], [M], [ω] and [þ]) now seem to us never to have merited the major-entry status we gave them in the first place, for they are not really standard in any tradition. Most of the other symbols that shift to minor-entry status are compositionally interpretable combinations of a roman letter and a diacritical mark that are often used by American phoneticians (e.g., [č], [ǰ], [š], and [ž]).

The change we have made permits the distinction between major and minor entries to do some work; the fact that a symbol has a major entry actually tells the reader something. Unlike the distinction between broadly more important symbols and broadly less important ones, or whatever other notion we were groping toward in the practice seen in the first edition, their definition of the set of approved IPA symbols is well defined. The user of this book can now read off whether a symbol is current (1993) IPA usage simply by looking to see whether its graphic representation is in a box edged with a double line. (Even in the case of the diacritical marks, which never have major entries, we place them in a double-edged box if and only if they have a current (1993) official IPA use.) All the other symbols treated in the first edition are still here (plus new ones), and their entries are just as detailed. They are not counter-recommended in virtue of being described in minor entries. And our chart of typical American usage in the transcription of consonants is still included (see p. 301). But the single-edged box enclosing their picture will serve as a reminder that they are not currently IPA official, so that IPA documents cannot be cited to specify their denotations. For example, under IPA conventions [c] is a lamino-palatal stop without affrication, while [tʃ] is a postalveolar affricate; the familiar American symbol [č] might be appropriately used for a sound of either type, but if it were important which was meant, the writer would have to state that explicitly, because the IPA's principles are silent on the topic.

Finally, the reader may be interested to see a list of the symbols for which entirely new entries have been added in this edition. There are sixty-one altogether. In order of appearance, they are:

Four	Eight
Left-Hook Four	Hooktop P
Hooktop C	Left-Hook P
Curly-Tail Stretched C	Small Capital P
Hooktop Right-Tail D	Rho
D-B Ligature	Hooktop Q
D-Z Ligature	Q-P Ligature
Looptail G	Reversed Small Capital R
Hooktop Small Capital G	Barred T
Greek Gamma	Hooktop T
Front-Tail Gamma	Curly-Tail Turned T
Back-Tail Gamma	T-S Ligature
Ram's Horns	Barred Glottal Stop
Curvy Turned H	Curly-Tail Inverted Glottal Stop
Right-Tail Curvy Turned H	Barred Reversed Glottal Stop
Small Capital H	Ampersand
Long-Leg Turned Iota	Chao Tone Letters
Right-Tail Turned Iota	Superscript Cross
Small Capital K	Subscript Turned Bridge
Turned Small Capital K	Subscript Box
Reversed Small Capital L	Advancement Sign
H-M Ligature	Retraction Sign
Small Capital M	Up Arrow
Pi	Down Arrow
Reversed Polish-Hook O	Northeast Arrow
Sigma	Southeast Arrow
Double-O Ligature	Left Pointer

Right Pointer
Subscript Right Pointer
Period
Reversed Comma

Right Half-Ring
Subscript Seagull
Rhoticity Sign

Phonetic Symbol Guide

LOWER-CASE A

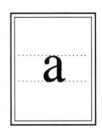

IPA USAGE

Cardinal Vowel No. 4: front unrounded. Described in *Principles* (p. 8) as the vowel sound of Northern English *back* or Parisian French *patte.* In the speech of Chicago, Illinois (and in various other varieties of American English), the word *pop* is pronounced as IPA [pap]. In the speech typical of Boston, Massachusetts, the pronunciation of the word *park* is approximately [pa:k].

AMERICAN USAGE

Same as IPA for many writers (see, e.g., Bloch and Trager 1942 (p. 22); Pike 1947 (p. 5); and Smalley 1963 (p. 263)); but many American linguists (see, e.g., Gleason 1955 (p. 8) and Chomsky and Halle 1968) do not distinguish [a] from [ɑ], either one being used for any low unrounded vowel distinct from [æ], the choice depending on typographical considerations. Thus in some American writings, [a] is used as a low back unrounded vowel, as in *pop,* which is IPA [pɑp] in many American dialects, but may be transcribed [pap]. In Crothers 1978 (p. 137) it is used for a low central vowel, IPA [ɐ].

OTHER USES

Universally used by Indologists for the short mid (or lower-mid) central unrounded vowel of Indic languages such as Hindi. Thus, for example, Fairbanks and Misra (1966) write ⟨kab⟩ for the Hindi word meaning 'when', IPA [kəb] or [kɐb].

COMMENTS

While many American linguists refer to [æ] as a low front vowel, the IPA and most careful American authorities are in agreement that [æ] represents a vowel slightly higher than fully low (between Cardinal 3

3

and Cardinal 4), while IPA [a] is defined as the most open front vowel possible (Cardinal 4).

The IPA's effort to establish ⟨a⟩ and ⟨ɑ⟩ as separate symbols "has not met with the success originally hoped for" (*Principles,* 19). The fluent reader of roman letters is too accustomed to ignoring the difference between them when switching between fonts or between handwriting and printing or typing. No orthography has adopted the two symbols as contrasting letters, though they are used as contrasting symbols in Isaac Pitman's 1845 phonotypic alphabet (cf. Pitman and St. John 1969 (p. 82) and some dictionary pronunciation guides.

SOURCE

Roman alphabet, lower case (as usually found in typesetters' fonts and typewriter elements).

Overdot A

Not in general use, but following the recommendations of Boas et al. (1916, 10) for the use of an overdot as a diacritic for central vowels, used by Bloch and Trager (1942, 22) for a low unrounded central vowel, approximately IPA [ɐ˞]. It is used for a low central *rounded* vowel in Crothers 1978 (p. 137), where "[a]" is used for Bloch and Trager's [ȧ].

Umlaut A

IPA Usage: According to *Principles* (p. 16), an open central unrounded vowel, though the current interpretation of the umlaut diacritic makes it an open central*ized* front unrounded vowel. *American Usage:* According to the widely followed recommendation of Boas et al. (1916, 9) on the use of the umlaut with vowel symbols, if [a] is a low back vowel, [ä] would be a low front unrounded vowel, i.e., IPA [a] (or perhaps [æ]). Used in this sense in Crothers 1978 (p. 137). Where [a] is used for a low front unrounded vowel (e.g., Bloch and Trager 1942 (p. 22) [ä] is a low back unrounded vowel. The symbol is not in common use, but is occasionally found. *Comments:* The result of the change in the IPA's interpretation of the umlaut and its common use with a different sense in American practice is a rather confusing situation in which [ä] may denote a centralized front vowel (official IPA), a central vowel (*Principles*), or a back vowel (e.g., Bloch and Trager).

Right-Hook A

IPA Usage: Recommended in *Principles* (p. 14) for a vowel with the quality of [a] (i.e., Cardinal 4) with rhotacization (*r*-coloration). Approval of the right-hook diacritic was withdrawn in 1976 (*Journal of the International Phonetic Association* 6 (p. 3)) in favor of a digraph such as [aɹ] or [aʴ]. *American Usage:* Not used. *Comments:* The rightward hook used by the IPA for indicating rhotacization should not be confused with the centered "Polish hook"; for example, ⟨ą⟩ is used in Polish orthography and Americanist transcription (e.g., Smalley 1963 (p. 333)) for nasalized vowels.

TURNED A

IPA USAGE

A not quite fully open, central unrounded vowel; higher than Cardinal 4, lower than Cardinal 3. Illustrated by the unstressed short open final syllable in the British English word *sofa,* pronounced [səʊfɐ].

AMERICAN USAGE

Not used.

COMMENTS

This symbol is rather rare in practice. None of the editions of Gimson's *Introduction to the Pronunciation of English* (1962, 1970, 1980) use it, for example.

SOURCE

Roman alphabet lower-case *a,* turned (rotated 180°).

SCRIPT A

IPA USAGE

Cardinal Vowel No. 5: open back unrounded.

AMERICAN USAGE

Standardly, same as IPA if used; but for many linguists not distinct from ⟨a⟩, either being used for any low unrounded vowel distinct from [æ], the choice depending on type font, and thus usually ⟨a⟩ when printed or typewritten.

Pike (1947, 5) and Smalley (1963, 174) show [ɑ] for a low *central* unrounded vowel. Pike has no symbol for a low back unrounded vowel, and Smalley proposes ⟨ɒ⟩ (rather misleadingly; see the entry for Turned Script A).

COMMENTS

The IPA's effort to establish ⟨ɑ⟩ and ⟨a⟩ as separate symbols "has not met with the success originally hoped for" (*Principles,* 19). The fluent reader of roman letters is too accustomed to ignoring the difference between them. No orthography has adopted the two symbols as contrasting letters, though they are used as contrasting symbols in Isaac Pitman's 1845 phonotypic alphabet (cf. Pitman and St. John 1969 (p. 82)) and some dictionary pronunciation guides.

SOURCE

Roman alphabet lower-case *a* as handwritten.

Alpha

Boas et al. (1916, 2) recommend ⟨α⟩ to represent the vowel sound in English *but,* which they classify as an upper-mid back unrounded vowel. This is confusing; although there is quite a bit of variation among dialects regarding the vowel sound of *but,* it is seldom taken to be back and upper-mid, i.e., close to Cardinal 15, IPA [ɣ]. And it is unclear why such a vowel would not be described by the familiar Schwa, which is clearly the least controversial transcription of the vowel in question for most dialects. Additionally confusing is the fact that under stress the word *but* has (in many dialects) the vowel usually transcribed by IPA [ʌ], which is lower-mid (and back in its cardinal form, Cardinal 6, though what most English speakers use is a much more central vowel broadly transcribed with [ʌ]). Alpha is sometimes found as a typographical substitute for Script A, ⟨ɑ⟩; in particular, Smalley (1963, 261) uses what appears to be ⟨α⟩ but refers to it as "'written *a*' or 'script *a*'." However, Smalley's chart places the symbol ⟨α⟩ not under the back vowels but in the "lower-low central" position (with [ʌ] one step higher at "low central"). The idea of using Alpha for an open central unrounded vowel has been revived by a group of linguists at the Summer Institute of Linguistics in England, where dissatisfaction with the 1989 IPA inventory of symbols for central vowels (particularly the hard-to-write Turned A) has led to the adoption of ⟨α⟩ for a vowel between Cardinals 4 and 5 (see Hunt 1992). Crothers (1978, 137) uses ⟨α⟩ for a low back rounded vowel (Cardinal 13, IPA [ɒ]), but this seems to be idiosyncratic. The source is the Greek alphabet, lower case.

TURNED SCRIPT A

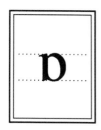

IPA USAGE

Cardinal Vowel No. 13: open back rounded. The secondary cardinal vowel corresponding to Cardinal 5.

AMERICAN USAGE

Standardly, same as IPA if used (cf. Pike 1947 (p. 5)); but Smalley (1963, 261) regards the vowel in question as *un*rounded, IPA [ɑ] (rounding is all but neutralized for very low vowels), and many linguists do not use the symbol at all, using [ɑ] or [a] for low back unrounded vowels and Open O (i.e., ⟨ɔ⟩) for low back rounded vowels.

The transcription system of Kurath 1939 (p. 126) seeks to remedy variation in the use of the turned script *a* for both unrounded and rounded low back vowels (e.g., by Bernard Bloch) through the use of a reversed turned script *a* to unambiguously represent an unrounded low back vowel, Turned Script A being reserved for rounded vowels.

COMMENTS

The IPA (*Principles,* 7–9) distinguishes between a fully open, fully back vowel with lip rounding, as in Southern British English *hot* (/hɒt/), and a slightly closer vowel, as in Southern British *caught* (/kɔːt/) or the Scottish pronunciation of *hot* (/hɔt/). Because American dialects generally do not show a /ɔ/-/ɒ/ phonological distinction (and even in Southern British there is a concomitant length difference), the need for both symbols is not felt by many American linguists.

SOURCE

Roman alphabet lower-case *a* as handwritten, turned (rotated 180°).

Overdot Turned Script A

Not in general use, but following the recommendations of Boas et al. (1916, 10), used by Bloch and Trager (1942, 22) for a low central rounded vowel. Trager (1964, 16) suggests [ɐ] as an alternative (conflicting with the IPA definition of this symbol). The *Principles* transcription for a low central rounded vowel would be [ɒ̈], which Bloch and Trager use for a low front rounded vowel.

Umlaut Turned Script A

IPA Usage: According to *Principles* (p. 16), an open central rounded vowel, basically [ɒ+], though the current interpretation of the umlaut diacritic makes it an open central*ized* back rounded vowel. *American Usage:* According to the widely followed recommendation of Boas et al. (1916, 9) on the use of the umlaut with vowel symbols, if [ɒ] is taken to be a low back rounded vowel, [ɒ̈] would represent a low front rounded vowel, i.e., a vowel with all of the properties of [ɒ] but front instead of back. The IPA transcription would be [œ]. The symbol is not in general use, but is listed by Bloch and Trager (1942, 22). Trager (1964, 16) proposes a ligature of the small capitals ⟨ᴀ⟩ and ⟨ᴏ⟩ as an alternative symbol. *Comments:* The result of the change in the IPA's interpretation of the umlaut and its common use with a different sense in American practice is a rather confusing situation in which [ɒ̈] may denote a centralized back vowel (official IPA), a central vowel (*Principles*), or a front vowel (e.g., Bloch and Trager).

Inverted Script A

Not in general use. Kurath (1939, 126) reports that some of the field workers for the *Linguistic Atlas of New England* (e.g., Bloch) had used Turned Script A indifferently for both rounded and unrounded low back vowels. This character was invented by analogy to unambiguously denote an unrounded low back vowel so that Turned Script A could be reserved for a rounded low back vowel in future work. Extremely rare.

ASH

IPA USAGE

A not quite fully open, front unrounded vowel; higher than Cardinal 4 (IPA [a]), more open than Cardinal 3 (IPA [ɛ]). Illustrated in *Principles* (p. 9) by Southern British English *cat* ([kæt]) and Russian *pjat'* ('five').

AMERICAN USAGE

Standardly, same as IPA. Many American linguists refer to [æ] as a low front vowel. See, e.g., Gleason 1955 (p. 8), Chomsky and Halle 1968 (p. 176), and Halle and Mohanan 1985 (p. 57). However, many American works on phonetics, e.g., Bloch and Trager 1942 (p. 22), Pike 1947 (p. 5), and Maddieson 1984 (p. 251), are in agreement with the IPA in using [æ] to represent a vowel slightly higher than fully low ("higher-low," "raised low," etc.). Smalley (1963, 263) reconciles the American terminology with the IPA usage by calling [æ] "low" and [a] "lower-low."

SOURCE

Taken from Old English orthography, where the *a-e* ligature was used to represent the sound of the runic symbol with the mnemonic name *æsc* 'ash'. The upper-case form is ⟨Æ⟩. The letter is used occasionally in modern English printing for certain words of Latin origin (e.g., 'formulæ' and 'encyclopædia'), though it does not represent [æ] in these words.

Overdot Ash

Not in general use, but following the recommendations of Boas et al. (1916, 10) for the use of an overdot as a diacritic for central vowels, used by Bloch and Trager (1942, 22) for a higher-low unrounded central vowel, approximately IPA [ɐ]. It is used with this sense in Crothers 1978 (p. 137).

Umlaut Ash

IPA Usage: According to *Principles* (p. 16), a semi-open central unrounded vowel, between Cardinals 3 and 4 in height and between Cardinals 3 and 6 in backness, similar to [ɐ]. The current interpretation of the umlaut diacritic makes it a semi-open central*ized* front unrounded vowel, between [æ] and [ɐ]. *American Usage:* According to the widely followed recommendation of Boas et al. (1916, 9) on the use of the umlaut with vowel symbols, this would represent a vowel with all of the properties of [æ] but back instead of front. Trager (1964, 16) suggests [ä] or [ʌ] as alternative transcriptions for such a vowel. The symbol is rarely found. The IPA would use [ʌ−] or [ɑ+] for Bloch and Trager's [ä]. *Comments:* The change in the IPA's interpretation of the umlaut and its common use with a different sense in American practice has resulted in a rather confusing situation in which [ä] with the umlaut diacritic may denote a centralized front vowel (official IPA), a central vowel (*Principles*), or a back vowel (Bloch and Trager).

A-O Ligature

Proposed by Trager (1964, 16) for a higher-low front rounded vowel, an alternative to the transcription [ö] suggested by Bloch and Trager (1942, 22). A Trager suggestion that never caught on. Front rounded vowels lower than IPA [œ] are in any case essentially unattested, though the IPA now provides [Œ] for a low front rounded vowel.

Small Capital A

IPA Usage: Mentioned in *Journal of the International Phonetic Association* 5 (p. 52) as having been proposed, and occasionally used, as a symbol for a fully open central unrounded vowel. *American Usage:* No standard use, but used in various ways by early Americanists, especially in the *Handbook of American Indian Languages* (Boas 1911). Thus Jones (1911, 744) uses ⟨ᴀ⟩ for IPA [ʌ], and Thalbitzer (1911, 975) uses it for "uvularized ɑ," i.e., [ɑ] when adjacent to a uvular consonant. The recommendations of Boas et al. (1916, 10) concerning the use of small capital letters would make ⟨ᴀ⟩ the transcription of a voiceless [a]. *Source:* Roman alphabet, small capital font.

Capital A

American Usage: Boas et al. (1916, 10) recommend the use of small capitals to represent the voiceless versions of normally voiced sounds (either vowels or sonorants), and following this, Pike (1947, 5) and Smalley (1963, 392) both use a general convention of capital letters for voiceless vowels; thus the transcription [A] might be used for IPA [a̯]. *Other uses:* Used also in various ways in phonological work. For example, Capital A represents the morphophoneme proposed by Hamp (1951) as the trigger of the initial consonant mutation Aspiration in Old Irish and Welsh. It represents an *a*-coloring laryngeal in some Indo-Europeanist work (see Hamp 1965a (p. 123, note 3). And in Chomsky and Halle 1968 (chapters 2–4) it is used to represent informally the vocalic nucleus that is realized as [æ] when lax and [ey] when tense.

Four

Used occasionally by Mayanists as a substitute for Left-Hook Four, which colonial-period grammarians in Guatemala used as a notation for ejectives; see, e.g., *International Journal of American Linguistics* 52 ((1986), 233). As a subscript or superscript, used to indicate pitch levels, stress levels, or tones. Often, though not always, higher numerals indicate lower levels (as in, e.g., Pike 1947, where pitch 4 is the lowest in English intonation, and Chomsky and Halle 1968, where stress level 4 is one lower than tertiary).

Left-Hook Four

Used, often rather inconsistently, by colonial-period (18th-century) Spanish grammarians as a notation for several ejective stops in Mayan languages of colonial highland Guatemala. The consonants represented included /ts'/, /tʃ'/, and [k'], and the symbol is still used occasionally in this way by some modern Mayanists when citing data from colonial sources; see, e.g., Robertson 1986 (p. 229). Not strictly a phonetic symbol or even a phonological one, but rather orthographic.

Inverted Small Capital A

Proposed by Trager (1964, 16) to represent a higher low central unrounded vowel, as an alternative to the transcription [æ] suggested by Bloch and Trager (1942, 22). Trager suggests that [ɐ] should be used for a back unrounded vowel that is "higher low" (between Cardinals 5 and 6) and [ʌ] should be used for the corresponding central vowel. The suggestion apparently never caught on. We have been told that this symbol was in use in IPA circles a century ago for a close mid back unrounded vowel, current IPA [ɤ], but we have not seen it thus used ourselves.

Capital Ash

Boas et al. (1916, 10) recommend the use of small capitals to represent the voiceless versions of normally voiced sounds (either vowels or sonorants) and following this, Pike (1947, 5) and Smalley (1963, 392) both use a general convention of capital letters for voiceless vowels; thus the transcription [Æ] might be used for IPA [æ̥].

Small Capital A-O Ligature

Proposed by Trager (1964, 16) for a low front rounded vowel, as an alternative to the transcription [ɒ̈] suggested by Bloch and Trager (1942, 22). *Principles* does not give a symbol for representing a vowel of the sort this symbol was intended for. Chomsky and Halle (1968, 191–92) use [œ] for it. In 1976 the IPA added ⟨œ⟩ to its chart of secondary vowel symbols (*Journal of the International Phonetic Association* 6 (p. 2)) for a low front rounded vowel. Such vowels are essentially unattested in natural languages, so none of these symbols are used in practice.

TURNED V

Cardinal Vowel No. 14: open mid back unrounded (but see also comments below). The secondary cardinal vowel corresponding in height and backness to Cardinal 6.

AMERICAN USAGE

Usually same as IPA, but some variation is encountered (see below).

COMMENTS

The IPA transcription [ʌ] is specified in *Principles* as the symbol for the fully back vowel Cardinal 14. However, its most common use is to represent the vowel sound of, e.g., Southern British English *cup,* and descriptions of English generally agree that this sound is closer to central than back for most speakers. Adding to the confusion, *Principles* (p. 9) makes the remark that [ʌ] can be heard in the pronunciation of *cup* in *Northern* England; but in the majority of Northern British dialects we have heard, *cup* has the vowel [ʊ] (nearly close back rounded, between Cardinals 7 and 8). For further discussion of this vowel in English and other languages, see Gimson 1962 and subsequent editions and Henton 1990.

Caution must be exercised in interpreting American uses of [ʌ], too. Bloch and Trager (1942, 22) assign it a value corresponding to the IPA value (lower-mid back); but Pike (1947, 5) considers it lower-mid central, and Smalley (1963, 363) defines it as low central (where his "low" is higher than the "lower-low" series). In many American dialects there is no phonological distinction between [ʌ] and [ə], and American linguists often treat these two symbols as if they were interchangeable (see, e.g., the confusing note provided by Cartier and Todaro (1983, 17)). Gleason (1955) does not use [ʌ] at all. The chart of segment types provided by Chomsky and Halle (1968, 176) shows [ʌ] as a mid back unrounded lax vowel ([−high, −low, +back, −round, −tense]). This apparently does not allow for it to be distinguished from Schwa.

Occasionally, [ʌ] has been used to represent other vowels. For example, in Sánchez and Castro 1977 it denotes a high back unrounded vowel (IPA [ɯ]).

Turned V is referred to as "Wedge" by some phoneticians, but this seems inadvisable to us, because the *háček* accent ⟨ˇ⟩ is also called that in names like Wedge C for ⟨č⟩. Another name sometimes used for Turned V is "Caret," but this is best reserved for the much smaller typesetter's proof correction mark ⟨‸⟩.

Notice that ⟨ʌ⟩ is not the same symbol as either ⟨Λ⟩ (upper-case Greek *lambda*) or ⟨∧⟩ (the logical conjunction symbol). Not all typesetters have appreciated this; for example, the Mohawk transcriptions in Postal 1964 contain numerous occurrences of the logical conjunction symbol, all of which should have been set as Turned V.

SOURCE

Roman alphabet lower-case *v*, turned (rotated 180°). This is visually suggestive of a small capital *a*, i.e., without its crossbar (which is perhaps intended to hint at some kind of low back tongue position; see the entry for Small Capital A).

Small Capital Delta

Proposed by Trager (1964, 16) to represent a mid back unrounded vowel, as an alternative to the transcription [ɛ̇] suggested by Bloch and Trager (1942, 22). A Trager suggestion that never caught on. The reason for the choice of symbol may have been the visual similarity between ⟨ᴅ⟩, ⟨ʌ⟩, and ⟨a⟩. It is a small capital from the Greek alphabet. It is used in syntactic literature as a dummy terminal symbol, but not generally as a phonetic symbol.

LOWER-CASE B

IPA USAGE

Voiced bilabial stop.

AMERICAN USAGE

Same as IPA.

COMMENTS

Not always used for a phonetically voiced stop; in languages like Mandarin Chinese and Icelandic, it may be used in broad transcription or in orthography for an unaspirated voiceless stop that contrasts with an aspirated one.

SOURCE

Roman alphabet, lower case.

Underdot B

Used by Trager (1964, 22) to represent a labiodental stop (an alternative to his ⟨ɓ⟩), following the general recommendation of Boas et al. (1916, 10) of underdot as a retraction sign for consonants. The symbol is hardly ever used, not least because labiodental stops seem never to contrast with bilabial stops in any language.

Crossed B

Widely used by Indo-Europeanists, e.g., Brugmann (1904; see page 1 for his symbol chart), Prokosch (1939, 35 etc.), and Wright (1910, 54 etc.), for a voiced bilabial fricative ("spirant"), IPA [β], and also in Romance philology; see, e.g., the transcriptions in Quilis and Vaquero 1973 or Fontanals 1976.

Barred B

Not standard; but used by Pike and Smalley for a voiced bilabial fricative (IPA [β]), and still sometimes found: see, e.g., the transcriptions in Danesi 1982. By a general convention, barred stop symbols (with a superimposed hyphen or short dash through the body of the letter) are often used to represent those fricatives for which the IPA symbols are not used. The resultant symbols have the advantage of being easy to type on an unmodified typewriter. The symbol is used with this sense by Meillet and Cohen (1952, xiii).

Slashed B

Occasionally found for a voiced bilabial fricative, IPA [β], as a typographical variant of a barred or crossed *b;* see, e.g., Joos 1966 (pp. 400–404), where the Crossed B of an earlier source is reset in a way looking more like Slashed B.

Soft Sign

Used for the Indo-European "shva secundum," the reduction of a short vowel, in contrast to [ə], the "shva primum," the reduction of a long vowel (Prokosch 1939 (p. 94)). Also used by Hamp (see, e.g., Hamp 1965b (p. 225)) for a postulated sixth vowel in Proto-Keltic. The character is taken from the Cyrillic alphabet. In Russian orthography, the soft sign indicates that the preceding consonant has a palatal articulation.

Hard Sign

Proposed by Trager (1964, 16) to represent a lower high back un-rounded vowel; an alternative to ⟨ï⟩. Taken from the Cyrillic alphabet, lower case. In Bulgarian orthography, the hard sign corresponds to a vowel of similar quality to the one that the symbol denotes in the Trager system, which may have been the motivation for this choice. The symbol has seldom if ever been used in phonetic work.

D-B Ligature
An amalgam of the shapes of ⟨d⟩ and ⟨b⟩, listed as a variant of its first component, ⟨d⟩; see page 41.

HOOKTOP B

IPA USAGE

Voiced glottalic ingressive (i.e., implosive) bilabial stop.

AMERICAN USAGE

Usually same as IPA.

OTHER USES

Trager (1964, 22) makes the idiosyncratic proposal that this symbol should be used for a pulmonic egressive voiced labiodental stop. (The IPA recognizes no symbol for such a segment.)

COMMENTS

The IPA usage of Hooktop B is well established in both IPA and American traditions and has been used in some African orthographic systems. Since labiodental stops have not been found to contrast with bilabial stops (or even to occur systematically at all) in any language, Trager's suggestion about using this symbol for labiodental stops was never taken up, and is not likely to be.

Voiced bilabial implosives are attested in some South Asian languages (notably Sindhi, which is Indo-European); in some Southeast Asian languages (Karen, Khmer, and Vietnamese, for example); in a few Amerindian languages (Maidu, formerly spoken in California, and some languages of Central America); and in numerous Nilo-Saharan and Niger-Congo languages of Africa.

SOURCE

Roman alphabet lower-case *b*, modified by hooking the vertical stroke rightward at the top. *Principles* (p. 14) uses the expression "ɓ, ɗ, etc." in introducing this symbol, apparently with the intention of encouraging the construction of analogously modified symbols for other implosives that might be identified.

23

SMALL CAPITAL B

IPA USAGE

IPA USAGE

Voiced bilabial trill.

OTHER USES

According to the recommendations of Boas et al. (1916, 10) on the uses of small capitals, this symbol could be used for a labial stop that is "intermediate . . . between sonant and surd," i.e., partially but not fully voiced. A report by a working group of British clinical phoneticians in 1983 (PRDS Group 1983; see also Ball 1987) proposed a set of conventions according to which Small Capital B is used, in transcribing disordered speech, to represent a voiced linguolabial stop (current IPA [d̼]). The IPA declined to adopt Ball's suggestion and incorporate the PRDS Group proposals, apparently to avoid adding a suite of six new symbols to represent sounds that are extremely rare, and added the Subscript Seagull diacritic instead.

COMMENTS

The voiced bilabial trill that this symbol represents in the IPA is often shown as "Brr!" under the conventions of written English, and used as an exclamation about the weather or the speaker being cold. Heffner (1950, 136), using [ʙ] to transcribe it, notes that "German teamsters still use this trill, accompanied by a high pitched and very loud voice note, to induce their draft horses to stop," and says that the sound is known in German as the "Kutscher R"). Heffner added, "I know of no language in which it is a regular speech sound." In the late 1970s, such languages were discovered to exist. They include Kele and Titan (spoken in New Guinea), and [ʙ] seems to have first been used to transcribe this sound in Ladefoged 1982 (pp. 154–55). The transcription was approved officially by the IPA in 1989. Smalley (1963, 456) writes [b̃] for the sound (this transcription would be meaningless under IPA conventions, since [˜] denotes nasalization, i.e., lowering of the velum, and [b] is an oral stop, with velum raised). Suarez (1983, 46), reporting that it occurs in the word meaning 'ant lion' in Amuzgo and Isthmus Zapotec (but in no other words!), transcribes it [bʳ] (using the IPA suggestion that "small index letters may be used to indicate shades of sound" (*Principles*, 17)).

SOURCE

Roman alphabet, small capital font. Notice that [ʀ] also represents a trill in the IPA alphabet.

IPA USAGE

Voiced bilabial fricative.

AMERICAN USAGE

Same as IPA, if used; Barred B (⟨ƀ⟩), Crossed B (⟨ƀ⟩), or occasionally Slashed B (⟨ƀ⟩) may be found instead.

COMMENTS

As in Spanish *iba* 'was (3rd sing.)'. Contrasts with labiodental [v] in some languages, e.g., Avatime, Ewe, and Logba in the Kwa group in West Africa (see Ladefoged 1968 (p. 25)).

SOURCE

Greek alphabet, lower case.

LOWER-CASE C

Voiceless palatal stop. As represented by *ty* in Hungarian orthography.

AMERICAN USAGE

Sometimes as IPA, but since 1934, commonly used for an alveolar affricate, IPA [ts], following the recommendations of Herzog et al. (1934, 631).

Recommended by Boas et al. (1916, 5) for a voiceless palato-alveolar fricative, IPA [ʃ], but this was supplanted by the later recommendations of Herzog et al. that [š] be used for [ʃ] and [c] be reserved for [ts] in those cases where it functions as a single affricate consonant. Smalley (1963, 275) uses it for a voiceless alveopalatal stop.

OTHER USES

Boas (1911, 23) gives [c] for a voiceless "dental" fricative, though it is given as "alveolar" in his Chinook paper (p. 565). Jones (1911, 743) uses it for IPA [ʃ]. The variation may be as much in descriptive terminology as denotation. The most likely use of unadorned ⟨c⟩ in this period is for some voiceless coronal fricative.

Indologists use ⟨c⟩ for the palato-alveolar affricates of such languages as Hindi as well as for true palatal stops (and generally refer to such consonants as "palatals" even if they are produced with palato-alveolar contact). Cf. Whitney 1889 (p. 2).

COMMENTS

Hungarian *ty* represents IPA [c]. German *z* represents American [c] (= IPA [ts]).

Roman alphabet, lower case. It seldom denotes IPA [c] in the languages in whose orthographies it appears. It is fairly close in Italian *ciao,* and hence was a natural choice for scholars transliterating Sanskrit च.

Acute-Accent C

Proposed by Trager (1964, 22) to represent a voiceless prepalatal affricate; an alternative to Trager's [ç] (not the same as IPA [ç]). The IPA equivalent of Trager's [ç] = [ć] would be [tʃ] = [tʃʲ]. Found in some European works with a similar denotation to the one Trager suggests; for instance, Trubetzkoy (1932, 38) uses ⟨ć⟩ for the affricate corresponding to palatalized ("mouillert") [s], which he writes with ⟨ś⟩. Since the prime, an acute accent placed after the symbol ([´]), is also used to indicate palatalization among American and continental European linguists, [c´] is likely to have a similar interpretation to [ć] when found. Also used in the Polish and Serbo-Croatian orthographies.

Barred C

Proposed by Smalley (1963, 455) for a voiceless flat (i.e., not grooved) "alveopalatal" (palato-alveolar) fricative (IPA [ç]). The symbol is also used by Meillet and Cohen (1952, xiii) for a voiceless palatal fricative, the "*ich*-laut," presumably IPA [ç]. By a general convention, barred stop symbols (with a superimposed hyphen or short dash through the body of the letter) are often used to represent those fricatives for which the IPA symbols are not used. The resultant symbols have the advantage of being easy to type on an unmodified typewriter.

Slashed C

American Usage: Voiceless alveolar or dental centrally released affricate (IPA [ts]). Used in both Gleason 1955 and Pike 1947. Note that some other sources (e.g., Herzog et al. 1934 (p. 631) and Hockett 1955) use ⟨c⟩ instead. *Other uses:* Used in Boas 1911 (p. 23) as a voiceless "linguo-dental" or "linguo-labial" fricative, a use supplanted by [θ] or [s̪] in later work. *Comments:* We have analyzed this character as a roman alphabet lower-case *c* with a superimposed oblique stroke. In some fonts the superimposed stroke is vertical rather than oblique, but this is never a distinctive feature of the symbol. An effectively equivalent symbol is usually available on American typewriter keyboards as the "cent sign." Its absence as a character on computer terminal keyboards and non-U.S. typewriters favors our decision to treat it as a *c* with a superimposed stroke.

Wedge C

American Usage: Voiceless palato-alveolar affricate, IPA [tʃ]. The recommendation of Herzog et al. (1934, 631) that [č] be used for IPA [tʃ] has gained almost universal currency among American linguists. *Source:* Roman alphabet lower-case *c,* with the wedge diacritic. As

used in the orthography for Czech, where the diacritic is called the
háček ('little hook').

 Open O
*Typographically a turned ⟨c⟩, but actually a vowel symbol,
listed (and named) as a variant of ⟨o⟩; see page 143.*

C CEDILLA

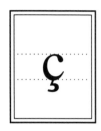

IPA USAGE

Voiceless palatal median fricative. Articulated further back than [ʃ] (palato-alveolar) or [ç] ("alveolo-palatal") but not as far back as [x] (velar).

AMERICAN USAGE

Generally not used. Palatal fricatives are generally transcribed with symbols for fronted velar fricatives. Hence Pike (1947, 7) and Gleason (1955, 7) give [x̟] for a voiceless palatal central fricative, and Smalley (1963, 359) specifies [x̣].

COMMENTS

Illustrated by the initial segment of English *hue* in some pronunciations, by the final sound of German *ich,* and by the initial segment of Japanese *hito.*

Used in Boas 1911 (p. 23) as a voiced "linguo-dental" or "linguo-labial" fricative, a use supplanted by [ð] or [z̠] in later work.

The cedilla is used in French and formerly in Spanish to indicate a fricative value as opposed to a stop or affricate value for the letter *c* in contexts where the stop value would otherwise be expected. Thus in French, *c* = [k] in *cas* but [s] in *ça.* The letter *c* with a cedilla is also used in Turkish orthography, to denote a voiceless palato-alveolar affricate, IPA [tʃ]. Note that it does not actually denote a palatal fricative in any of these orthographic uses.

SOURCE

Roman alphabet lower-case *c* (used for a palatal stop), with the cedilla diacritic.

Hooktop C

IPA Usage: Approved during the period 1989–93 for a voiceless glottalic ingressive (i.e., implosive) palatal stop; approval was withdrawn in 1993. *Comments:* Implosives tend, for aerodynamic reasons, to be voiced, but as pointed out in many works on phonetics (Pike 1947 (p. 40); Smalley 1963 (p. 381); Ladefoged 1971 (p. 25); and Catford 1988 (p. 27)), voiceless implosives are easy enough to produce. They are occasionally encountered in languages—but they are very rare; and although Maddieson (1984), Pinkerton (1986), and Henton, Ladefoged, and Maddieson (1992, 81) give some citations, they give no example of a language claimed to have a voiceless implosive at the palatal place of articulation. Thus Hooktop C appears never to have been used at all in the literature during its brief period of official recognition. Typographically, this is a case of good riddance, because the hooktop modification does not work well for this letter shape: the symbol ⟨c⟩ has no upright to support the hooktop. Thus the effect, especially when the symbol is handwritten, is that it looks like a deformed Epsilon. The most obvious transcription for a voiceless palatal implosive under currently approved IPA transcription principles would be [ʄ̥]. *Source:* By obvious visual analogy with [ɓ] and [ɗ], the symbols originally established by the IPA for voiced implosives.

CURLY-TAIL C

IPA USAGE

Voiceless "alveolo-palatal" median laminal fricative. Articulated further forward than [ç] (true palatal) but not as far forward as [ʃ] (palato-alveolar), and articulated laminally (with the flat blade of the tongue) rather than apically (with the tip of the tongue, as in the retroflex [ʂ]).

AMERICAN USAGE

Not in general use. Listed in Halle and Clements 1983 (p. 29) as a voiceless palatal central fricative, i.e., IPA [ç].

COMMENTS

Illustrated (*Principles,* 12) by the sound represented as *ś* in Polish *geś,* and as *hs* in the Wade romanization for Mandarin Chinese (*x* in the Pinyin system).

The IPA's distinction between "alveolo-palatal" place of articulation (closer to palatal) and palato-alveolar (closer to alveolar) has not gained wide currency. The term *palato-alveolar* is standard, but the term *alveolo-palatal* is not, and in fact is rarely encountered. The term *alveopalatal* used by Gleason, Pike, and Smalley corresponds to the IPA's *palato-alveolar.*

SOURCE

Roman alphabet lower-case *c* (used by IPA for a palatal stop), modified with the same curly tail used for ⟨ʑ⟩ (IPA's voiced "alveolo-palatal" central fricative).

Stretched C

IPA Usage: Formerly denoted a velaric ingressive postalveolar stop) (i.e., click) with "retroflex" place of articulation (but see below). Approval withdrawn in 1989.   *Comments:* Illustrated by the click that *q* represents in the Zulu orthography, which is generally referred to as "palatal" in the literature, but has also been called "retroflex," especially in earlier work.

The sound is similar to the pop of a cork being drawn from a bottle. It has been described by Ladefoged and Traill (1984, 2), after a careful investigation of the articulation, as "alveolar" rather than "retroflex" or "palatal." As they acknowledge (p. 6), this is a departure from earlier works, and may cause some confusion, since there is another click (written [≠] in the local orthography for Hottentot and by many linguists) that has been called alveolar but which Ladefoged and Traill claim is palatal. The difficulty apparently stems not so much from a disagreement about how the sound is made as from the conceptual problem of what should be called the primary place of articulation of a sound with velar closure, apico-alveolar closure, and oral airflow into a palatal cavity.

Printed as ⟨C⟩ in some sources, e.g., Chomsky and Halle 1968 (p. 320), and as ⟨ᴄ⟩ in Beach 1938 (p. 289).   *Source:* Perhaps a visual compromise between ⟨c⟩ on the one hand and the rightward-swept tail of retroflex consonant symbols like ⟨ʈ⟩ and ⟨ɖ⟩ on the other.

Curly-Tail Stretched C

Proposed by Beach (1938, 289) for a nasalized version of the alveolar velaric ingressive stop (or click) represented by Stretched C, but never officially approved by the IPA. Under modern conventions, which use a two-character combination of [ŋ] plus a click symbol to represent a nasalized click, the representation of a nasalized alveolar click would be [ŋ͡!].

Capital C

Sometimes found as a typographical compromise for [ɕ]; see, e.g., Chomsky and Halle 1968 (p. 320) and the occurrence of "Chū" for "ɕhū:" in the bibliography of Cole 1966 (p. 470).

Also used by phonologists to represent an arbitrary consonant of any sort; thus "CV syllable structure" means "consonant-vowel syllable structure," and so on.

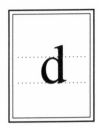

LOWER-CASE D

Voiced dental or alveolar stop. [d̪] indicates definitely dental; [d] may represent either articulation.

AMERICAN USAGE

Same as IPA.

COMMENTS

The exact place of articulation for an apical stop can be indicated with diacritics. For example, American phoneticians may mark dental artic-ulation with a subscript arch (or the IPA subscript bridge diacritic), and may indicate retroflex articulation with an underdot.

The symbol is not always used for a phonetically voiced stop; in languages like Mandarin Chinese and Icelandic, it may be used in broad transcription or in orthography for an unaspirated voiceless stop that contrasts with an aspirated one.

SOURCE

Roman alphabet, lower case.

Crossed D

Sometimes found representing a voiced interdental fricative, but stan-dard American usage for this is [ð], as in IPA. Widely used to represent a voiced interdental fricative in transliterations of early Germanic languages (e.g., by Wright (1910, 54) for Gothic and generally by Brugmann (1904; see page 1 for his symbol chart)). Also found in works on Romance linguistics; see, e.g., the transcriptions in Quilis and Vaquero 1973 and Fontanals 1976. Appears with this sense in Meillet and Cohen 1952 (p. xiii). A typographical substitute for ⟨ð⟩, whose capital form is ⟨Đ⟩.

Barred D

Not standard, but sometimes used (e.g., by Pike (1947, 7) and Smalley (1963, 454)) for a voiced interdental fricative (IPA [ð]), and still sometimes found; see, e.g., the transcriptions in Danesi (1982). Barred stop symbols (with a superimposed hyphen or short dash through the body of the letter) are often used to represent those fricatives for which the IPA symbols are not used. The resultant symbols have the advantage of being easy to type on an unmodified typewriter. In the case at hand, there is no difficulty in finding a suitable symbol for the voiced grooved alveolar fricative, since ⟨z⟩ is on every English-language typewriter; Barred D provides a way of representing a dental or interdental slit (flat) fricative.

Slashed D

May occasionally be found for a voiced interdental fricative, IPA [ð], though we have not been able to locate a printed source.

Front-Hook D

Used by Daniel Jones in early transcriptions to indicate a voiced retroflex stop, in particular for Sinhalese. According to Jones, the IPA symbol [ɖ] was introduced in 1927 (see Jones and Laver 1973 (p. 202, note 36)), replacing this character and the traditional [ḍ].

HOOKTOP D

IPA USAGE

Voiced glottalic ingressive (i.e., implosive) alveolar, dental, or post-alveolar stop.

COMMENTS

Voiced alveolar or dental implosives are attested in some South Asian languages (notably Sindhi, which is Indo-European), in some Southeast Asian languages (Karen, Khmer, and Vietnamese, for example), in a few Amerindian languages (Maidu, formerly spoken in California, and some languages of Central America), and in numerous Nilo-Saharan and Niger-Congo languages of Africa.

The Subscript Bridge diacritic can be used to indicate dental rather than alveolar place of articulation, and the Underbar diacritic can be employed to specify postalveolar place.

SOURCE

Roman alphabet lower-case *d,* modified by hooking the vertical stroke rightward at the top. *Principles* (p. 14) uses the expression "ɓ, ɗ, etc." in introducing this symbol, apparently with the intention of encouraging the construction of analogously modified symbols for other implosives that might be identified.

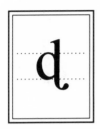

RIGHT-TAIL D

Voiced retroflex (i.e., apico-postalveolar) stop.

AMERICAN USAGE

Not normally used; [ɖ] is used instead.

COMMENTS

As in the sound represented by Hindi ⟨ड़⟩.

SOURCE

Roman alphabet lower-case *d,* modified by the addition of the rightward long tail used by the IPA for retroflex consonant symbols. Introduced in 1927, according to Daniel Jones (Jones and Laver 1973 (p. 202, note 36)).

Hooktop Right-Tail D

IPA Usage: Not actually on the IPA chart, but permitted implicitly under IPA conventions for the representation of a voiced retroflex implosive. *Comments:* The IPA's recommendation in *Principles* (p. 14) is that "ɓ, ɗ, etc." should be used for voiced implosives. The intention was apparently to encourage the construction of analogously modified letters for other implosives that might be identified. Thus the symbol is within the IPA tradition; we treat it as a minor entry rather than a major entry here solely because it is not one of the five voiced implosive symbols listed on the 1993 revision of the IPA chart (*Journal of the International Phonetic Association* 23, number 1, unpaginated centerfold). Sindhi (an Indic language of northern India) does in fact have a voiced retroflex implosive, according to Henton, Ladefoged, and Maddieson (1992, 93). The transcription that appears in their printed paper is in fact a ⟨ɖ⟩ with a right superscript circumflex ⟨ˆ⟩; the authors obviously intended a ⟨ɗ⟩ with a hooktop modification but the manuscript copy was not set as intended. The sound denoted by this symbol is extremely rare, for obvious reasons: one would only expect to find it in languages that make use of both the retroflex position of articulation for stops and the glottalic ingressive airstream mechanism, and neither is particularly common.   *Source:* Roman alphabet lowercase *d* modified by both the right tail for retroflex consonants and the right hook on the top of the upright for implosives.

D-B Ligature

Proposed early in the 20th century, apparently by Clement Doke (see the chart in Doke 1926b (p. 41)), as the symbol for a voiced labiodental stop. Adopted by Ladefoged and Maddieson (1996) for representing this sound, which occurs in such African languages as Zulu and the XiNkuna dialect of Tsonga, though not, apparently, in contrast with bilabials. Guthrie (1948, 61) reported minimal pairs like [ȸar] "shine" versus [bar] "give birth to" in a language that he called Tonga (Nyanja-Tumbuka family), but Ladefoged and Maddieson are not able to confirm this observation. Laver (1994, 215) points out that the sound may be heard in English in some pronunciations of the phrase *head first*. (Laver uses the transcription [π] for the sound; see entry for Pi.) *Source:* An invention designed to harmonize with IPA characters, perhaps due to Doke. The symbol looks like a *b* with an additional left-facing loop. The voiceless counterpart, also used by Doke, is Q-P Ligature.

D-Z Ligature

IPA Usage: Not in the current IPA chart, but formerly recognized as a one-symbol way of representing a voiced alveolar affricate. The current practice is to use the two-symbol sequence [dz]. If any ambiguity were to arise, the affricate could be represented by [d͡z] to distinguish it from a sequence consisting of [d] followed by [z]. *Source:* Roman alphabet, lower case; a ligature composed of the shapes ⟨d⟩ and ⟨z⟩.

D-Yogh Ligature

IPA Usage: Not in the current IPA chart, but formerly recognized as a one-symbol way of representing a voiced palato-alveolar affricate. The current practice is to use the two-symbol sequence [dʒ]. If any ambiguity were to arise, the affricate could be represented by [d͡ʒ] to distinguish it from a sequence consisting of [d] followed by [ʒ]. *American Usage:* Not used; [dž] or [ǰ] would be used for a voiced palato-alveolar affricate. *Source:* A ligature of the shapes ⟨d⟩ and ⟨ʒ⟩. A voiced palato-alveolar affricate has an alveolar stop component (transcribed [d]) and a palato-alveolar fricative component (transcribed [ʒ]).

ETH

IPA USAGE

Voiced apico-dental or interdental median fricative.

AMERICAN USAGE

Same as IPA. Sometimes [ɖ] or [đ] is found instead.

SOURCE

The letter *eth* originated in Old English orthography as a crossed Irish *d*. The symbols *thorn* (⟨þ⟩) and *eth* were used indifferently in Late Old English manuscripts to represent the interdental fricative phoneme which was voiced between two voiced sounds and voiceless elsewhere. Cf. Quirk and Wrenn 1957 (pp. 6–7). The character was borrowed for Scandinavian orthographies and survives in Modern Icelandic. The upper-case form is ⟨Ð⟩.

Delta

Not generally used, but if found it is probably for a voiced interdental fricative, IPA [ð]. Cf. Sapir 1925 (p. 43) and Firth 1948 (p. 140).

Recommended by Boas et al. (1916, 11) for a voiced "dorsal" stop. Transcriptions using the symbols for such a dorsal series are seldom found.

Delta represents IPA [ð] in Modern Greek.

Capital D

American Usage: Often used to represent the voiced alveolar flap of American pronunciations of, e.g., the word *pity;* thus American [pɪDi] = IPA [pɪɾi]. Cf. Chomsky 1964 (p. 90).   *Source:* Roman alphabet, upper case.

LOWER-CASE E

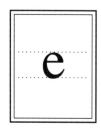

Cardinal Vowel No. 2: close mid front unrounded.

AMERICAN USAGE

Standardly, same as IPA; but commonly also used for Cardinal 3 (IPA [ɛ]). Thus in transcribing English, the mid vowel of *bait* may be distinguished from that of *bet* by length ([be:t] vs. [bet]) or diphthongization ([beyt] vs. [bet]—IPA [beit] or [beɪt] vs. [bɛt]).

SOURCE

The letter *e* is commonly a symbol for a vowel like Cardinal 2 in the writing systems of European languages (e.g., French, Spanish, and Italian).

Umlaut E

IPA Usage: According to *Principles* (p. 16), a close mid unrounded central vowel (between Cardinals 2 and 15 in backness, i.e., between [e] and [ɤ]). The current interpretation of the umlaut diacritic makes it a central*ized* close mid unrounded vowel.   *American Usage:* According to the widely followed recommendation of Boas et al. (1916, 9) on the use of the umlaut with vowel symbols, [ë] would represent an unrounded higher-mid back vowel, i.e., a vowel with all of the properties of [e] but back instead of front. The IPA transcription would be [ɤ].

Cf. Bloch and Trager 1942 (p. 22), and Trager 1964 (p. 16). Abercrombie (1967, 161) suggests [ə] for the original IPA [ë] (cf. *Journal of the International Phonetic Association* 5 (p. 52)). Catford (1977, 178) and Trager (1964, 16) use it also. *Comments:* The result of the change in the IPA's interpretation of the umlaut and its common use with a different sense in American practice is a rather confusing situation in which [ë] may denote a centralized front vowel (official IPA), a central vowel (*Principles*), or a back vowel (e.g., Bloch and Trager).

Polish-Hook E

American Usage: Nasalized [e]. Boas et al. (1916, 8) recommend the use of a centered subscript rightward hook as a nasalization diacritic, and this is still used (instead of the IPA's tilde diacritic) by some authorities, e.g., Smalley (1963, 333). The diacritic is found indicating nasalization in Polish orthography, hence our name for it. *Other uses:* Used by some editors of Old English texts (e.g., Bright (1935) and Sweet (1882)) to distinguish orthographic *e*'s (IPA [ɛ]) which resulted from umlaut. Does not occur in the original manuscripts. Cf. Moore and Knott 1955 (p. 12).

Right-Hook E

IPA Usage: Recommended in *Principles* (p. 14) for a vowel with the quality of [e] (i.e., Cardinal 2) with rhotacization (*r*-coloration). Approval of the right-hook diacritic was withdrawn in 1976 (*Journal of the International Phonetic Association* 6 (p. 3)) in favor of a digraph such as [eɹ] or [eˀ], but it was then reintroduced in the 1989 revision. *American Usage:* Not used. The rightward hook used by the IPA for indicating rhotacization should not be confused with the centered "Polish hook"; for example, [ą] is used in Polish orthography and Americanist transcription for nasalized vowels.

SCHWA

IPA USAGE

Mid central unrounded vowel.

AMERICAN USAGE

Same as IPA.

OTHER USES

Used by Jerzy Kuryłowicz, and by other Indo-Europeanists subsequently, to represent Saussure's "laryngeals." Kuryłowicz wrote $\langle ə_1 \rangle$, $\langle ə_2 \rangle$, etc., for distinct postulated laryngeals. See Polomé (1965) for a thorough discussion and references to the literature.

COMMENTS

Used for a range of distinguishable non-peripheral vowels for which other symbols could also be used; thus [ə] may represent in broad transcriptions a retracted and only slightly rounded [œ] in French, [ɐ] in word-final position in British English, [ɜ] in stressed positions in British English, [ɨ] in many American dialects, and so on.

There is a wide range of variation in the articulatory descriptions given to Schwa by American phoneticians. Bloch and Trager (1942, 22) define it as mean-mid central. Pike (1947, 5) gives it as upper-mid central. Smalley (1963, 363) shows it as lower-mid central. Gleason (1955, 8) does not distinguish [ə] from [ʌ] and describes [ə] as mid central or back. On the distinction between [ə] and [ʌ], see the unintendedly confusing note by Cartier and Todaro (1983, 17).

Following in this tradition, Chomsky and Halle (1968, 176) do not include [ə] in their chart showing the feature composition of English segments, though they use the symbol [ə] throughout. This is because they write [ə] for a totally unstressed vowel and deliberately take no position on the question of its precise phonetic realization (59, note 1; 245, note 7). Hence they espouse no phonetic description corresponding to [ə], though they note (59, note 1) that for many speakers it may be [ɨ]. Their feature system apparently does not allow for the representation of a distinction between IPA [ɨ], [ə], and [ʌ].

SOURCE

Roman alphabet lower-case *e,* turned (rotated 180°). The name *schwa* or *shva* (Hebrew *sh'wa*) comes from traditional Hebrew grammar (Prokosch 1939 (p. 94)).

Right-Hook Schwa

IPA Usage: Formerly recommended (*Principles,* 14) for a mid central unrounded vowel with rhoticity (i.e., *r*-coloration). Described as "another way of writing frictionless ɹ when used as a vowel." Approval of the general use of the right-hook diacritic was withdrawn in 1976 (*Journal of the International Phonetic Association* 6 (p. 3)) in favor of a digraph such as [əɹ] or [əˑ], though this character was deemed useful enough to be retained, along with Right-Hook Reversed Epsilon. However, the 1993 revision no longer recognizes either of them as letters. Instead, they can be composed by means of the rhoticity sign. *Source:* Schwa, with the addition of the IPA right-hook diacritic devised by Daniel Jones and formerly recommended for indicating rhotacization, now slightly modified as Rhoticity Sign. The secretary of the IPA said in 1975 of the symbols formed with Right Hook: "I think no one but Jones ever really liked these symbols, and even he was not enthusiastic" (*Journal of the International Phonetic Association* 5 (p. 57)).

REVERSED E

IPA USAGE

Close-mid central unrounded vowel, midway between [e] and [ɤ]. Used by Abercrombie (1967, 161) and Catford (1977, 178), and finally made an official IPA symbol in 1993.

AMERICAN USAGE

Not generally used, though Kurath 1939 (p. 123) and Trager 1964 (p. 16) list it with an interpretation that agrees with the IPA usage.

COMMENTS

This symbol is an ⟨e⟩ reversed left-to-right, i.e., the mirror image of ⟨e⟩. It should not be confused with the much more common symbol ⟨ə⟩ (Schwa), which is an ⟨e⟩ that has been turned (i.e., rotated 180°).

SOURCE

Roman alphabet, lower-case *e,* modified by lateral reversal.

Small Capital E

Recommended by Bloch and Trager (1942, 22) for a front unrounded vowel at exactly the mid point ("mean-mid"), i.e., between Cardinal 2 and Cardinal 3. Used in this way in Crothers 1978 (p. 137). The recommendations of Boas et al. (1916, 10) concerning the use of small capital letters would make [ᴇ] the transcription of voiceless [e]. The character is a roman alphabet small capital *e*. Note that the character is distinct from both ⟨ɛ⟩ and ⟨E⟩.

Umlaut Small Capital E

Proposed by Bloch and Trager (1942, 22) for a "mean-mid" (i.e., mid) back unrounded vowel (i.e., between Cardinals 6 and 7 but unrounded). See also Trager 1964 (p. 16), where alternative transcriptions [Ė] and [ʌ] are suggested for this vowel. The corresponding IPA transcription would be [ɤ˗] or [ʌ˖].

Capital E

Boas et al. (1916, 10) recommend the use of small capitals to represent the voiceless versions of normally voiced sounds (either vowels or sonorants), and following this, Pike (1947, 5) and Smalley (1963, 392) both use a general convention of capital letters for voiceless vowels; thus the transcription [E] might be used for IPA [e̥]. In Indo-Europeanist work, used for a non-*a*-coloring laryngeal (see Hamp 1965a (p. 123, note 3)), and in Chomsky and Halle 1968 (chapters 2–4) to represent informally the vocalic nucleus that is realized as [ɛ] when lax and [iː] when tense.

EPSILON

IPA USAGE

Cardinal Vowel No. 3: open mid front unrounded.

AMERICAN USAGE

Same as IPA, when used.

OTHER USES

Al-Ani (1970, 29) uses ⟨ɛ⟩ for the voiced pharyngeal fricative (IPA [ʕ]), presumably for its visual similarity to the Arabic character ⟨ع⟩. Cf. the entry for Turned Three.

As a superscript, used by early Americanists (e.g., in the *Handbook of American Indian Languages* (Boas 1911)) to indicate a glottal stop. Thus the transcription [ᵋa´tcī] by William Jones (1911, 742) corresponds to something like IPA [ˈʔatʃiːʲ].

Used by Chomsky and Halle (1968, 161, 176, 228n, 229, 245n) for a hypothetical mid front glide in English which causes certain phonological effects (e.g., the change of [t] to [s] in the alternation *resident/residence,* the latter having an underlying final /ɛ/) but is always removed by an elision rule in derivations so that it never surfaces phonetically.

SOURCE

Greek *epsilon* (in some fonts). The other way of printing *epsilon,* ⟨ε⟩, (which is common in mathematical texts as the set membership sign) is not generally used, though it may be found (cf. Sapir 1925 (p. 43)). The character occurred as a vowel symbol (with the value IPA [i]) in Isaac Pitman's 1845 phonotypic alphabet (cf. Pitman and St. John 1969 (p. 82)).

Overdot Epsilon

Not in general use, but following the recommendations of Boas et al. (1916, 10), used by Bloch and Trager (1942, 22) for a lower-mid central unrounded vowel; cf. also Trager (1964, 16), who gives [ɜ] (Reversed Epsilon) as an alternative. The corresponding *Principles*-type transcription would be [ɛ̈].

Right-Hook Epsilon

IPA Usage: Recommended in *Principles* (p. 14) for a vowel with the quality of [ɛ] (i.e., Cardinal 3) with rhotacization (*r*-coloration). Approval of the right-hook diacritic was withdrawn in 1976 (*Journal of the International Phonetic Association* 6 (p. 3)) in favor of a digraph such as [ɛɹ] or [ɛ˞]. *American Usage:* Not used. The rightward hook used by the IPA for indicating rhotacization should not be confused with the centered "Polish hook"; for example, [ą] is used in Polish orthography and Americanist transcription for a nasalized vowel.

CLOSED EPSILON

Open-mid central rounded vowel.

AMERICAN USAGE

Not in common use, but occurs in Kurath 1939 (p. 125) for a rounded lower-mid front vowel, IPA [œ]. Used chiefly to transcribe the vowel sound in the pronunciation of English *bird* in some dialects which do not have rhotacized central vowels.

COMMENTS

Oddly, although the IPA council decided to accept the argument that a new letter was needed for this value (see *Journal of the International Phonetic Association* 23 ((1993), 32–34)), the letter introduced was not the symbol already in use by Abercrombie (1967, e.g., p. 161) and Catford (1977, e.g., p. 178); nor was it the one proposed by Catford (1990), where Barred Open O was suggested. Instead, the IPA council chose to introduce a symbol shape that was apparently invented (perhaps by Kurath) for use in the *Linguistic Atlas of New England.*

SOURCE

Derived from the shape of Greek lower-case *epsilon,* ⟨ɛ⟩, by closing the curve.

Note: Since the second edition of this book went to press, the IPA has changed its policy on the status of Closed Epsilon, announcing (see *Journal of the International Phonetic Association* 25, no. 1, p. 48; dated June 1995 but published in 1996) that it was approved unintentionally owing to a typographical error. The IPA's intent was to approve Closed Reversed Epsilon (see p. 57). The entry on this page should thus have been a minor entry.

REVERSED EPSILON

IPA USAGE

Sanctioned in *Principles* (p. 7) as "another variety of central vowel."
Listed under "Other Symbols" below the 1979 revised chart (see
Cartier and Todaro 1983 (p. 84)) as a "variety of ə." Used by Abercrombie (1967, 161) and Catford (1977, 178) to represent a central unrounded vowel of the same height as Cardinal 3.

AMERICAN USAGE

Seldom used, but Kurath (1939, 123) and Trager (1964, 22) use it for a
lower-mid central unrounded vowel, as an alternative to [ɛ].

OTHER USES

Used as a typographical compromise for Yogh in the transliterations of
texts in Jones 1972 (chapter 2) and in Trubetzkoy 1969 (p. 73).

COMMENTS

Reversed Epsilon was introduced primarily to represent the vowel of
educated Southern British English ("received pronunciation" or RP, in
the terminology of Daniel Jones (see Jones 1918)) in such words as
bird. Jones did not use the symbol, writing [ə:] instead (see, e.g., 1962,
88–91, and 1956, 47), but it does appear in Gimson 1962 (pp. 116–18),
and later editions. Jones suggests in various places (see especially
1962, 64) that [ə:] is higher than [ə] in RP, which might indicate that
[ɜ:] should be taken as somewhat higher than mid. This disagrees with
Trager, with Catford (1977, 178), and with Kurath and McDavid
(1961, 1). However, Gimson (1962, 116) notes that a wide range of
variants of the RP /ɜ/ phoneme are found, some lower than Cardinal 3
and some higher than Cardinal 2; he assigns /ə/ a very similar range
(1962, 119) and questions the correctness of assuming distinct /ɜ/ and

/ə/ phonemes (1962, 116). The assignment of the symbol ⟨ə⟩ to represent a mid vowel, ⟨ɘ⟩ to represent an upper-mid vowel, and ⟨ɜ⟩ to represent a lower-mid vowel (on which Trager and Catford have settled) should be regarded as arbitrary, and not directly connected to Gimson's use of ⟨ɜ⟩ and ⟨ə⟩ in describing RP phonetics and phonemics.

SOURCE

Greek alphabet, lower-case *epsilon,* modified by left-right reversal.

Right-Hook Reversed Epsilon

IPA Usage: Suggested (*Journal of the International Phonetic Association* 5 (p. 57)) as useful enough to be retained for the rhotacized (*r*-colored) version of [ɜ] when general approval of the right-hook rhotacization diacritic on vowels was withdrawn in favor of digraphs. The symbol is given in Cartier and Todaro's (1983, 11) English vowel chart, though not in their revised IPA chart (1983, 84). *American Usage:* Not in general use, but found, e.g., in Kenyon 1950. *Comments:* The IPA's decision to withdraw recognition from the general use of the rhotacization diacritic was prompted by an opinion of the secretary of the IPA, who said of the symbols for rhotacized vowels: "I think no one but Jones ever really liked these symbols, and even he was not enthusiastic" (*Journal of the International Phonetic Association* 5 (p. 57)). *Source:* Greek alphabet lower-case *epsilon,* laterally reversed, with the IPA's right-hook diacritic for rhotacization.

Closed Reversed Epsilon

IPA Usage: Never officially approved, but considered (*Journal of the International Phonetic Association* 5 (p. 52)) for an open mid central rounded vowel, intermediate between [œ] and [ɔ], and used in just this way by Abercrombie (1967, 161) and Catford (1977, 178): for a central rounded vowel of the same height as Cardinal 3. However, when the IPA finally approved a symbol for this sound in 1993, it approved Closed Epsilon. *American Usage:* Not generally used, though it occurs in Kurath 1939 (p. 123), denoting a lower-mid central rounded vowel. *Source:* Apparently created by closing the shape of a laterally reversed Greek lower-case *epsilon,* ⟨ɛ⟩.

Note: Since the second edition of this book went to press, the IPA has changed its policy on the status of Closed Epsilon, announcing (see *Journal of the International Phonetic Association* 25, no. 1, p. 48; dated June 1995 but published in 1996) that Closed Epsilon (see p. 54) was approved unintentionally owing to a typographical error. Closed Reversed Epsilon is now the official IPA symbol for an open-mid central rounded vowel, so the entry on this page should have been a major entry.

LOWER-CASE F

Voiceless labiodental fricative.

Same as IPA.

May be used for [ɸ] in languages like Japanese which have [ɸ] but no [f]. However, some languages, e.g., Ewe and Logba of the Kwa group in West Africa, have a [ɸ]-[f] contrast (see Ladefoged 1968 (p. 25)).

Roman alphabet, lower case.

Script Lower-Case F

Used in the International African Institute's orthography for African languages for a voiceless bilabial fricative, IPA [ɸ]. Cf. *Practical Orthography of African Languages* (International African Institute 1930) and Tucker 1971. Also used in Westermann and Ward 1933 (pp. 77–79).

Small Capital F

Given by Kurath (1939, 140) for a sound "resembling *f* . . . but with less friction and usually shorter," the voiceless correspondent to Script V, and therefore presumably a voiceless frictionless labiodental approximant. Used by Danish Eskimologists for a voiceless [w] (IPA [ʍ]); see Thalbitzer et al. 1952.

Barred Dotless J
Typographically, a turned ⟨f⟩, but used (like ⟨j⟩ and several other symbols) to represent a palatal articulation, and listed as a variant of ⟨j⟩; see page 96.

LOWER-CASE G

IPA USAGE

Voiced velar (or advanced velar) stop.

AMERICAN USAGE

Voiced velar stop.

COMMENTS

Not always used for a phonetically voiced stop; in languages like Mandarin Chinese and Icelandic, it may be used in broad transcription or in orthography for an unaspirated voiceless stop that contrasts with an aspirated one.

A little-known IPA recommendation (*Principles,* 14) suggests using the symbol ⟨ɡ⟩ for advanced velar stops and the symbol ⟨g⟩ for ordinary velar stops where the two are distinguished. This does not seem to have struck phoneticians as a good idea, and the two variants of this letter are generally regarded as interchangeable. Cf. Albright 1958 (p. 59).

Something like this contrast (but with the symbols switched) is used by Wright (1910, 50) in his transcription of "Indogermanic." The symbols ⟨k⟩ and ⟨g⟩ are given as "palatal" stops and ⟨q⟩ and ⟨ɡ⟩ as "true velars."

SOURCE

Roman alphabet, lower case.

Barred G

Not standard; but both Pike and Smalley suggest Barred G to represent a voiced velar fricative (IPA [ɣ]). (N.B.: Pike 1947 seems to have a typo, ⟨g⟩ for ⟨g̶⟩, at several points in the chart on page 7). Barred stop symbols (with a superimposed hyphen or short dash through the body of the letter) are often used to represent those fricatives for which the IPA symbols are not used. The resultant symbols have the advantage of being easy to type on an unmodified typewriter.

Crossed G

Occasionally found for a voiced velar fricative (IPA [ɣ]). By a general convention, barred stop symbols (with a superimposed hyphen or short dash through the body of the letter) are often used to represent those fricatives for which the IPA symbols are not used. The resultant symbols have the advantage of being easy to type on an unmodified typewriter. The superimposed dash crosses the descender of ⟨g⟩ in, e.g., Jespersen 1949 (p. 22) and Meillet and Cohen 1952 (p. xiii). Presumably this character was formed by analogy with Crossed D and Crossed B.

HOOKTOP G

Voiced glottalic ingressive (i.e., implosive) velar stop.

COMMENTS

Voiced velar implosives are not as common as bilabial or alveolar ones; there is a rather clear tendency for the rarity of implosives to be proportional to the backness of their articulation. But they are attested (not necessarily in phonological contrast with [g]) in some African languages; Maddieson 1984 (p. 217) mentions Ik, Hamer, Maasai, Nyangi, and Swahili. (The implosive articulation of Swahili voiced stops has long been noted; see, e.g., the statement by Ashton (1944) that all the voiced stops are pronounced implosively except where immediately preceded by a nasal.) Some English speakers may produce a voiced velar implosive when imitating the "glug-glug" sound of wine being poured from a bottle (with decreasing lip rounding used to make it sound as if the bottle is being emptied; notice that voiceless sounds can also be used for the "glug-glug" sound effect).

SOURCE

Roman alphabet lower-case *g*, modified by adding a rightward-oriented hook at the top by analogy with Hooktop B and Hooktop D. *Principles* (p. 14) uses the expression "ɓ, ɗ, etc." in assigning symbols for implosives, apparently with the intention of encouraging the construction of analogously modified symbols for other implosives that might be identified, and Hooktop G appears on official IPA charts from 1979 on.

Looptail G

Frequently found as a substitute for the IPA symbol ⟨g⟩, but not recommended. See the entry for Lower-Case G for details of two ways in which the transcriptions [g] and [ɡ] have been distinguished. The source is the roman alphabet, lower case. Looptail G is the normal letter shape in such fonts as Times Roman, while the open-tail version we have called Lower-Case G is found in fonts such as Helvetica and Courier.

SMALL CAPITAL G

IPA USAGE

Voiced uvular stop.

AMERICAN USAGE

Same as IPA, if used; recommended by Trager (1964, 22) for a voiced postvelar (i.e., uvular) stop.

COMMENTS

Voiced correspondent of [q]. Encountered in Eskimo, and (allophonically) in Teherani Persian (Farsi) (*Principles,* 35). Contrasts with both [q] and [qʰ] in Burushaski according to Catford (1977, 160).

Smalley regards uvular stops like [ɢ] as "backed velars," and transcribes them using velar symbols with the underdot diacritic.

SOURCE

Roman alphabet, small capital font.

HOOKTOP SMALL CAPITAL G

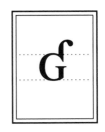

IPA USAGE

Voiced glottalic ingressive (i.e., implosive) uvular stop.

AMERICAN USAGE

Not in general use.

COMMENTS

The sound for which the IPA approved this symbol in 1989 is extremely rare. There is a rather clear tendency for the rarity of implosives to be proportional to the backness of their articulation, and the uvular position is as far back as is feasible for an implosive. Maddieson 1984 (p. 113) reports the sound's occurrence in the sound system of just one African language: Ik, spoken in Uganda. However, Maddieson does not use this symbol; he transcribes the sound with the left-facing superscript pointer diacritic thus: [ɢˁ]. Hooktop Small Capital G itself seems never or seldom to have been used in published work as yet. The sound may be extremely rare, but it is not that difficult to produce; some English speakers may produce it, in fact, when doing the exaggerated stage gulp that is written "GULP!" in comic strips, or when imitating the "glug-glug" sound of wine being poured from a bottle (with decreasing lip rounding used to make it sound as if the bottle is being emptied; notice that voiceless sounds can also be used for the "glug-glug" sound effect).

SOURCE

By obvious visual analogy with [ɓ] and [ɗ], the symbols originally established by the IPA for voiced implosives (*Principles* (p. 14) says "ɓ, ɗ, etc.," clearly intending to encourage such analogical invention).

Capital G

May be found as a typographical substitute for the small capital ⟨G⟩ (voiced uvular stop); see, e.g., Pike 1947. Used for the morphophoneme proposed by Hamp (1951) to represent the trigger of Gemination, an initial consonant mutation in Old Irish.

GAMMA

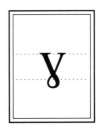

IPA USAGE

Voiced velar median fricative.

Used as a right superscript, it is the official IPA diacritic for velarized sounds. See the chart for IPA diacritics.

AMERICAN USAGE

When used, same as IPA.

OTHER USES

Doke (1926a, 1926b) used Gamma for a voiced dental click in languages that have that sound but do not have a voiced velar fricative (e.g., Zulu and various Khoisan languages), but this usage is never found in recent work.

COMMENTS

Principles (p. 10) originally specified that this symbol should be used for a voiced velar approximant as well as for a fricative (just as the symbol ⟨j⟩ was originally recommended for both the voiced palatal approximant, IPA [j], and the palatal fricative, current IPA [ʝ].) This was changed in 1979, the symbol [ɰ] being introduced for the approximant and [ɣ] being restricted to the fricative. The voiced velar fricative occurs intervocalically in languages like Spanish (e.g., *hago* 'I make') and German (e.g., *sagen* 'to say'). It is the Modern Greek value of the Greek letter *gamma,* ⟨γ⟩, on which the shape of the IPA symbol is based. Note, however, that the IPA symbol is distinct in shape from the latter, which we call Greek Gamma, and which often occurs in American transcriptions, as, e.g., in Sapir 1925 (p. 43).

It is particularly important not to confuse IPA Gamma ([ɣ]) with Baby Gamma, now replaced by IPA Ram's Horns ([ɤ]), since the two have little in common phonetically, Ram's Horns being the symbol for a close mid back unrounded vowel. This error is found, however; see, e.g., Hockett 1955 (p. 194).

SOURCE

Greek alphabet, lower case, modified to harmonize with the typography of other IPA characters.

Greek Gamma

American Usage: Voiced velar fricative. See entry for Gamma on the difference between this Greek letter and the IPA symbol we have called Gamma. *Source:* Greek alphabet, lower case.

Front-Tail Gamma

Suggested by Trager (1964) for a voiced prevelar slit spirant, i.e., a fronted velar fricative. The suggestion never caught on. The Greek alphabet lower case *gamma,* with modified tail.

Back-Tail Gamma

Suggested by Trager (1964) for a voiced postvelar slit spirant, i.e., a retracted velar (or uvular) fricative. The suggested never caught on. The Greek alphabet lower case *gamma,* with modified tail.

Baby Gamma

IPA Usage: Not currently used (superseded by Ram's Horns), but encountered in pre-1989 IPA transcriptions for Cardinal 15, a close mid back unrounded vowel. *American Usage:* When used, denotes an upper mid back rounded vowel. *Comments:* This character was well established in earlier IPA usage (see *Principles* (p. 6)), but it has often been confused with Gamma, not only by beginning students but by typesetters and proofreaders; for example, the [ɤ] seen on page 72 of Bleek 1926 is an error for [ɣ], and the same error occurs in the chart on page 17 of Baldi 1983. Smalley (1963, 363) actually calls this symbol "gamma" (admitting that it "is not strictly speaking a Greek *gamma,* but looks enough like it so that we call it that for want of a better term"; no conflict with IPA [ɣ] arises for Smalley, since he uses Barred G for the voiced velar fricative). There is perhaps some phonetic kinship between Gamma and Baby Gamma: Catford (1977, 183) points out that Cardinal 15 [ɤ] is the vowel obtained by opening the air passage of a velar fricative [ɣ] until there is no friction; thus there is a sense in which Cardinal 15 and the voiced velar fricative are phonetically related. Nonetheless, for the most part the confusion between Gamma and Baby Gamma is undesirable, and with this in mind the IPA redesigned the character in 1989, and Ram's Horns (see next entry) became the current name for the new letter shape. *Source:* Used as a vowel symbol (with the phonetic value [au]) in Isaac Pitman's 1845 phonotypic alphabet (see Pitman and St. John 1969 (p. 82)). The name Baby Gamma is due to Kenneth Pike, according to Trager (1964, 15).

RAM'S HORNS

IPA USAGE

Cardinal Vowel No. 15: close mid back unrounded. The secondary cardinal vowel corresponding to Cardinal 7, [o].

AMERICAN USAGE

When used, same as IPA.

COMMENTS

This symbol should be carefully distinguished from IPA Gamma, [ɣ]. Gamma is a descender, and denotes a fricative consonant. Ram's Horns is not a descender; its base sits on the line of writing, and the horn-like protuberances above its small loop extend only as high as the top of an [o]. It was partly in an effort to differentiate the two symbols more sharply that the IPA redesigned the symbol for Cardinal 15 in 1989, giving it slightly longer horns that curl apart at the top (compare the serifs at the top of Baby Gamma in the previous entry); the name *Ram's Horns* was mentioned at the 1989 Kiel convention, and became current for it soon thereafter.

SOURCE

Derived from Baby Gamma by slight shape modification.

LOWER-CASE H

Voiceless glottal fricative or approximant.

Used as a right superscript, it is the official IPA diacritic for aspirated sounds. See the chart for IPA diacritics.

AMERICAN USAGE

Same as IPA.

OTHER USES

Indo-Europeanists write ⟨h⟩ for a voiceless velar fricative in some cases, e.g., in Germanic languages, where an earlier velar fricative has become glottal in modern dialects (cf. Old vs. Modern English).

In working transcriptions for Australian indigenous languages, *h* is often used after alveolar consonant symbols to indicate dentals; thus *th* may be used for [t̪], *nh* for [n̪], and so on.

COMMENTS

A segment broadly represented as [h] may have a very wide range of phonetic variation, e.g., between [ɸ], [ç], [ḁ], [e̥], and [o̥] in Japanese.

SOURCE

Roman alphabet, lower case.

Underdot H

IPA Usage: In principle, should represent a "closer" variety of the glottal fricative [h], but this has no clear phonetic meaning. *American Usage:* Occasionally found representing a voiceless pharyngeal fricative, IPA [ħ], particularly in transliterations of Arabic. Recommended by Boas et al. (1916, 14) for such a sound, in this instance apparently conflicting with their general interpretation of the underdot as a retraction diacritic.

H-V Ligature

Recommended by Boas et al. (1916, 12) for a voiceless [w], following the use for Gothic. Used as the roman alphabet transliteration of the 25th letter of the Gothic alphabet. Described as "either a labialized **h** or else a voiceless **w**" (cf. Wright 1910 (p. 11)). A ligature composed of *h* and *v,* created to emphasize the fact that the sound patterns as a single consonantal unit in the Gothic sound system.

H-M Ligature
See page 113.

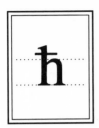

CROSSED H

IPA USAGE

Voiceless pharyngeal fricative.

AMERICAN USAGE

Same as IPA, if used.

COMMENTS

It was recommended to the IPA (see *Principles,* 19) that ⟨ħ⟩ be replaced by Turned Two, ⟨ƨ⟩, which is visually reminiscent of Arabic ⟨ƨ⟩ (*ḥa*), but the suggestion has not found its way into practice.

SOURCE

Roman alphabet lower-case *h,* with superimposed crossbar.

HOOKTOP H

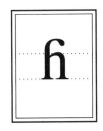

Voiced (or murmured, or whispery, or breathy-voiced) glottal fricative.

Heffner (1950, 150) states that this symbol is used for an Arabic sound that is "not infrequent in words like *behind, beheld, behave, perhaps*" in English. The Arabic sound traditionally known as *'ain* is generally described as a voiced pharyngeal fricative, IPA [ʕ]. To be more precise, according to Catford (1977, 163) [ʕ] is a "faucal" or "transverse" or "upper" pharyngeal voiced fricative (distinguished in recent phonetic research from the "epiglottal" or "lower" pharyngeal fricatives, current IPA [ʜ] and [ʢ], that Catford calls "linguo-pharyngeal"). Heffner appears to regard Arabic *'ain,* which he calls "the voiced congener of hâ," as a sound more like the English [ɦ]. Later, on page 153, where he calls [ɦ] a "laryngeal fricative," he refers to the Arabic sounds traditionally called *Hâ* and *Gain* as "originally emphatic pharyngeal consonants [ħ] and [ʕ]." There is thus some apparent disagreement about the phonetics of Arabic between Heffner and later sources like Catford. The IPA-approved value of Hooktop H seems not to be in question in the dispute, however.

As a right superscript, Hooktop H is used by Pike (1947, 7) with voiced stops as a digraph for murmured or voiced aspirated stops; cf. also Ladefoged 1982 (p. 258). The current IPA usage for murmured stops is the subscript umlaut diacritic.

This sound is heard in English when the pronunciations of words like *behave* or *behind* are voiced throughout ([bɪɦeɪv], [bɪɦaɪnd]). The sound is often described as a voiced glottal fricative, but there is no aspect of this description that is uncontroversial. First, it is a matter of debate among phoneticians whether [h]-like sounds are fricatives or approximants. And second, the glottis is not fully in a state of voicing during the production of [ɦ]; it is generally in the "murmur" or "breathy voice" state characteristic of the release of the breathy-voice ("voiced aspirate") stops of Indic languages. A right superscript Hooktop H is used to represent that kind of release (with or without the subscript diacritic [..] under the stop symbol to indicate the murmur state of the glottis).

Normally the rightward-oriented hooked top on a consonant symbol indicates that it represents an implosive stop, but that analogical pattern is not relevant here. Thus the initial Hooktop B in the Sindhi word [ɓəni] 'field' represents a glottalic ingressive stop, but the superscript Hooktop H of the initial stop in [bɦənən̪u] 'lamentation' indicates a pulmonic egressive stop with breathy-voiced release. Of course, there is no ambiguity here, since a glottalic ingressive glottal fricative is essentially an articulatory impossibility and certainly never occurs in languages or needs symbolization.

SOURCE

Roman alphabet lower-case *h,* modified by bending the vertical stroke rightward at the top.

Right-Tail Hooktop H

Used by Prokosch (1939, 50) for a voiceless fortis velar fricative in his discussion of Grimm's Law. He contrasts [fþɦ] (voiceless fortis) with [φθχ] (voiceless lenis). The symbol seems to be Hooktop H with a rightward turning tail. It occurs in Prokosch only in italic font, and so it could simply be a form of an italic Hooktop H which has an exaggerated right leg.

Heng

This symbol was suggested (only half seriously) by Yuen-Ren Chao (1934, 52) as the symbol for a putative phoneme uniting English /h/ (which only occurs at the beginnings of syllables) and /ŋ/ (which only occurs at the ends of syllables). This symbol does not occur in phonetic transcriptions because it is not associated with any fixed set of phonetic properties—which is exactly the point of Chao's discussion. Included here for typographical continuity in the family of *h*-based characters (and because calling it *Heng* allowed us to devise a name for the otherwise unnameable ⟨ɧ⟩).

HOOKTOP HENG

Recommended (*Principles*, 14) for a "combination of **x** and ʃ (one variety of Swedish *tj, kj,* etc.)." Still recognized in the 1993 chart.

AMERICAN USAGE

Not used.

COMMENTS

The IPA description appears to mean that *tj* and *kj* in the Swedish orthography may correspond to a voiceless fricative articulated with simultaneous velar and palato-alveolar friction.

The symbol is rarely seen, and would need a note of explanation if used.

SOURCE

A visual blend of ⟨h⟩ and ⟨ʃ⟩?

TURNED H

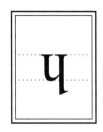

IPA USAGE

Voiced rounded palatal median approximant. (Rounded counterpart of [j]; the semivowel corresponding to [y].)

AMERICAN USAGE

Not used.

COMMENTS

As heard in French *lui* [lɥi], not the same as *Louis* [lwi].

SOURCE

Roman alphabet lower-case *h,* turned (rotated 180°). Visually suggestive of ⟨y⟩, the IPA symbol for the corresponding vowel.

Curvy Turned H

In use for some years by phoneticians in China to represent a non-open central or back rounded "apical" vowel with friction that occurs in some varieties of Chinese; for example, the chart on page 7 of Yuan et al. 1960 makes it fairly clear that this symbol is the rounded analog of Long-Leg Turned Iota. The sound denoted is essentially a syllabic [zʷ], which is why the IPA does not recognize any special symbol for this sound. Possibly (according to a Chinese linguist from Beijing consulted by John Renner, p.c.) introduced into China by German linguists in the 1950s. Clearly in the IPA tradition of character design, the letter is a clever visual amalgam of several others: Iota, which suggests some kind of close unrounded vowel; a laterally reversed ⟨r⟩, which suggests an apico-alveolar articulation; and ⟨u⟩, which suggests rounding. It is also visually similar—perhaps too similar—to the distinct IPA symbol Turned H, ⟨ɥ⟩, which denotes a rounded palatal median approximant and is also used in the description of Chinese phonetics.

Right-Tail Curvy Turned H

In use for some years by phoneticians in China to represent a rhotacized (or retroflex) non-open central or back rounded "apical" vowel with friction that occurs in some varieties of Chinese; for example, the chart on page 7 of Yuan et al. 1960 makes it fairly clear that this symbol is the rounded analog of Curvy Turned H. The sound denoted is essentially a syllabic [ʐʷ], which is why the IPA does not recognize any special symbol for this sound. Possibly (according to a Chinese linguist from Beijing consulted by John Renner, p.c.) introduced into China by German linguists in the 1950s. Clearly in the IPA tradition of character design, the letter is a clever visual amalgam of several others: Iota, which suggests some kind of close unrounded vowel; a laterally reversed ⟨r⟩, which suggests an apico-alveolar articulation; ⟨u⟩, which suggests rounding; and the right-tail modification characteristic of symbols for retroflex sounds. It also looks—perhaps misleadingly— like a right-tail version of the distinct IPA symbol Turned H ⟨ɥ⟩, which denotes a rounded palatal median approximant and is also used in the description of Chinese phonetics.

SMALL CAPITAL H

IPA USAGE

Voiceless epiglottal fricative.

AMERICAN USAGE

Not used.

COMMENTS

Catford (1977, 163) distinguishes "faucal" or "transverse" or "upper" pharyngeal voiced fricatives from "epiglottal" or "lower" or "linguo-pharyngeal" fricatives. IPA [ʜ] is the approved symbol for the voice-less variety of the latter, added to the official symbol inventory in 1989. Epiglottal fricatives are produced by narrowing the pharynx in a front-back direction by moving back the root of the tongue and thus the epiglottis.

Catford suggests some example of the occurrence of the voiced counterpart of this sound (IPA [ʕ]), but gives no examples of voiceless epiglottal fricatives in any language. In particular, he emphasizes that the Arabic pharyngeal fricatives [ħ] and [ʕ] are faucal, not epiglottal.

SOURCE

Roman alphabet, upper case.

Capital H

Sometimes used (e.g., by Smalley (1963, 181)) to represent the putative phoneme in the Trager and Smith analysis of English that has
[h] as its realization in prevocalic position and is realized as [ə] in
postvocalic position. Not found in phonetic transcriptions; purely a
phonological abstraction. Also used by Holger Pedersen, and by other
Indo-Europeanists subsequently, to represent Saussure's "laryngeals."
Pedersen used ⟨H₁⟩ and ⟨H₂⟩ to represent specific distinct phonemes of
Proto-Indo-European. ⟨H⟩ is used to refer to the class including both
of them, or, in a theory propounded by L. L. Hammerich, to represent
a conjectured unique PIE laryngeal. See Polomé 1965 for a thorough
discussion and references to the literature.

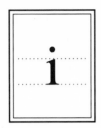

LOWER-CASE I

IPA USAGE

Cardinal Vowel No. 1: close front unrounded.

AMERICAN USAGE

Same as IPA.

COMMENTS

Not the same as ⟨ɩ⟩ or ⟨ɪ⟩.

SOURCE

Roman alphabet, lower case. ⟨i⟩ represents [i] in most languages that use the letter (with the exception of English, where it represents [i] in *machine,* but [aɪ] in *shine,* [ɪ] in *shin,* and so on).

Umlaut I

IPA Usage: According to *Principles* (p. 16), a close central unrounded vowel, an alternative to [ɨ], though the current interpretation of the umlaut diacritic makes it a central*ized* close front unrounded vowel between [i] and [ɨ].   *American Usage:* According to the widely followed recommendation of Boas et al. (1916, 9) on the use of the umlaut with vowel symbols, [ï] would represent a high back unrounded vowel, i.e., a vowel with all of the properties of [i] but back instead of front. The IPA transcription would be [ɯ]. Cf. Pike 1947

(p. 5) and Trager 1964 (p. 16). *Comments:* The result of the change in the IPA's interpretation of the umlaut and its common use with a different sense in American practice is a rather confusing situation in which [ï] may denote a centralized front vowel (official IPA), a central vowel (*Principles*), or a back vowel (e.g., Bloch and Trager). *Source:* The character is a roman alphabet lower-case *i,* with the umlaut diacritic. When the umlaut is added to a dotted letter, it is customary for it to replace the dot, though sometimes in typewritten work one may encounter ⟨ï⟩.

Dotless I

Used occasionally as a typographical substitute for ⟨ɪ⟩ or ⟨ɩ⟩. Occurs in Turkish orthography, representing IPA [ɯ], and thus should ideally not be used for IPA [ɪ] if ⟨ɪ⟩ or ⟨ɩ⟩ is available. The character is a lower-case *i* with its dot removed. It was introduced into the Turkish alphabet in the 1928 orthography reform that replaced the earlier Arabic-based writing system.

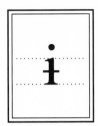

BARRED I

Close central unrounded vowel, between Cardinal 1 and Cardinal 8.

AMERICAN USAGE

Often same as IPA, but there is some variation: Pike (1947, 5) agrees with the IPA, but Smalley (1963, 284) lists the symbol as denoting an unrounded central vowel that is "lower-high," i.e., semi-high like [ɪ] and [ʊ]; and some sources collapse central high vowels with back: Gleason (1955, 8) cites [ɨ] as either central or back, and Halle and Clements (1983, 29) state that [ɨ] represents the same sound as [ɯ], which is definitely not the case under the IPA's definition of the latter. They give no symbols for any back unrounded vowels other than [ɑ], which is quite peculiar.

COMMENTS

Barred I has often been used by American scholars in the transcription of English, for words with a schwa that is pronounced somewhat higher than the mid line; for example, the word *just* has been transcribed [ǰɨst].

SOURCE

Roman alphabet lower-case *i,* modified with superimposed hyphen.

SMALL CAPITAL I

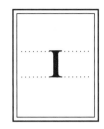

Near-close near-front unrounded vowel, between Cardinal 1 and Cardinal 2.

Same as IPA.

Sometimes [ɪ] is regarded as differing from [i] in tenseness rather than height, [i] being tense and [ɪ] lax.

The recommendations of Boas et al. (1916, 10) on the use of small capital letters would make [ɪ] the transcription of a voiceless [i].

Roman alphabet, small capital font.

Umlaut Small Capital I

IPA Usage: Given the adoption of Small Capital I as the official symbol for a near-close, near-front unrounded vowel and the interpretation of the umlaut diacritic for centralized vowels, this would symbolize a near-close vowel midway between [ɪ] and [ɨ] in backness. *American Usage:* According to the widely followed recommendations of Boas et al. (1916, 9) on the use of the umlaut with vowel symbols, [ï] would represent a semi-high back unrounded vowel (between [ï] and [ë]), i.e., a vowel with all of the properties of [ɪ] but back instead of front. Cf. Bloch and Trager 1964 (p. 22). The IPA transcription for such a vowel would be [ɯ]. Pike (1947, 5) suggests the very similar symbol ⟨ï⟩ for this sound. Trager (1964, 16) proposes ⟨ъ⟩ as an alternative.

Barred Small Capital I

Not common, but given by Bloch and Trager (1942, 22) for a lower-high central unrounded vowel, a logical extension of the character [ɪ] (lower-high front unrounded) by use of the superimposed hyphen on analogy with [ɨ]. Used by Halle and Mohanan (1985, 91) for a high back unrounded vowel, IPA [ɯ].

Capital I

Pike and Smalley both suggest the use of capital letters for voiceless vowels; thus the transcription [I] might be used for IPA and standard American [i̥]. ⟨I⟩ is also sometimes found as a typographical substitute for Small Capital I or the former IPA symbol Iota, because it is available in all roman typewriter and printer fonts. In Chomsky and Halle 1968 (chapters 2–4), Capital I is used to represent informally the vocalic nucleus that is realized as [ɪ] when lax and [ay] (in their transcription) when tense.

Iota

IPA Usage: Formerly denoted a near-close near-front unrounded vowel, between Cardinal 1 and Cardinal 2. Approval withdrawn in 1989. *American Usage:* Same as IPA if used (as it is in, e.g., Smalley 1963, where the name *Iota* is also used), though [ɪ] is perhaps more frequent in American transcriptions. *Comments:* The IPA decided at the 1989 Kiel convention to adopt [ɪ] and [ʊ] for the vowels of English *pit* and *put,* withdrawing recognition from [ɩ] and [ɷ]. Since American phoneticians had often preferred [ɪ] over [ɩ] (and had virtually never used [ɷ]), this brought IPA and American usage somewhat closer together. *Source:* Greek alphabet, lower case.

Long-Leg Turned Iota

In use for some years by phoneticians in China to represent a non-open central or back unrounded "apical" vowel with friction that occurs in many varieties of Chinese (including Mandarin); see, for example, the chart on page 7 of Yuan et al. 1960. The sound denoted is essentially a syllabic [z], which is why the IPA does not recognize any special symbol for this sound. The transcriptional decision made in *Principles* (p. 42) is in fact to use [ə]; the accompanying explanatory note reads: "The letter **ə** is used here with two special values; after **s, ts, tsh** it has a value of the **ɯ**-type with some accompanying friction (thus resembling **z**); after **ʃ, c, ch** it is accompanied by some friction, and resembles **ʒ**." Thus, the note continues, "**sə** . . . might also be written **sz**." Possibly (according to a Chinese linguist from Beijing consulted by John Renner, p.c.) introduced into China by German linguists in the

1950s. Clearly in the IPA tradition of character design, the letter is visually reminiscent of both Iota, suggestive of some kind of close unrounded vowel, and a laterally reversed ⟨r⟩, suggesting an apico-alveolar articulation.

Right-Tail Turned Iota

In use for some years by phoneticians in China to represent a rhota-cized (or retroflex) non-open central or back unrounded "apical" vowel with friction that occurs in many varieties of Chinese (including Mandarin); see for example the chart on page 7 of Yuan et al. 1960. The sound denoted is essentially a syllabic [ʐ] or perhaps [ʒ], which is why the IPA does not recognize any special symbol for this sound. The transcriptional decision made in *Principles* (p. 42) is in fact to use [ə]; the accompanying explanatory note reads: "The letter ə is used here with two special values; after **s, ts, tsh** it has a value of the ɯ-type with some accompanying friction (thus resembling **z**); after **ʃ, c, ch** it is ac-companied by some friction, and resembles **ʒ**." Thus, the note contin-ues, "**ʃə** . . . might also be written "**ʃʒ**." Possibly (according to a Chi-nese linguist from Beijing consulted by John Renner, p.c.) introduced into China by German linguists in the 1950s. Clearly in the IPA tradi-tion of character design, the letter is visually reminiscent of both Iota, suggestive of some kind of close unrounded vowel, a laterally reversed ⟨r⟩, suggesting an apico-alveolar articulation, and the right-tail modification characteristic of the retroflex series of letters. (Typo-graphically, it resembles a laterally reversed ⟨ʃ⟩, but it is in fact set lower, and we have named it to reflect its relationship to Long-Leg Turned Iota.)

Pipe
Visually similar to Capital I in sans serif fonts, but listed with other nonalphabetical symbols; see page 221.

LOWER-CASE J

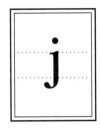

Voiced palatal median approximant.

As a right superscript, indicates a coloration of [j] quality, i.e., modification in the direction of high, front, unrounded (palatal approximant) articulation. Thus [tʲ] would be equivalent to [t̡]: a palatalized [t].

AMERICAN USAGE

No standard use. The following uses have been found in American linguistics literature:

Sometimes used with the same value as the IPA recommends, though [y] is the most frequently found American transcription for the voiced palatal approximant.

Sometimes written for IPA [dʒ] (voiced palato-alveolar affricate), especially in broad transcription of English, though [ǰ] should be regarded as standard for the voiced palato-alveolar affricate.

Boas (1911, 23): voiced dental fricative, IPA [ð].

Boas et al. (1916, 5): voiced palato-alveolar fricative, IPA [ʒ]. (This usage was supplanted by the later recommendations of Herzog et al. (1934) that [ž] be used for [ʒ].)

Sapir (1925, 23): voiced palato-alveolar fricative, IPA [ʒ].

Smalley (1963, 275): voiced alveopalatal stop, IPA [ɟ+].

OTHER USES

Standardly used by Indologists and Dravidianists for voiced palatal or palato-alveolar stops or affricates in languages such as Sanskrit, Hindi, and Tamil. See, e.g., Whitney 1889 (p. 2).

In a rare case of sanctioned ambiguity, *Principles* (p. 13) recommends use of the same symbol for a voiced fricative and a frictionless approximant at the palatal place of articulation "since the two varieties have not been found to exist as separate phonemes in any language." Thus it appears in two positions in pre-1989 IPA consonant charts.

However, the reasoning expressed in *Principles* is now known not to be phonetically justified (see the entry for Curly-Tail J). And by 1976 there was actually agreement in the council of the IPA that the ambiguity should be resolved (*Journal of the International Phonetic Association* 6 (1976), 2–3). Nonetheless, resolution of the ambiguity between the approximant and fricative values for IPA [j] was deferred because the council split on whether to retain [j] as a palatal approximant or to use [y] instead. The 1979 chart leaves the symbol ambiguous. The 1989 revision fixed the denotation as the palatal approximant (adding Curly-Tail J as the fricative).

The disagreement between the IPA and other systems on the use of ⟨y⟩ and ⟨j⟩ is an ongoing problem. *Principles* notes that the "World Orthography" described in *Practical Orthography of African Languages* (International African Institute 1930) differs from the IPA *only* in "that *j* and *y* are taken to have their English consonantal values."

The letter ⟨j⟩ represents a variety of consonants in different orthographies: [ʒ] in French, [x] in Spanish, [dʒ] in English, and, agreeing with its IPA value, [j] in German and the Scandinavian languages (note the Norwegian loanword *fjord* in English).

SOURCE

Roman alphabet, lower case; as used for various Germanic languages. The phonological unit corresponding to ⟨j⟩ is sometimes referred to as "jod" by Germanicists and other linguists.

Hooktop J

American Usage: Proposed by Smalley (1963, 378) for an "alveopalatal" implosive, but this seems to be his term for palatal, for he uses it in all cases where other systems would use "palatal." *Other uses:* The sound in question is reported in Sindhi (Ladefoged 1971 (p. 26)), and in Kadugli, Swahili, Maasai, Nyangi, Ik, Yulu, and Angas (Maddieson 1984 (p. 217)).

Barred J

Proposed by Smalley (1963) for a voiced flat (i.e., not grooved) "alveopalatal" (palato-alveolar) fricative, and listed by Hyman (1975, 241) as a voiced palatal stop, i.e., IPA [ɟ]. The symbol is not in general use. Smalley's use of Barred J is probably supposed to be equivalent to IPA [ʑ]. His use is consistent with a general convention that assigns barred stop symbols (with a superimposed hyphen or short dash through the body of the letter) to represent those fricatives for which the IPA symbols are not used. The resultant symbols have the advantage of being easy to type on an unmodified typewriter. Hyman's use seems to be merely a typographical compromise.

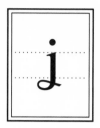

CURLY-TAIL J

IPA USAGE

Voiced palatal median fricative.

AMERICAN USAGE

Not used.

COMMENTS

The IPA's *Principles* states that the symbol ⟨j⟩ could be used for both
the voiced palatal approximant and its corresponding fricative, since
the two were not known to contrast in any language. But it is now
known that some languages have a phonological contrast between the
two sounds. In 1975, the IPA secretary stated in its journal that such a
contrast was found in "Gaelic, some varieties of German and Spanish,
and perhaps Modern Greek," and that some phoneticians were using
[ʝ] for the fricative (*Journal of the International Phonetic Association*
5 (p. 54)); and earlier than that, Hoffman (1963) had reported a voiced
palatal fricative in contrast with [j] in Bura and Margi (Ladefoged
(1968, 28) and (1971, 59–60) confirms this for Margi). Thus a new
symbol is needed not just for representing fine phonetic detail about
degrees of frication, but by virtue of the position of *Principles* that
separate letters should be available for distinct phonological units.
Catford (1977) recognized this need and introduced his own symbol
for the fricative, namely [ʝ] (see entry for Small Capital J). In 1989 the
IPA council at last recognized the lack, and approved the symbol [ʝ].

SOURCE

Roman alphabet lower-case *j*, with a curly-tail modification similar
(but turning in the opposite direction) to the one seen in Curly-Tail C,

[ɕ], which also represents a fricative (though alveolo-palatal rather than pure palatal).

Wedge J

American Usage: Voiced palato-alveolar affricate with central fricative release (IPA [dʒ]).   *Comments:* The recommendations of Herzog et al. (1934, 631), which formalized the use of the wedge diacritic in American transcription, used [ǯ] as the transcription for IPA [dʒ]. The regular analogic pattern of their recommendations was interrupted by the replacement of [ǯ] by [ǰ], presumably as a typographical compromise. As an example, Hoijer (1945, 8) uses a transcription which is otherwise consistent with previous recommendations except in the use of ⟨ǰ⟩ for ⟨ǯ⟩. Cf. also Bloomfield (1933, 129), who uses ⟨ǰ⟩ for IPA [dʒ].   *Source:* Roman alphabet lower-case *j,* with the *haček* ('little hook') or wedge used for certain palato-alveolar consonants in the Czech orthography.

BARRED DOTLESS J

IPA USAGE

Voiced palatal stop.

AMERICAN USAGE

Not generally used.

COMMENTS

As represented by *gy* in the Hungarian word *Magyar* 'Hungarian'.

SOURCE

Typographically, a turned lower-case *f,* but better thought of as a variant of ⟨j⟩, since in English words like *job* a *j* represents a palato-alveolar affricate [dʒ] that is at least somewhat similar to IPA [ɟ], though not identical.

HOOKTOP BARRED DOTLESS J

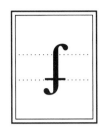

IPA USAGE

Voiced glottalic ingressive (i.e., implosive) palatal stop.

COMMENTS

This symbol was added to the official IPA chart after the 1989 Kiel convention and was retained in the 1993 revision. It had been used occasionally before 1989, e.g., in Ladefoged 1971 (see page 26, where the Sindhi word [bəʄu] 'run' is cited). The sound is not common, but Maddieson 1984 (p. 217) reports its occurrence in several African languages: Angas, Ik, Kadugli, Maasai, Nyangi, Swahili, and Yulu. Greenberg 1970 suggests that languages with implosives tend to have a laryngealized pulmonic egressive palatal approximant [j̰] when they lack the palatal member of the implosive series, but Maddieson 1984 (p. 114) disagrees.

SOURCE

By obvious visual analogy with [ɓ] and [ɗ], the symbols originally established by the IPA for voiced implosives (*Principles* (p. 14) says "ɓ, ɗ, etc.," clearly intending to encourage such analogical invention). Typographically, the symbol comes out looking like a barred Esh (as in Maddieson 1984; see, e.g., pages 112–13), or like Double-Barred Esh in serifed variants of the IPA font (see, e.g., Henton, Ladefoged, and Maddieson 1992 (p. 93)). This may be visually compatible with the rest of the IPA character set, but it is not helpful mnemonically, and in the case of the variant that looks like Double-Barred Esh it is potentially confusing, since that symbol was used by Beach (1938), and recommended (unsuccessfully) to the IPA for adoption, to represent the velaric ingressive palato-alveolar stop [ǂ], and Beach's recommended symbol has been used elsewhere in the literature (see, e.g., Chomsky and Halle 1968 (pp. 319–20)).

Small Capital J

Used by Catford (1977, 120) for a "voiced dorso-palatal fricative."
Catford uses this symbol without remark, though it is not standard. The
IPA has now introduced Curly-Tail J for the voiced palatal fricative.

Fish-Hook R
*Typographically, a turned Small Capital J, but used to repre-
sent an ɾ-sound and listed as a variant of ⟨r⟩; see page 161.*

LOWER-CASE K

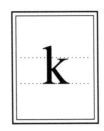

IPA USAGE

Voiceless velar stop.

AMERICAN USAGE

Same as IPA.

COMMENTS

Note [kʰ] for aspirated variant, [k'] for ejective (glottalic egressive) velar stop, [kʲ] for palatalized variant, etc.

Wright 1910 (p. 51) gives [k] as a voiceless "palatal" stop in contrast to [q], a "true velar." What is considered the dividing line between "palatal" and "velar" sounds has apparently changed over time. Cf. also Boas et al. 1916. Presumably the denotations are the same; only the descriptive terminology has changed.

SOURCE

Roman alphabet, lower case.

Crossed K

Used in Meillet and Cohen 1952 (p. xiii) for a voiceless "velar" fricative. A logical extension of the convention for using barred forms of stop symbols for the homorganic fricatives.

Hooktop K

IPA Usage: Approved during the period 1989–93 for a voiceless glottalic ingressive (i.e., implosive) velar stop; approval withdrawn in 1993. *American Usage:* Sometimes used with the IPA value (see, e.g., the reference to Smalley below). *Other uses:* Represents a velar ejective (voiceless glottalic egressive stop, IPA [k']) in the orthographies of some African languages, e.g., Hausa, and thus may sometimes be found in phonetic or quasi-phonetic transcriptions by Africanists, but with a different denotation from the one for which it was temporarily approved by the IPA. *Comments:* Implosives tend, for aerodynamic reasons, to be voiced; but as pointed out in many works on phonetics (Pike 1947 (p. 40); Smalley 1963 (p. 381); Ladefoged 1971 (p. 25); and Catford 1988 (p. 27)), voiceless implosives are easy enough to produce. Pike (1947, 40) notes that some people use a voiceless velar implosive to imitate the "glug-glug" sound of wine being poured from a bottle (with decreasing lip rounding used to make it sound as if the bottle is being emptied; notice that voiced sounds can also be used for the "glug-glug" sound effect). Smalley (1963, 381) diagrams its production and uses Hooktop K to represent it; Catford (1988, 27) gives instructions for producing it (transcribing it "[k'↓]"). Pike notes that although in some cases voiceless implosives might be confused with clicks, i.e., velaric ingressive stops, confusion is precluded in the velar case because velar clicks are articulatorily impossible (see Turned K, below). Voiceless implosives have been attested in some languages, but never velar ones, it seems, so this symbol is not likely ever to be encountered in transcriptions with its former IPA-approved denotation. The most obvious transcription for a voiceless velar implosive under currently approved IPA transcription principles would be [ɠ̊]. *Source:* By obvious visual analogy with [ɓ] and [ɗ], the symbols originally established by the IPA for voiced implosives.

Turned K

IPA Usage: Originally recommended (*Principles,* p. 14) for a velar click, i.e., a velaric ingressive velar stop. However, articulatory studies of how the click consonants are produced have revealed that such a thing is not an articulatory possibility. A click is produced by creating a velar closure simultaneously with a more anterior closure, creating suction between the two by sliding back the velar closure, and then releasing the anterior closure to create the click. The two closures must be separated by at least a centimeter or two, so a velar click is a contradiction in terms (see Ladefoged and Traill 1984 for further phonetic details). Hence the IPA's recommendation was simply a mistake, and the symbol could never be validly used. It was dropped from the IPA chart with the 1979 revision.   *Other uses:* Used in some early work by Dorsey on Ponca (a Siouan language) to represent unaspirated [k], so that ⟨k⟩ could be used for the aspirated [kʰ] (see Boas and Swanton 1911 (p. 881).   *Comments:* Though obsolete for decades, this symbol seems to have taken the fancy of some designers of phonetic typefaces, and appears needlessly in a number of modern phonetic fonts, e.g., the one built into WordPerfect for Windows 6.0 and the LaserIPA font from Linguist's Software.   *Source:* Roman alphabet lower-case *k,* turned (rotated 180°).

Small Capital K

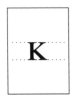

Used by some earlier (pre-1950) Eskimologists, following the orthography proposed for Greenlandic Eskimo by Samuel Kleinschmidt in the 19th century, to represent a voiceless uvular stop. Some works may set this symbol as a capital *k* for convenience, but a small capital seems to have been the original intent. This symbol has now given way almost everywhere to the transcription [q], as proposed by Thalbitzer et al. 1952 for Eskimo and Aleut, and officially sanctioned by the IPA.

Turned Small Capital K

IPA Usage: Not used, but specifically mentioned in *Principles* (p. 19) as having been suggested for use as a "general symbol" for any consonant that has no current IPA symbol. For this reason, the symbol is included in the LaserIPA font marketed by Linguist's Software.

LOWER-CASE L

IPA USAGE

Voiced alveolar lateral approximant.

Used as a right superscript, it is the official IPA diacritic for lateral release sounds. See the chart for IPA diacritics.

AMERICAN USAGE

Same as IPA.

COMMENTS

Takes various diacritics to show phonetic modifications: [l̥] (voiceless), [l̩] (syllabic), [ɫ] (velarized, as in English "dark" postvocalic /l/), [lʲ] (palatalized), [ḷ] (retroflex, in American usage), etc.

Kurath (1939, 138) gives [l̦] as a distinctly "clear *l*" with no velarization at all.

SOURCE

Roman alphabet, lower case.

Tilde L

IPA Usage: Velarized ("dark") voiced alveolar lateral approximant, as in English postvocalic laterals, e.g., in *all.* *American Usage:* Same as IPA. Sometimes found as a substitute for Barred L (the IPA's Belted

L), i.e., a voiceless alveolar lateral fricative. This substitution can lead to ambiguity and is best avoided.

Barred L

American Usage: Voiceless alveolar lateral fricative (IPA [ɬ]). The character is used by Boas et al. (1916, 7) as an alternative to Small Capital L for the voiceless version of [l]. *Comments:* As represented by ⟨ll⟩ in Welsh and in Greenlandic Eskimo. The character is sometimes used with the bar slanted, i.e., ⟨ł⟩, a character used in the Polish orthography for a sound like IPA [w]; see, e.g., Chomsky and Halle 1968 (p. 317). Tilde L is also sometimes substituted. The original form (cf. Boas et al. 1916 (p. 7)), however, is an *l* with a superimposed horizontal dash or hyphen, and it seems best to use it to avoid confusion with these other characters. *Source:* Roman alphabet lower-case *l*, with superimposed hyphen.

BELTED L

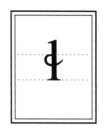

IPA USAGE

Voiceless alveolar lateral fricative.

AMERICAN USAGE

Same as IPA, if used. Barred L is sometimes used instead.

COMMENTS

As represented by ⟨ll⟩ in Welsh and in Greenlandic Eskimo.

SOURCE

Roman alphabet lower-case *l,* with superimposed curved belt.

RIGHT-TAIL L

IPA USAGE

Voiced post-alveolar (retroflex) lateral approximant.

AMERICAN USAGE

Not used. The usual equivalent is [ḷ], using the underdot diacritic of Boas et al. (1916, 10) to indicate retracted articulation.

COMMENTS

The retroflexion diacritic used by the IPA in [ʂ] and [ʐ] is echoed by the rightward-swept elongation of the rightmost vertical stroke of a character in the IPA's special symbols for other retroflex consonants: [ɳ], [ʈ], [ɖ], and [ɽ]. In the interests of terminological consistency, we recognize in this family resemblance an IPA retroflexion indicator, which we call "right tail."

SOURCE

Roman alphabet lower-case *l*, modified with the IPA diacritic for retroflexion.

L-YOGH LIGATURE

IPA USAGE

Voiced alveolar lateral fricative.

AMERICAN USAGE

Same as IPA, if used.

COMMENTS

As represented by ⟨dhl⟩ in Zulu orthography. Found in a number of African languages, e.g., Bura and Margi (Chadic; Ladefoged 1968 (p. 29)) as well as Zulu and Xhosa (Southern Bantu; see *Principles* (pp. 50–51) for Xhosa).

SOURCE

This symbol is in origin a ligature of ⟨l⟩ and ⟨ʒ⟩, though this was not entirely evident from the versions of it in some IPA fonts, including the one used for printing *Principles* itself. The symbol was redesigned in 1989 to look more like a combination of the shapes of its component characters. In *Principles,* its shape was as shown below.

SMALL CAPITAL L

Voiced velar lateral approximant.

Not standard, but where used, mostly same as IPA.

This symbol was approved by the IPA in 1989 after the Kiel convention (*Journal of the International Phonetic Association* 19 (p. 71)), but by then it had been in occasional use for some time. Wells (1982, xvii; volume 3, section 6.5.9) had used it for "a lip-rounded vocoid with close back tongue position and unilateral velar closure" (volume 3, p. 551), and this is one variety of velar lateral approximant (Wells cites Caffee 1940 for the original description of the sound in Southern U.S. English). Wells' choice of symbol may have been influenced by Bloch and Trager 1942 (p. 16), where the symbol is given as the transcription for a "dorsal lateral," or Trager 1964 (p. 22), where it is proposed for a "medio-velar" lateral, suggesting an articulation distinct from the one Wells mentions, one in which the dorsum makes a closure against the median line of the velum but there is no contact at the sides. (Both of these works actually use a capital *l*, but since Trager calls the symbol "small-cap *l*," the intent was presumably to advocate the small capital.)

Boas et al. (1916, 10) recommend that small capital letters be used for the voiceless versions of normally voiced sounds, and hence [ʟ] might sometimes be found representing a voiceless lateral approximant (IPA [l̥]), especially in early 20th-century Amerindianist work.

Roman alphabet, small capital font.

Capital L

American Usage: Not standard, but may be found for a voiceless alveolar lateral. *Other uses:* Among Celticists, used to indicate a nonmutated *l* in, e.g., Carmody 1945. Used for the morphophoneme proposed by Hamp (1951) to represent the triggers of Lenition, an initial consonant mutation in Celtic languages. Cf. also McCloskey 1979 (p. 8–9). *Comments:* The standard transcription for a voiceless [l] would be [l̥] or [ɬ]. Following the recommendation of Boas et al. (1916, 10) that small capital letters be used for the voiceless versions of normally voiced sounds, Pike (1947, 7) and Smalley (1963, 217) both suggest [L] for IPA [l̥]. *Source:* Roman alphabet, upper case.

Reversed Small Capital L

Proposed by Bloch and Trager (1942, 26) for a labial lateral approximant. It is perfectly possible to form such a sound (basically, a [w] with the lips in contact at the median line but slightly apart at the sides), but languages do not seem to exploit this possibility, so this symbol has not been in use and is not likely to see use in the future.

Lambda

American Usage: Voiced alveolar laterally released affricate: IPA [dl]. *Other uses:* Recommended by Boas et al. (1916, 13) for a "dorsal" (i.e., palatal) lateral approximant, presumably IPA [ʎ]. *Source:* Greek alphabet correspondent of ⟨l⟩. Used for [dl] in early work on Eskimo by Jenness, and recommended for standard Americanist use by Herzog et al. (1934, 631). Note that we take IPA [ʎ] to be a Turned Y rather than a laterally reversed lambda.

Crossed Lambda

American Usage: Voiceless alveolar laterally released affricate (IPA [tɬ]). *Comments:* The character is a Greek *lambda* with a superimposed short slash. Invented on analogy with Barred L as the voiceless correspondent of [λ] by Herzog et al. (1934, 631).

Turned Y
Typographically similar to a reversed Lambda, but actually a turned ⟨y⟩, listed as a variant of ⟨y⟩; see page 200.

Turned V
Typographically the same as a small capital version of Greek capital lambda, ⟨Λ⟩, *and also the same as a turned ⟨v⟩, but actually a vowel symbol with a similar use to the less common Small Capital A, hence listed as a crossbarless variant of ⟨ᴀ⟩; see page 18.*

LOWER-CASE M

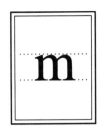

IPA USAGE

Voiced bilabial nasal.

AMERICAN USAGE

Same as IPA.

COMMENTS

Takes various diacritics to show phonetic modifications: [m̥] (voiceless), [m̩] (syllabic), etc.

SOURCE

Roman alphabet, lower case.

MENG

IPA USAGE

Voiced labiodental nasal.

AMERICAN USAGE

When used, same as IPA.

COMMENTS

Labiodental nasals occur in many languages as phonetically conditioned variants of bilabial or other nasals before labiodental fricatives (Spanish *m* before *f*, for example, is usually labiodental, and the same is often true in relaxed English speech). What is extraordinarily rare is for a labiodental nasal to contrast with a bilabial nasal phonologically; indeed, it appears that when this symbol was approved by the IPA, and for a long time afterward, no instance was known. However, a language with such a contrast has since been described: Paulian (1975) reports that the Kukuya dialect known as Teke has [ɱ] contrasting with both [m] and a labiodental fricative.

Catford 1977 (p. 192) uses this symbol for a palatalized [m], but this appears to be a printer's error for [mʲ], i.e., [m] with the IPA's palatalization diacritic Left Hook.

SOURCE

Roman alphabet, lower-case, with the same left-facing tail modification of the bottom of the rightmost upright that is seen in Eng ⟨ŋ⟩. We have taken the liberty of coining the name *Meng* for this symbol because of its Eng-like shape; but note that while the left-facing tail is associated with velar articulation in ⟨ŋ⟩ and ⟨g⟩, it does not mean anything of that sort here.

H-M Ligature

IPA Usage: Not used, but mentioned in *Principles* (p. 19) as having been suggested as a symbol for a voiceless bilabial nasal stop, IPA [m̥].   *Comments:* Using a ligature created by combining ⟨h⟩ and ⟨m⟩ is a clever idea for transcribing [m̥]; note that when *Principles* gives a transcription for a language that has voiceless bilabial nasals (Burmese, p. 40), it does not use [m̥], but rather, for readability and avoidance of diacritics, [hm] (exactly the letter sequence that is used in the orthography of English for the thoughtful interjection "hmm," IPA [m̥mː] = [hmm]). But clever or not, the symbol was never given official sanction and is not in the current IPA chart. It is, however, included in the LaserIPA font from Linguist's Software.   *Source:* Roman alphabet, lower case; combination of the shapes of ⟨h⟩ and ⟨m⟩.

TURNED M

IPA USAGE

Cardinal Vowel No. 16: close back unrounded. The secondary cardinal vowel corresponding to Cardinal 8.

AMERICAN USAGE

Standardly the same as IPA, if used; but various alternatives, including [ï] and [ɨ], are found.

COMMENTS

As represented by ⟨ı⟩ in Turkish orthography. The Japanese vowel transliterated as ⟨u⟩ is similar to this, having virtually no rounding.

Halle and Clements (1983, 29) assert that "ɯ = ɨ," but this is definitely not the case under the IPA's definitions, or in standard American. It can only be regarded as a defensible claim under the analysis of vowels in the Chomsky and Halle tradition, where all vowels are treated phonologically as either front or back ([−back] or [+back]).

In the seven-volume compendious grammar of French by Damourette and Pichon (1911–27), Turned M is used nonstandardly to represent [u] (see, e.g., volume 1, section 139, page 168). This was apparently necessitated by some other changes that were part of an attempt to follow French orthography more closely than the IPA does: to represent IPA [ʒ] they use ⟨j⟩ (as in *je* 'I'); to represent IPA [j] they use ⟨y⟩ (as in *yeux* 'eyes'); and to represent IPA [y] they use ⟨u⟩ (as in *tu* 'you (sing)'); so some other letter had to be found for IPA [u] (as in *ou* 'or'), and they made the fairly reasonable decision to use Turned M (which is associated with all the right phonetic features except for rounding).

Roman alphabet lower-case *m,* turned (rotated 180°). Visually suggestive of two *u*'s, or of *w,* and thus hinting at high back tongue position.
The character was used as a vowel symbol (with the value IPA [u]) in
Isaac Pitman's 1845 phonotypic alphabet (cf. Pitman and St. John
1969 (p. 82)).

LONG-LEG TURNED M

щ

IPA USAGE

Approved in 1976 (*Journal of the International Phonetic Association* 6 (p. 3)) for a voiced velar median approximant, the glide corresponding to [ɯ]. The symbol resolves the ambiguity of [ɣ], which has only its fricative value now.

AMERICAN USAGE

Not in use, but recommended by Trager (1964, 16) for a back unrounded semivowel.

COMMENTS

Despite the differing terminology above, the 1979 IPA system and Trager's 1964 system are in agreement. The sound in question can be described either as a semivowel (glide) with the properties "high," "back," and "unrounded," or as a median approximant consonant with velar place of articulation. The sound can be regarded as an unrounded [w].

This symbol has not seen much use. Ladefoged (1968, 26) suggests that Bini has such a sound, but transcribes it as [ɣ˔]. Likewise, Maddieson (1984) lists five languages (Kanakuru, Aranda, Adzera, Wiyot, and Cofan) claimed to have the segment in question, but transcribes it [ɣ].

SOURCE

Invention, possibly by Trager, involving the addition of a tail to the IPA's ⟨ɯ⟩, to suggest on the one hand ⟨ɯ⟩ and on the other hand the IPA's ⟨ɥ⟩. Trager calls the symbol "double-turned *h*."

Small Capital M

Recommended by a working group on the phonetic representation of disordered speech for a voiced linguo-labial nasal stop (see PRDS Group 1983; Ball 1987). Linguo-labial consonants, including the linguo-labial nasal, do occur in nonpathological speech in some languages (see Maddieson 1987), but they are extremely rare. The IPA ignored the plea of Ball (1987) to adopt the PRDS Group's policy (which introduces six new letters), declining to recognize a whole suite of new symbols for a class of sounds that are so seldom encountered in ordinary speech. The IPA chose instead to introduce the Subscript Seagull diacritic, which is used below alveolar consonant symbols.

Capital M

Following the recommendation of Boas et al. (1916, 10) that small capital letters be used for the voiceless versions of normally voiced sounds, Pike (1947, 7) and Smalley (1963, 192) both suggest [M] for a voiceless bilabial nasal, i.e., IPA [m̥].

Turned W
Somewhat similar to ⟨ᴍ⟩ or ⟨M⟩, but actually a turned ⟨w⟩, listed as a variant of ⟨w⟩; see page 193.

LOWER-CASE N

Voiced dental or alveolar nasal. [n̪] indicates definitely dental; [n] may be either if no contrast is to be indicated, but will be taken to be alveolar as a default assumption.

Used as a right superscript, it is the official IPA diacritic for nasal release sounds. See the chart for IPA diacritics.

AMERICAN USAGE

Same as IPA.

COMMENTS

Takes various diacritics to show phonetic modifications: [n̥] (voiceless), [n̩] (syllabic), [n̪] (dental), etc. Note that some diacritics indicate more radical differences in denotation: [ñ] is a common transcription for an alveopalatal or palatal nasal stop, [ń] is used in the orthography of Polish for a palatal nasal stop, IPA [ɲ].

SOURCE

Roman alphabet, lower case.

Acute-Accent N

Suggested by Trager (1964, 22) for a prepalatal (i.e., fronted palatal) nasal. Following the orthography of some Slavic languages (e.g.,

Polish), [ń] might be found as a transcription for the palatal nasal, IPA [ɲ].

Front-Bar N

Proposed by Trager (1964, 22) for a dental nasal, IPA [n̪] or American [n̠].

Pi

Proposed by Laver (1994, 215) for a voiced labiodental oral stop, such as will sometimes be heard in a casual pronunciation of British English *head first:* in Laver's symbolization, [hɛπfɜst] is sometimes heard instead of [hɛdfɜst] (we correct an apparent typographical error: Laver has [ə] for [ɛ]). For the voiceless labiodental stop, Laver suggests [π̥]. Other symbols for these sounds have been in use among Africanists for some time (see D-B Ligature and Q-P Ligature), so it is not clear why Laver thought it appropriate to propose this new invention. There appear to be no attested cases of languages making use of labiodental stops in contrast with bilabial ones, so the symbol is not likely to see a great deal of use. Greek alphabet, lower case. Pi stands for IPA [p] in modern Greek, not a labiodental.

Long-Leg N

IPA Usage: Proposed in *Principles* (p. 14) for representing a syllabic alveolar nasal, particularly as in Japanese, or as a digraph for nasal vowels (p. 16). IPA approval was withdrawn in 1976 (*Journal of the International Phonetic Association* 6 (p. 3)) because the symbol is purely phonological, being realized in Japanese by a number of different sounds. The symbol ⟨n̩⟩ is normally used for a syllabic [n].

Tilde N

American Usage: Voiced palato-alveolar or palatal nasal. Gleason, Pike, and Smalley use ⟨ñ⟩ for a palato-alveolar nasal ("alveopalatal" in their terms), using ⟨ŋ⟩ (Gleason) or ⟨ṇ⟩ (Smalley) for a true palatal one. Used throughout Boas 1911 and recommended by Boas et al. (1916) as a typographical compromise for the voiced velar nasal. Eng (⟨ŋ⟩) is the standard symbol. *Source:* Roman alphabet lower-case *n,* with tilde (as in Spanish orthography).

LEFT-HOOK N

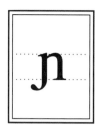

IPA USAGE

Voiced palatal nasal.

AMERICAN USAGE

Same as IPA, if used, but various alternatives are commonly employed: ⟨ŋ̟⟩ (Gleason 1955), ⟨ŋ̡⟩ (Smalley 1963), and very commonly ⟨ñ⟩.

COMMENTS

Illustrated by the sound represented as *gn* in French and Italian, *ñ* in Spanish, etc.

SOURCE

Roman alphabet lower-case *n,* modified with the leftward-facing tail or hook used by the IPA for symbols denoting palatal or palatalized sounds.

IPA USAGE

Voiced velar nasal.

AMERICAN USAGE

Same as IPA.

COMMENTS

Illustrated by the sound represented as *ng* in the English word *thing* and *n* in the word *think*.

SOURCE

Roman alphabet lower-case *n,* modified with a tail reminiscent of the tail of a ⟨g⟩. The symbol is known as either "eng" or "angma" and occurred in this form with this value in Isaac Pitman's 1845 phonotypic alphabet (cf. Pitman and St. John 1969 (p. 82)). Albright (1958, 11) suggests that it goes back to Holder in 1669. Brugmann (1904, 1) uses a similar symbol.

Eta

The Greek alphabet character *eta* is used by some printers as a substitute for ⟨ŋ⟩, especially in italic fonts. The typesetter of *American Anthropologist* unfortunately did this in Herzog et al. 1934 (pp. 630–31).

We assume that their recommendation is that Eng and not Eta is to be used for the velar nasal. A symbol like [η] or [ŋ] has been used by Danish Eskimologists for a uvular nasal (IPA [ɴ]). In Modern Greek, Eta represents the vowel [i].

RIGHT-TAIL N

IPA USAGE

Voiced retroflex (i.e., apico-postalveolar) nasal.

AMERICAN USAGE

Not used.

COMMENTS

Illustrated by the sound represented ⟨ण⟩ in Hindi, Marathi, etc. American and Indological practice uses [ṇ] for this sound.

The retroflexion diacritic used by the IPA in [ṣ] and [z̙] is echoed by the rightward-swept elongation of the rightmost vertical stroke of a character in the IPA's special symbols for other retroflex consonants: [ʈ], [ɖ], [ɭ], and [ɽ]. In the interests of terminological consistency, we recognize in this family resemblance an IPA retroflexion indicator, which we call "right tail."

SOURCE

Roman alphabet *n,* modified with the IPA diacritic for retroflexion.

SMALL CAPITAL N

IPA USAGE

Voiced uvular nasal.

AMERICAN USAGE

Same as IPA, if used, but usually not found, [ŋ] often being used instead.

Boas et al. (1916, 10) recommend that small capital letters be used for the voiceless versions of normally voiced sounds and hence [N] could be found for a voiceless alveolar nasal (IPA [n̥]).

COMMENTS

Found according to *Principles* (p. 36) in Persian (Farsi), as an allophone of /n/ before /q/. It occurs in Central West Greenlandic Inuit as an allophone of /q/ under enclitic sandhi and, geminated, as a reflex of earlier /nʀ/ or /mʀ/ (the orthographic representation of [NN] being *rng*); see Fortescue 1984 (p. 334). (Fortescue uses ⟨N⟩ for the IPA symbol ⟨ɴ⟩.)

Following the terminology of Boas et al. (1916, 4), Smalley (1963) does not recognize uvular consonants as such, but uses the term "backed velar" instead. For the backed velar nasal, Smalley uses ⟨ŋ⟩.

SOURCE

Roman alphabet, small capital font.

Capital N

American Usage: Following the recommendation of Boas et al. (1916, 10) that small capital letters be used for the voiceless versions of normally voiced sounds, Pike (1947, 7) and Smalley (1963, 192) both suggest [N] for IPA [n̥]. *Other uses:* Used by Eskimologists as a substitute for ⟨ŋ⟩; see, e.g., Fortescue 1984. Some phonemic representations for languages with retroflex consonants use capital letters for them; thus, e.g., the ⟨N⟩ used in Fairbanks and Misra (1966) denotes IPA [ɳ]. Capital N has other uses in phonology. It is found in lexical and phonological representations representing a nasal "archiphoneme," i.e., to denote a segment that is a nasal stop unspecified for place of articulation (and realized phonetically in various ways depending on the properties of adjacent segments). Thus the lexical representation of English *think* might be given as /θiNk/. Among Celticists, used to indicate a nonmutated [n] (cf. Carmody 1945). Used for the morphophoneme proposed by Hamp (1951) to represent the triggers of the initial consonant mutation Nasalization in Celtic languages. Cf. also McCloskey 1979 (pp. 8–9).

LOWER-CASE O

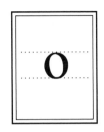

Cardinal Vowel No. 7: close-mid back rounded.

AMERICAN USAGE

Same as IPA.

COMMENTS

As in French *beau,* IPA [bo]. The English vowel in *toe* is generally diphthongal, varying between [ow] and [əʊ], but standardly represented as [oʊ] in broad transcription.

SOURCE

Roman alphabet, lower case.

Overdot O

Not in general use. Following the recommendations of Boas et al. (1916, 10) for the use of an overdot as a diacritic for central vowels, used by Bloch and Trager (1942, 22) for a "higher-mid" rounded central vowel. Trager (1964, 16) suggests [ɵ] as an alternative. The equivalent IPA transcription is [θ], [θ̞], or [ɵ˕].

Umlaut O

IPA Usage: According to *Principles* (p. 16), a rounded close-mid central vowel (between [ø] and [o]); equivalent to [ɵ]. The current interpretation of the umlaut diacritic makes it a central*ized* rounded close-mid back vowel, between [o] and [ɵ]. *American Usage:* According to the widely followed recommendation of Boas et al. (1916, 9) on the use of the umlaut with vowel symbols, [ö] would be a rounded higher-mid front vowel, i.e., a vowel with all of the properties of [o] but front instead of back. The IPA transcription would be [ø]. Cf. Bloch and Trager 1942 (p. 22) and Trager 1964 (p. 16). *Other uses:* The symbol is used in the orthographies for a number of Germanic languages with essentially its American value. *Comments:* The result of the change in the IPA's interpretation of the umlaut and its common use with a different sense in American practice is a rather confusing situation in which [ö] may denote a centralized back vowel (official IPA), a central vowel (*Principles*), or a front vowel (e.g., Bloch and Trager).

Polish-Hook O

American Usage: Boas et al. (1916, 8) recommend the use of a centered subscript rightward hook as a nasalization diacritic. Sometimes used instead of the IPA's tilde diacritic, as by Smalley (1963, 333). *Other uses:* Used by some editors of Old English texts (e.g., Bright (1935) and Sweet (1882)) to distinguish orthographic *o*'s (IPA [ɔ]) which developed from [a]. Does not occur in the original manuscripts (Moore and Knott 1955 (p. 33)). Used for Old Norse to represent IPA [ɔ], which developed from [a] by *u*-mutation (Prokosch 1939 (p. 110)).

Source: The symbol is roman alphabet lower-case *o* with the hook used in Polish orthography to mark nasal vowels.

Reversed Polish-Hook O

IPA Usage: Not in general use or included in the IPA chart, but specifically mentioned in the "Other letters" section of *Principles* (p. 14) as a symbol for a labialized [z] or [ð], i.e., what would in current IPA be transcribed [zʷ] or [ðʷ]. *Comments:* Intended as a voiced counterpart of Sigma. Though never actually included in the IPA chart, this symbol did get included in the LaserIPA font from Linguist's Software. *Source:* Roman alphabet, lower-case *o* (or perhaps Greek alphabet, lower-case *sigma*) modified with a reversed Polish hook.

Sigma

IPA Usage: Not in general use or included in the IPA chart, but specifically mentioned in the "Other letters" section of *Principles* (p. 14) as a symbol for a labialized [s] or [θ], i.e., what would in current IPA be transcribed [sʷ] or [θʷ]. *Other uses:* In much recent (post-1977) metrical and prosodic phonology, Sigma is now widely used as a variable over syllables or as the label of the root node of the tree representation for a syllable. This, however, is not a phonetic use. *Comments:* Since the phonetic value of Greek *sigma* is [s] and the ⟨o⟩-like shape suggests rounding, the symbol is cleverly iconic. But although Doke (1926b) used it (see page 291, footnote 4), it did not receive official sanction and was never included in the IPA's chart. However, because of its mention in *Principles,* it is included in the LaserIPA font from Linguist's Software. *Source:* Greek alphabet, lower case.

Capital O

American Usage: Pike and Smalley both suggest the use of capital letters for voiceless vowels; thus the transcription [O] might be used for IPA [o̥]. *Other uses:* In Chomsky and Halle 1968 (chapters 2–4), Capital O is used to represent informally the vocalic nucleus that is realized as [ɔ] when lax and [ow] when tense. Used in Crothers 1978 (p. 137) for a mid back rounded vowel (Bloch and Trager's "mean-mid" vowel [ʊ]).

Female Sign

Proposed by Trager (1964, 22) for a voiced pharyngeal stop. Pharyngeal plosives had not in fact been attested when Trager was writing, but they have since been described in certain Hebrew and Arabic speakers' enunciations of what are normally pharyngeal fricatives (Laufer and Condax 1981). However, Laufer (1991) argues that it is phonetically impossible for such a plosive to be voiced (the IPA symbol Barred Glottal Stop is reserved for representing pharyngeal plosives without specification for voicing in the 1993 IPA chart), so Trager's suggestion was destined never to be adopted.

Uncrossed Female Sign

Proposed by Trager (1964, 22) for a voiceless pharyngeal stop. Voiceless pharyngeal plosives are attested in certain Hebrew and Arabic dialects (see previous entry), but Trager's suggestion was not the one adopted by the IPA; the 1993 IPA chart shows Barred Glottal Stop as the symbol for a pharyngeal plosive.

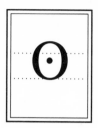

BULLSEYE

IPA USAGE

Bilabial click, i.e., velaric ingressive stop with bilabial place of articulation for the front closure.

AMERICAN USAGE

Same as IPA.

COMMENTS

This sound is not mentioned in *Principles*, but the symbol was approved by the IPA in 1976 (*Journal of the International Phonetic Association* 6 (p. 2)). A bilabial velaric ingressive stop is essentially a kiss. The sound occurs as a consonant in a number of southern Khoisan languages, though not in any other language family. Doke (1926b, 126) denied the existence of such segments, defining clicks solely in terms of lingual (i.e., coronal) articulation, and asserting that the sounds just mentioned were labiovelar plosives [k͡p]. But current phonetic research (see Laver 1994 (pp. 173–74) for a useful introduction and some references) accepts the existence of the bilabial click, distinct from the voiceless bilabial plosive [p], the voiceless labiovelar plosive [k͡p], and the voiceless implosive [ɓ̥].

All clicks are double articulations. Recent research on their detailed phonetic description (see, e.g., Ladefoged and Traill 1984) has introduced a practice of transcribing all of them with digraphs. (Indeed, given that clicks very often have following "accompaniments" such as aspiration, not discussed here, quite often it will be a trigraph that is used.) These composite symbols are constructed from a click symbol, now construed as the symbol for the characteristic front closure of the click, and an additional preceding velar or uvular consonant symbol, linked to it with a tie bar, to indicate the superimposed glottis and velum states and the articulatory character of the back closure. Thus the click symbols never occur alone in the transcriptions seen in recent work. Suppose ⟨ξ⟩ were the symbol for a given type of click (or rather, for its front closure). Then [g͡ξ] would be the transcription for a voiced click with ξ articulation, [ŋ͡ξ] would be used to denote a voiced nasal ξ-type click, and so on. The voicelessness and lack of nasality of a plain voiceless oral click with front closure of ξ type would be indicated by [k͡ξ].

SOURCE

Attributed by Doke (1926b, 126) to W. H. I. Bleek (no reference cited). Introduced into the IPA chart in the 1979 revised version. The symbol has hitherto mostly been set as a circle ⟨○⟩ with a dot in the center (see, e.g., Laver 1994 (pp. 174–75)), but the latest (1993) IPA chart has graduations of shape in the circular part indicating that it is officially the capital letter ⟨O⟩. This is in keeping with the IPA tradition of making symbols typographically harmonious with a Times Roman type font wherever possible.

BARRED O

Rounded close-mid central vowel; intermediate between [ø] and [o].

AMERICAN USAGE

Not used. Following the recommendation of Boas et al. (1916, 10) on the use of the overdot diacritic, [ȯ] would be a central round vowel intermediate between [o] and [ö]. Gleason (1955, 2), Pike (1947, 5), and Halle and Clements (1983, 31) use ⟨ö⟩ for IPA [ø], and offer no symbol for a rounded mid central vowel.

COMMENTS

As in Swedish *dum,* according to *Principles* (p. 9) which also sanctions transcribing [ө] as [ö] (though see the entry for ⟨ö⟩).

SOURCE

Roman alphabet lower-case *o,* modified by superimposed hyphen. The character occurs as a vowel symbol (with the value IPA [ɔ]) in Isaac Pitman's 1845 phonotypic alphabet (cf. Pitman and St. John 1969 (p. 82)).

THETA

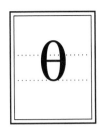

IPA USAGE

Voiceless interdental median fricative.

AMERICAN USAGE

Same as IPA (but see comments about script *theta* below).

COMMENTS

It is very important to distinguish ⟨θ⟩ from ⟨ɵ⟩ (Barred O) if the latter is used.

It is also important to distinguish ⟨θ⟩ from the rarely found script version of the letter, ⟨ϑ⟩. Boas et al. (1916, 5) proposed that script *theta* should be used for voiced interdental fricatives, IPA [ð], and very occasionally this may be found in Americanist literature (see, e.g., Spier 1946 (p. 17)). However, ⟨ð⟩ has since become standard among Americanists as it has among almost all linguists.

SOURCE

Greek alphabet, as printed. *Principles* (p. 2) explicitly rejects the script form ⟨ϑ⟩ which, according to the *Chicago Manual of Style,* Fourteenth Edition (p. 350), is "usually used in mathematical formulas" and "should not be combined with other fonts." *Theta* represents IPA [θ] in Modern Greek.

SLASHED O

Cardinal Vowel No. 10: close-mid front rounded. The secondary cardinal vowel corresponding to Cardinal 2.

AMERICAN USAGE

Same as IPA, if used. But Gleason (1955, 2), Pike (1947, 5), and Halle and Clements (1983, 31), for example, use ⟨ö⟩ instead.

COMMENTS

Illustrated by French *peu* and German *schön*.

This symbol should be carefully distinguished from Phi and Null Sign, though not all typesetters have appreciated this: in Quirk and Wrenn 1957 (p. 122), [ø] is set as ⟨φ⟩, and in Ingram 1976 (p. xvi), [ɸ] is set as [ø]; these occurrences should be regarded as typesetting and editing errors.

SOURCE

Roman alphabet lower-case *o,* with superimposed oblique stroke; as used in Danish orthography.

Null Sign

This symbol has no phonetic value, but is used by phonologists to notate a zero morpheme, or to indicate nothing—e.g., to show the effect of a deletion, or to represent epenthesis rules as replacement of nothing by some specified segment. Dinnsen (1974, 43) uses the slightly different null set symbol ⟨∅⟩ as the notation for a phonological segment "specified minus for all features" and thus not endowed with any phonetic properties, and argues that this null segment nonetheless plays a role in the phonology of some languages.

Mentioning the null sign here allows us to stress that it is distinct from all four of the following visually rather similar characters: Phi (⟨ɸ⟩), Barred O (⟨ɵ⟩), Slashed O (⟨ø⟩), and Theta (⟨θ⟩). Typesetting errors in connection with these symbols are unfortunately fairly common.

IPA USAGE

Voiceless bilabial fricative.

AMERICAN USAGE

Same as IPA.

COMMENTS

The *f* of the usual romanization of Japanese represents [ɸ]. In some languages, e.g., Ewe (West Africa), [ɸ] and [f] contrast.

The typographical variant symbol ⟨φ⟩ and the upper-case correspondent ⟨Φ⟩ are not used in transcription; the ⟨Φ⟩ found in Hughes and Trudgill 1979 (p. ix) is an error. The symbol ⟨ɸ⟩ should also be carefully distinguished from ⟨ø⟩ and ⟨Ø⟩; Ingram 1976 (p. xvi) has [ø] as an error for ⟨ɸ⟩, and Quirk and Wrenn 1957 (p. 122) has the converse error, using a variety of Phi where [ø] is intended.

SOURCE

Greek alphabet, lower case.

O-E LIGATURE

IPA USAGE

Cardinal Vowel No. 11: open-mid front rounded. The secondary cardinal vowel corresponding to Cardinal 3.

AMERICAN USAGE

Same as IPA, if used (as it is, e.g., by Smalley). But Pike, Halle and Clements, and others use ⟨ɔ⟩ instead.

COMMENTS

Illustrated by the vowel sounds in French *œuf* (short [œ]) and *veuve* (long [œ:]), and by German *zwölf.*

SOURCE

Ligature of *o* and *e,* as used in French orthography.

SMALL CAPITAL
O-E LIGATURE

IPA USAGE

Approved in 1976 for Cardinal Vowel No. 12: open front rounded. The secondary cardinal vowel corresponding to Cardinal 4.

AMERICAN USAGE

Not in use, but proposed by Trager (1964, 16) for a mid front rounded vowel. The transcription in the Bloch and Trager system (1942) would be [ö].

COMMENTS

The IPA initially provided no symbol for an open front rounded vowel, "since this sound has not as yet been found to occur in any language as a phoneme separate from *æ*" (*Principles,* 6), but the 1979 revision added this symbol.

SOURCE

Ligature of small capitals *o* and *e. Journal of the International Phonetic Association* 6 ((1976), 54) attributes the symbol to the text accompanying Daniel Jones's 1956 recording of the cardinal vowels.

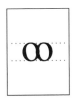

Double-O Ligature

Created by the 17th-century Massachusetts missionary John Eliot as a notation for a mid to high back rounded vowel in certain Algonquian languages of the Northeastern United States. The vowel in question tends to have a phonetic value similar to the one that the sequence ⟨ou⟩ orthographically represents in French, and in some manuscripts by French missionaries, ⟨ou⟩ is used instead; in others, an *omicron-upsilon* digraph from Byzantine Greek manuscripts is used for this purpose. Occasionally modern Algonquianists still use the symbol ⟨ꝏ⟩ when citing in print data from 17th-century manuscript sources. Substitutes and typographical compromises, like double *o* or double zero or ⟨∞⟩ (the mathematical symbol for infinity), are also found, and some Algonquianists have employed the symbol Eight, ⟨8⟩, for the same purpose. Not strictly a phonetic symbol or even a phonological one, but rather an orthographic one.

Eight

A report by a working group of British clinical phoneticians in 1983 (PRDS Group 1983; see also Ball 1987) proposed a set of conventions according to which Eight is used, in transcribing disordered speech, to represent a voiced linguolabial fricative (current IPA [ð̼] or [z̼]). The IPA declined to adopt Ball's suggestion and incorporate the PRDS Group proposals, apparently to avoid adding a suite of six new symbols to represent sounds that are extremely rare, and added the Subscript Seagull diacritic instead. Eight has been used occasionally by Algonquianists to represent in print a grapheme that appeared in early manuscript sources on Algonquian languages. French missionary linguists in the 17th century used a Byzantine Greek *omicron-upsilon* digraph (composed by writing ⟨υ⟩ above ⟨o⟩ as a notation for a mid to high back rounded vowel (similar to the one that the sequence ⟨ou⟩ orthographically represents in French; in some manuscripts, ⟨ou⟩ is used instead). The 17th-century Massachusetts missionary John Eliot created the symbol Double-O Ligature, ⟨ꝏ⟩, for the same or a similar purpose. The typographically more accessible ⟨8⟩ has been used as a substitute for both of these in work by modern Algonquianists; see, e.g., Cowan 1979 and the book by Gordon M. Day that Cowan reviews. Goddard and Bragdon (1988) use ⟨8⟩ quasi-phonetically in an idealized close-to-phonemic orthography for Massachusetts, but in general this is not strictly a phonetic or phonological usage, but rather an orthographic one.

OPEN O

IPA USAGE

Cardinal Vowel No. 6: open-mid back rounded.

AMERICAN USAGE

Same as IPA, following the recommendations of Boas et al. (1916, 2). Occasionally used (e.g., Pike 1947 (p. 5)) as a low (or upper-low) back rounded vowel, an alternative to IPA [ɒ].

COMMENTS

Illustrated by the vowel sound of the Scottish English pronunciation of *hot,* German *Sonne,* and (to a fair approximation) represented by *o* before *r* in French and most varieties of English (French *porte, fort;* English *corn*); cf. also the pronunciation of *caught* in educated Southern British English ("received pronunciation" or RP, in the terminology of Daniel Jones (see Jones 1918)).

SOURCE

Roman alphabet lower-case *o,* modified. Typographically, lower-case *c* turned (rotated 180°). The character appears in this form and with this value in Henry Sweet's *A Handbook of Phonetics* (1877).

Overdot Open O

Following the recommendations of Boas et al. (1916, 10) on the use of the overdot diacritic, used for a lower-mid central rounded vowel by Bloch and Trager (1942, 22). See also Trager 1964 (p. 16). Trager suggests [œ] as an alternative. The IPA transcription for an open-mid central rounded vowel is [ɞ].

Umlaut Open O

IPA Usage: According to *Principles* (p. 16), an open-mid rounded central vowel, between Cardinals 6 and 3, similar to a rounded [ɐ], though the current interpretation of the umlaut diacritic makes it a central*ized* lower-mid rounded back vowel, between [ɔ] and [ɒ]. *American Usage:* According to the widely followed recommendation of Boas et al. (1916, 9) on the use of the umlaut with vowel symbols, [ɔ̈] would represent a rounded lower-mid or low front vowel, i.e., a vowel with all of the properties of [ɔ] but front instead of back. The IPA transcription would be [œ]. Cf. Bloch and Trager 1942 (p. 22) where it is given as an alternative to [œ], Trager 1964 (p. 16), and Halle and Clements 1983 (p. 31). Pike (1947, 5), who uses [ɔ] as a "close" (i.e., upper-) low back vowel correspondingly uses [ɔ̈] as a close low front vowel, IPA [œ]. *Comments:* The result of the change in the IPA's interpretation of the umlaut and its common use with a different sense in American practice is a rather confusing situation in which [ɔ̈] may denote a centralized back vowel (official IPA), a central vowel (*Principles*), or a front vowel (e.g., Trager).

Barred Open O

Proposed by Trager (1964, 16) for a lower-mid central rounded vowel, as an alternative to the [ɔ] of Bloch and Trager 1942 (p. 22). The IPA equivalent is [ɞ]. The character is Open O with superimposed hyphen (as in other symbols for central vowels, e.g., ⟨ɨ⟩, ⟨ʉ⟩, and ⟨ɵ⟩).

Right-Hook Open O

IPA Usage: Recommended in *Principles* (p. 14) for a vowel with the quality of [ɔ] (i.e., Cardinal 6, open-mid back rounded) with rhotacization (*r*-coloration). Approval of the right-hook diacritic was withdrawn in 1976 (*Journal of the International Phonetic Association* 6 (p. 3)) in favor of a digraph such as [ɔɹ] or [ɔʲ]. *American Usage:* Not used. The rightward hook used by the IPA for indicating rhotacization should not be confused with the centered "Polish hook"; for example, [ą] is used in Polish orthography and Americanist (e.g., Smalley 1963 (p. 333)) transcription for nasalized vowels.

Open O-E Ligature

Suggested by Trager (1964, 16), departing from Bloch and Trager 1942 (p. 22), for a lower-mid front rounded vowel. The Bloch and Trager symbol for a low front rounded vowel is ⟨ö⟩ (1942, 22), and

Trager (1964, 16) suggests this or ⟨ʌ⟩. Adopted by Chomsky and Halle (1968, 191–92) to represent the underlying low front rounded vowel that they postulate for English. Under Chomsky and Halle's analysis, the abstract segment represented by this symbol undergoes several rules shifting vowel quality and adding glides, and emerges phonetically as the diphthong written [ɔy] by Chomsky and Halle (IPA [ɔɪ]). The IPA's *Principles* provides no symbol for an open front rounded vowel, "since this sound has not as yet been found to occur in any language as a phoneme separate from œ" (p. 6), but Small Capital O-E Ligature, ⟨ɶ⟩, was approved for such a vowel in 1976 (*Journal of the International Phonetic Association* 6 (p. 2)).

Omega

American Usage: Proposed by Bloch and Trager (1942, 16) following Boas et al. (1916, 10) for a higher-low back rounded vowel, between IPA [ɔ] and [ɒ]. *Other uses:* Used by Wells (1982, xvii) for an un-rounded [ʊ]: semi-high back unrounded. *Comments:* Not to be con-fused with ⟨w⟩, ⟨ɯ⟩, or ⟨ɷ⟩. The IPA transcription corresponding to Bloch and Trager's [ω] is [ɔ̜] or [ɒ̝]. *Source:* Greek alphabet, lower case.

Overdot Omega

Following the recommendation of Boas et al. (1916, 10) for the use of the overdot diacritic for central vowels, used by Bloch and Trager (1942, 22) for a higher-low central rounded vowel—the same height as IPA [æ], but central and rounded. Trager (1964, 16) suggests [ɷ] as an alternative. A suitable *Principles*-type transcription for Bloch and Trager's [ɷ̈] is [ɞ̈]). The current IPA transcription would be [ɞ].

Umlaut Omega

According to the widely followed recommendation of Boas et al. (1916, 9) on the use of the umlaut with vowel symbols, if [ɷ] represents a higher-low back rounded vowel, [ɷ̈] would represent a rounded higher-low front vowel, i.e., a vowel with all of the properties of [ɷ] but front instead of back. Cf. Bloch and Trager 1942 (p. 22). Not in general use. Not to be confused with ⟨w⟩, ⟨ɯ⟩ or, ⟨ɷ⟩. A suitable IPA transcription corresponding to Block and Trager's [ɷ̈] is [ɶ]). Trager (1964, 16) suggests [ɶ] as an alternative. Note that front rounded vowels lower than IPA [œ] are essentially unattested.

Inverted Omega

Proposed by Trager (1964, 16) for a higher-low central rounded vowel—the same height as IPA [æ] but central and rounded. An alternative to the [ɷ̈] of Bloch and Trager 1942 (p. 22). A Trager suggestion that never caught on. A suitable equivalent IPA transcription is [ɞ]).

Closed Omega

IPA Usage: Formerly approved for a vowel between Cardinal 7 and Cardinal 8; approval withdrawn in 1989. *Comments:* This symbol was common in IPA transcriptions of English for many years, representing the vowel usually found in the Southern British English words *look, put, full,* and *good* (which in Northern British English occurs also in a large class of other words, including *mud, blood, guts, luck,* and *muck,* where Southern British has [ʌ]). The IPA had always sanctioned the use of [ɷ] interchangeably with [ʊ] (and also [ɪ] interchangeably with [ɪ] in the front vowels), but Americans had never used [ɷ], and in 1989 the decision was made to withdraw its approval, leaving [ʊ] as the official symbol for this vowel and bringing IPA usage closer to American usage. *Source:* Used as a vowel symbol (but with the value IPA [o]) in Isaac Pitman's 1845 phonotypic alphabet (cf. Pitman and St. John 1969 (p. 82)), where it is the lower-case print form of a closed script *w.*

Small Capital Omega

Proposed by Bloch and Trager (1942, 22; see also Trager 1964 (p. 16)) for a mid back rounded vowel ("mean-mid" in Bloch and Trager's terms, i.e., between the height of Cardinals 6 and 7, IPA [ɔ] and [o]). The IPA transcription for such a vowel would be [o̞] or [ɔ̝]. A large capital *omega* is used by some Indo-Europeanists for an *o*-coloring laryngeal (see, e.g., Hamp 1965a (p. 123, note 3)).

Overdot Small Capital Omega

Following the recommendations of Boas et al. (1916, 10) on the use of the overdot as a diacritic for central vowels, used by Bloch and Trager (1942, 22; see also Trager 1964 (p. 16)) for a mid central rounded vowel ("mean-mid" in Bloch and Trager's terms, i.e., between the height of Cardinals 2 and 3, IPA [e] and [ɛ]). Trager suggests [ʚ] as an alternative. Neither symbol has gained currency. The IPA equivalent transcription is [ɵ].

Umlaut Small Capital Omega

According to the widely followed recommendation of Boas et al. (1916, 9) on the use of the umlaut with vowel symbols, where [ʊ] is Bloch and Trager's "mean-mid" back rounded vowel, [ʊ̈] would represent a rounded mean-mid front vowel, i.e., a vowel with all of the properties of [ʊ] but front instead of back, between the height of Cardinals 2 and 3, IPA [e] and [ɛ]. Cf. Bloch and Trager 1942 (p. 22) and Trager 1964 (p. 16). Trager suggests [œ] as an alternative, but note that this character has since been adopted by the IPA for an *open* front rounded vowel, i.e., Cardinal 12 (*Journal of the International Phonetic Association* 6 (p. 2)).

Barred Small Capital Omega

Following the convention of using the superimposed hyphen as a diacritic for central vowel symbols (cf. [ɨ], [ʉ], and [ɵ]), Trager (1964, 16) proposed this symbol for a mid central rounded vowel, as an alternative to the [ʊ̇] of Bloch and Trager 1942 (p. 22). A Trager suggestion that never caught on. The IPA equivalent is [ɵ].

Closed Epsilon
Looks like Closed Omega turned clockwise through 90 degrees, but listed as a variant of Epsilon; see page 54.

Closed Reversed Epsilon
Looks like Closed Omega turned counterclockwise through 90 degrees, but listed as a variant of Epsilon; see page 57.

Upsilon
See page 185.

LOWER-CASE P

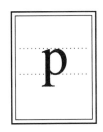

IPA USAGE

Voiceless bilabial plosive.

AMERICAN USAGE

Same as IPA.

COMMENTS

Note related sounds such as [pʰ] (aspirated), [p'] (ejective), [pʷ] (labialized), etc.

[p̌] is used in Trubetzkoy 1968 (p. 69) for a voiceless labiodental affricate, IPA [pf].

SOURCE

Roman alphabet, lower case.

Barred P

Used by both Pike (1947) and Smalley (1963) for a voiceless bilabial fricative (IPA [ɸ]). Barred stop symbols (with a superimposed hyphen or short dash through the body of the letter) are often used to represent those fricatives for which the IPA symbols are not used. The resultant symbols have the advantage of being easy to type on an unmodified typewriter. The form ⟨p̶⟩ is used by Meillet and Cohen (1952, xiii).

Hooktop P

IPA Usage: Approved during the period 1989–93 for a voiceless glottalic ingressive (i.e., implosive) bilabial stop; approval was withdrawn in 1993. *Comments:* Implosives are most commonly voiced for aerodynamic reasons, but as pointed out by, e.g., Pike (1947, 40), Smalley (1963, 381), and Ladefoged (1971, 25), voiceless implosives are easy enough to produce. They are occasionally encountered in languages, but they are very rare. Some Mayan languages are reported to have voiceless implosives as variants of the cognate ejectives found in sister languages (Pike 1963 (pp. 104, 107)). Pinkerton (1986) cites Tactic Pocomchi as having a voiceless bilabial implosive, but she uses [pᶜ] to represent it. Maddieson 1984 (pp. 106, 217) also uses this transcription. Henton, Ladefoged, and Maddieson (1992, 81) reproduce some data from Ladefoged et al. 1976 illustrating bilabial voiceless implosives in Owerri Igbo, and once more [pᶜ] is used rather than Hooktop P. (The occurrence of "[p<]" on page 94 is just a typesetter's error for [pᶜ].) Henton, Ladefoged, and Maddieson cite [ípᶜa] 'to gather' as contrasting with [íphá], [íbꞵa], [ípa], [íba], and [íɓa], all of which occur with other meanings in the language. Hooktop P seems to have appeared in the phonetic literature only a couple of times during its brief period of approval: Ikekeonwu (1991, 100), confirming the claims of Ladefoged et al. about voiceless implosives in Owerri, makes one use (strictly, one mention) of Hooktop P; and Laver (1994, 173) uses Hooktop P to transcribe the voiceless bilabial implosives in three illustrative forms from Tojolabal. The current official IPA transcription principles stipulate nothing about the transcription of voiceless bilabial implosives, but one obvious candidate transcription for the bilabial one would be [ɓ̥]. *Source:* By obvious visual analogy with [ɓ] and [ɗ], the symbols originally established by the IPA for voiced implosives.

Left-Hook P

Used by Doke (1926b, 291, note 4) as the voiced equivalent of the voiceless labialized dental (or alveolar) fricative sound for which he used [σ]. The current IPA equivalents for these sounds would be [sʷ], [s̪ʷ], or [θʷ] for the voiceless one and [zʷ], [z̪ʷ], or [ðʷ] for the voiced one. Doke was closely associated with the IPA tradition, but the IPA seems never to have considered sanctioning this symbol. It did, however, include a mention of a rather differently shaped symbol in this role; see the entry for Reversed Polish-Hook O. The two symbols may well have originated as typographical variants of a character that was never used enough to achieve a standardized shape.

Small Capital P

Recommended by a working group on the phonetic representation of disordered speech for a voiceless linguo-labial plosive (see PRDS Group 1983; Ball 1987). Linguo-labial consonants, including the voiceless linguo-labial plosive, do occur in ordinary speech in some natural languages (see Maddieson 1987), but they are extremely rare. The IPA ignored the plea of Ball (1987) to adopt the PRDS Group policy (which introduces six new symbols), declining to recognize a whole suite of new symbols for a class of sounds that are so extremely rare as segments in ordinary (non-disordered) speech in natural languages. Instead, the IPA introduced in 1989 (see *Journal of the International Phonetic Association* 19 (p. 71)) the Subscript Seagull diacritic, used beneath lingual consonant symbols for alveolar consonants to indicate linguo-labial articulation.

Capital P

Used for the morphophoneme proposed by Hamp (1951) to represent the triggers of Provection, an initial consonant mutation in Welsh and Breton.

Rho

Proposed by Heffner (1950, 136) for a voiced bilabial trill. Heffner notes the conventional spelling "Brr!" for this sound, and also notes that "German teamsters still use this trill, accompanied by a high-pitched and very loud voice note, to induce their draft horses to stop" (the sound being known in German as the "Kutscher R"). He confesses, "I know of no language in which it is a regular speech sound." Such languages were discovered to exist about a quarter of a century after Heffner wrote; they include Kele and Titan (spoken in New Guinea). Heffner's choice of symbol is rather ingenious: the letter shape ⟨ρ⟩ looks like ⟨p⟩, thus suggesting a bilabial articulation, yet its sound (in Modern Greek) is [r], thus suggesting a trill. But perhaps ⟨ρ⟩ has a disadvantage in that it looks too much like ⟨p⟩ and would constantly be confused with it in handwriting. Whatever the reason, when Ladefoged (1982) needed a symbol for the bilabial trill he did not pick up Heffner's symbol but instead proposed a new symbol, [ʙ], which is now approved by the IPA. A Greek alphabet, lower case *rho*.

Wynn

A runic symbol adopted for the Old English orthography which represented the voiced rounded labiovelar approximant (IPA [w]). Wynn is not a phonetic transcription symbol and most editors of Old English texts substitute ⟨w⟩ for it to forestall confusion of it with ⟨p⟩ or Thorn, ⟨þ⟩. The eighth of the runes of the Germanic futhark. Cf. Quirk and Wrenn (1957 (pp. 7–8)).

Thorn

IPA Usage: Not sanctioned, but see, e.g., the transcription scheme set out by Jespersen (1962, 235), which is broadly IPA throughout except that it has [þ] for [θ]. *American Usage:* Not used in modern work. *Other uses:* Used by historical scholars, especially Germanicists, as a phonetic symbol for a voiceless interdental fricative, IPA [θ]; see, e.g., Brugmann 1904, Prokosch 1939, Jespersen 1949, 1962, and many others. *Comments:* The symbols ⟨þ⟩ and ⟨ð⟩ were used indifferently in Late Old English manuscripts to represent the interdental fricative phoneme, which was voiced between two voiced sounds and voiceless elsewhere. Cf. Quirk and Wrenn 1957 (pp. 6–7). The character was borrowed into Scandinavian orthographies and is used in transliterations of other early Germanic languages; see, e.g., Brugmann 1904 (p. 1) and Wright 1910 (p. 4). *Source:* The third of the runes of the Germanic futhark. There is typographical variation, suggested below. Common attempts to produce the character on a typewriter are to overstrike *b* and *p,* or to position a lower-case *o* beside a slash (⟨/⟩). *Thorn*

was sometimes written like a ⟨y⟩, the source of ⟨yᵉ⟩, and later *ye,* for English *the.*

Q-P Ligature
An amalgam of the shapes of ⟨q⟩ and ⟨p⟩, listed as a variant of its first component, ⟨q⟩; see page 159.

LOWER-CASE Q

IPA USAGE

Voiceless uvular plosive.

AMERICAN USAGE

Same as IPA when used.

OTHER USES

Wright (1910, 5) uses [q] to represent the labialized voiceless "velar" (see below) stop in Gothic.

In the Pinyin transliteration of Mandarin Chinese, ⟨q⟩ does not represent anything like a uvular stop, but instead stands for an alveolo-palatal affricate, IPA [tɕ].

COMMENTS

Pike and Smalley regard uvular stops like [q] as "backed velars," and transcribe [q] as [k̲]. Wright (1910, 51) gives [q] as a "velar" stop and [k] as a "palatal" stop in his transcription for "Indogermanic." Boas et al. (1916, 4) consider [k] to be "palatal" and [q] to be "retracted palatal." What is considered the dividing line between "palatal" and "velar" sounds has apparently changed over time. Presumably the denotations are the same; only the descriptive terminology is different.

SOURCE

Roman alphabet lower-case *q,* traditionally used for transcribing the voiceless uvular stop of Arabic.

Hooktop Q

IPA Usage: Approved during the period 1989–93 for a voiceless glottalic ingressive (i.e., implosive) uvular stop; approval was withdrawn in 1993. *Comments:* Implosives are most commonly voiced for aerodynamic reasons, but as pointed out in many works on phonetics (Pike 1947 (p. 40); Smalley 1963 (p. 381); Ladefoged 1971 (p. 25); and Catford 1988 (p. 27)), voiceless implosives are easy enough to produce. Some English speakers may produce voiceless uvular implosives when imitating the "glug-glug" sound of wine being poured out of a bottle (with decreasing lip rounding used to make it sound as if the bottle is being emptied; notice that voiced sounds can also be used for the "glug-glug" sound effect). Campbell (1973), citing a number of earlier sources (see, e.g., Pike 1963 (pp. 104, 107)), notes the occurrence of this sound in several Mayan languages (he mentions Cakchiquel, Pokomam, Pokomchí, Quiché, Tzutujil, and Uspantec, adding "etc."), but he transcribes it [ˀq], following Greenberg (1970). Pinkerton 1986 reports on instrumental studies of voiceless uvular implosives in several of these languages (Cakchiquel, Chamelco K'ekchi, Coban K'ekchi, Quiché, Tactic Pocomchí, and Tzutujil), also transcribing it [qˁ] (see the entry for Left Pointer). Maddieson (1984, 106) uses the same transcription. Hooktop Q was seldom used in the published literature during its brief period of official recognition, though it is used once by Laver (1994, 173) in the transcription of a Cakchiquel form. The most obvious transcription for a voiceless uvular implosive under currently approved transcription principles would be [ɠ̥]. *Source:* By obvious visual analogy with [ɓ] and [ɗ], the symbols originally established by the IPA for voiced implosives.

Q-P Ligature

Proposed in the early 20th century as a symbolization for a voiceless labiodental stop, and in use at least as early as Doke (1926a). Adopted by Ladefoged and Maddieson (1996) for representing this sound, which occurs in such African languages as the XiNkuna dialect of Tsonga, though not, apparently, in contrast with bilabials. Laver (1994, 215) points out that the sound may be heard in English in some pronunciations of the phrase *head first*. (Laver uses the transcription [π̥] for the sound; see entry for Pi.) An invention designed to harmonize with IPA characters, perhaps due to Doke. The symbol looks like a *p* with an additional left-facing loop. It also resembles (perhaps too much) the style of Greek *phi*, ⟨φ⟩, that the IPA does not use for the voiceless bilabial fricative (the IPA symbol called Phi is ⟨ɸ⟩). The voiced counterpart, also used by Doke, is the D-B Ligature.

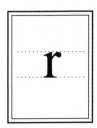

LOWER-CASE R

Voiced apico-alveolar trill.

AMERICAN USAGE

Usually same as IPA, but will often be used for other varieties of "*r*-sound," especially the English frictionless continuant, IPA [ɹ].

OTHER USES

In working transcriptions of Australian indigenous languages, ⟨r⟩ is often used before alveolar consonant symbols to indicate retroflex articulation; thus *rd* means [ɖ], *rt* means [ʈ], and so on.

COMMENTS

Being the easiest symbol to type or write, out of the many that are used for "*r*-sounds," this symbol will often be used in broad transcription to represent sounds other than the alveolar trill that it officially represents in IPA terms. The alveolar trill may be heard in Scottish English, or in most varieties of Spanish (the *rr* of *perro* 'dog').

The symbol ⟨r⟩ is combined with a number diacritics to indicate varieties of *r*-sound in American usage. The tilde, the wedge, and the underdot are particularly frequent. The (superscript) tilde often marks a trilled articulation (Pike 1947, 7; Smalley 1963, 456–57); the wedge may mark the articulation as flapped (Pike 1947 (p. 7); Smalley 1963 (pp. 456–57)) or fricative (Maddieson 1984 (p. 240)); the underdot generally marks the articulation as retracted, which may mean retroflex (Pike 1947 (p. 7); Maddieson 1984 (p. 241)) or uvular (Pike 1947 (p. 7); Smalley 1963 (p. 457)).

SOURCE

Roman alphabet, lower case.

FISH-HOOK R

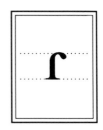

IPA USAGE

Voiced alveolar flap.

AMERICAN USAGE

Same as IPA, if used, but various alternatives are found. These include [d̆] (Smalley 1963 (p. 246)), [řř] (Gleason 1955 (p. 7); Halle and Clements 1983 (p. 29), but see page 11), and [D] (Chomsky 1964 (p. 90)).

COMMENTS

As in Spanish *pero* 'but': a single apical tap.

SOURCE

Roman alphabet lower-case *r*, modified by removal of the serif at top left.

Long-Leg R

IPA Usage: Formerly recommended (see *Principles,* 11) for a voiced alveolar fricative trill—the sound spelled ř in the Czech orthography (and heard in the native pronunciation of the name of the composer Dvořak); but approval was withdrawn in 1989, after the Kiel convention. *Comments:* This symbol, which represents an extremely rare sound and is not drawn from the regular orthography of any language, is seldom encountered, though it is used, of course, in the example transcription of Czech in *Principles* (p. 30). One obvious way to represent it would be to borrow from the Czech orthography and use [ř], and this is the representation most likely to be found in American transcriptions. The official IPA recommendation implicit in the discussion of the "Tiny T" diacritics in *Journal of the International Phonetic Association* 19 ((1989), p. 71), is to use [r] with the raising diacritic [˔] beneath it (i.e., indicating narrower constriction of the oral tract as raising of the primary articulator). As it happens, the resulting transcription, [r̝], looks rather reminiscent of Long-Leg R; but it is not a particularly intuitive way to represent the fricative trilling of the sound in question. *Source:* Roman alphabet lower-case *r,* modified by lengthening the upright to make the letter a descender.

RIGHT-TAIL R

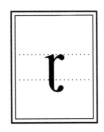

IPA USAGE

Voiced apico-postalveolar (i.e., retroflex) flap.

AMERICAN USAGE

Same as IPA, if used. [ɽ] may be used instead.

OTHER USES

Used in some work on African languages for a voiced alveolar flap, distinct from /l/ and /r/ in, e.g., Kreish (Gbaya). Also found in Indic languages such as Hindi/Urdu, Panjabi, and Bengali (see *Principles,* 36–37).

COMMENTS

The retroflexion diacritic used by the IPA in [ʂ] and [ʐ] is echoed by the rightward-swept elongation of the rightmost vertical stroke of a character in the IPA's special symbols for other retroflex consonants: [ɭ], [ɳ], [ʈ], and [ɖ]. In the interest of terminological consistency, we recognize in this family resemblance an IPA retroflexion indicator, which we call "right tail."

SOURCE

Roman alphabet lower-case *r,* with the IPA diacritic for retroflexion.

TURNED R

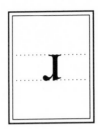

Voiced alveolar or postalveolar approximant.

AMERICAN USAGE

Same as IPA, if used.

COMMENTS

The *r*-sound of many British and American dialects of English, also found in a variety of other languages (Maddieson 1984 (p. 244)).

Essentially a nonsyllabic retroflex (i.e., rhotacized) central unrounded vowel. *Principles* (p. 14) refers to [ɚ] as "another way of writing frictionless ɹ when used as a vowel."

SOURCE

Roman alphabet lower-case *r*, turned (rotated 180°).

RIGHT-TAIL TURNED R

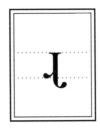

IPA USAGE

Voiced (median) retroflex approximant. Not given in *Principles,* but it appears in the 1979 chart (Cartier and Todaro 1983 (p. 84)).

AMERICAN USAGE

Not used.

COMMENTS

Often the *r*-sound of American English approximates a retroflex frictionless continuant. The sound is also encountered in many Australian languages and elsewhere (Maddieson 1984 (p. 245)).

The retroflexion diacritic used by the IPA in [ʂ] and [ʐ] is echoed by the rightward swept elongation of the rightmost vertical stroke of a character in the IPA's special symbols for other retroflex consonants: [ɭ], [ɳ], [ʈ], and [ɖ]. In the interest of terminological consistency, we recognize in this family resemblance an IPA retroflexion indicator, which we call "right tail."

SOURCE

Turned R, the IPA's symbol for the voiced alveolar approximant, with the IPA diacritic for retroflexion.

TURNED LONG-LEG R

IPA USAGE

Given in *Principles* (p. 14) for a "sound intermediate between d and l but distinct from ɭ"; a voiced alveolar lateral flap.

AMERICAN USAGE

Not in general use, though the symbol may be known from Ladefoged 1971. It was used in the sense described above by Kurath (1939, 138).

COMMENTS

The symbol was invented by Daniel Jones to represent a sound found in Tswana, which he describes as "sounding between l and d" (Jones and Laver 1973 (p. 193); see also Jones 1957 (p. xv)). It has often been used by others; see, e.g., Doke 1926a (p. 142), and Ladefoged 1971 (p. 52). The sound contrasts with IPA [ɾ], which *Principles* (p. 10) describes as "flapped" but Ladefoged calls a "tap" and Jones a "single flap." Ladefoged (1971, 51–52) says that "sounds having the characteristic gesture involved in making a flap may have in addition a distinctly lateral quality; when the articulation is formed there is contact only in the center of the mouth, so that momentarily there is a position similar to that of an l."

The sound is attested in Tswana according to Jones; in Ƈhỹ according to Doke; and in Haya and Chaga according to Ladefoged. It seems also to be a common variant of the /r/ sound of Japanese, though we have not seen this symbol used in the transcription of Japanese.

SOURCE

Apparently invented by Daniel Jones. The symbol is visually reminiscent of both ⟨l⟩ and ⟨r⟩.

SMALL CAPITAL R

IPA USAGE

Voiced uvular trill or flap, as in (one variety of) the Parisian French *r*-sound.

AMERICAN USAGE

Not generally used. Pike (1947, 7) and Smalley (1963, 246) use [r̃] for the trilled uvular *r*.

OTHER USES

Boas et al. (1916, 10) recommend that small capital letters be used for the voiceless versions of normally voiced sounds and hence [ʀ] could be found for IPA [r̥].

COMMENTS

Reserved for an actual trill; ⟨ʁ⟩ is used for the voiced uvular fricative.

SOURCE

Roman alphabet, small capital font.

Capital R

American Usage: Following the recommendation of Boas et al. (1916, 10) that small capital letters be used for the voiceless versions of normally voiced sounds, Pike and Smalley both suggest [R] for voiceless *r*-sounds like IPA [r̥], [ɹ̥], or [ʀ̥]. *Other uses:* Used to represent an unmutated *r* in Celtic languages in Carmody 1945.

Reversed Small Capital R

Proposed by Bloch and Trager (1942, 26) for a voiced bilabial trill. At the time, the IPA had no approved symbol for this sound. Later, Heffner (1950) proposed Rho for it. In 1989, the symbol [ʙ], which had already been used in Ladefoged 1982, was approved by the IPA. The sound is very rare, so none of these symbols has seen much use.

INVERTED SMALL CAPITAL R

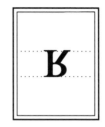

IPA USAGE

Voiced uvular fricative or frictionless approximant, as in some varieties of the French *r*-sound.

AMERICAN USAGE

Same as IPA, if used, but alternatives such as [ɣ] are found.

Note that Pike and Smalley do not recognize uvular obstruents as such, calling them "back[ed] velars," and using [ɡ̠] for the "backed velar" fricative.

COMMENTS

Reserved for a fricative or approximant; [ʀ] is used for the voiced uvular trill.

SOURCE

Roman alphabet small capital *r*, vertically inverted.

LOWER-CASE S

Voiceless alveolar median fricative.

Same as IPA.

Note [ṣ] for dental variant, [s'] for ejective variant, etc. Note that some diacritics indicate a more radical change of denotation: [š] is the American transcription for a voiceless palato-alveolar median fricative, IPA [ʃ], and [ś] is used in the Polish orthography and some comparative studies for a voiceless laminal palatal fricative, IPA [ç] (*Principles,* 12).

Roman alphabet, lower case.

Capital S

Used for the morphophoneme proposed by Hamp (1951) to represent the triggers of Spirantization, an initial consonant mutation in Welsh and Breton.

Wedge S

American Usage: Generally used in place of IPA's [ʃ] for a voiceless palato-alveolar median laminal fricative. *Comments:* The recommendation of Herzog et al. (1934, 631) on the use of the wedge in characters for palato-alveolar consonants required the substitution of [š] for the earlier use of [c], which came to be used for a voiceless alveolar affricate. This recommendation regarding [š] has been universally followed. Used by Brugmann (1904, 1) with this value. *Source:* Roman alphabet lower-case *s,* with wedge diacritic, as used in the Czech orthography. The diacritic is called the *haček* ('little hook') in Czech and called "wedge" by many American linguists.

RIGHT-TAIL S

IPA USAGE

Voiceless retroflex (i.e., apico-postalveolar) median fricative.

AMERICAN USAGE

Not used. [ʂ] would be used instead.

COMMENTS

The retroflexion diacritic used by the IPA in [ʂ] and [ʐ] is echoed by the rightward-swept elongation of the rightmost vertical stroke of a character in the IPA's special symbols for other retroflex consonants: [ɳ], [ɭ], [ɖ], and [ɽ]. In the interest of terminological consistency, we recognize in this family resemblance an IPA retroflexion indicator which we call "right tail."

SOURCE

Roman alphabet lower-case *s*, with the IPA's right-tail diacritic for retroflex consonants.

ESH

Voiceless palato-alveolar median laminal fricative.

Generally not used, ⟨š⟩ being used instead.

A modified ⟨s⟩. Similar to the "long *s*" of early English typesetters' fonts. It occurs in this form with this value in Isaac Pitman's 1845 phonotypic alphabet (cf. Pitman and St. John 1969 (p. 82)), where it functions as the (invented) lower-case print form of a Greek capital *sigma.*

Double-Barred Esh

Invented by D. M. Beach (1938, 289), modifying the previously established symbol ⟨≠⟩ for a "denti-alveolar implosive" click consonant. Beach states (1938, 77–78) that the symbol has been "derived from the symbol in current use by adding curves to the ends of the upright traversal in order to conform in general style and appearance to the other phonetic symbols employed by the International Phonetic Association" and adds: "I am recommending the symbol ʄ for official adoption by the I.P.A." Apparently his recommendation was never officially accepted, for Double-Barred Esh did not appear in the 1949 or 1979 charts, or even merit a mention in the "Further Improvements" section of *Principles* (p. 19). Beach suggests ⟨ɟ⟩ for the nasalized variety.

Looptop Reversed Esh

IPA Usage: Recommended in *Principles* (p. 14) for a labialized variety of [ʃ] or [ç], i.e., voiceless palato-alveolar or palatal fricative with lip rounding. This symbol is recommended for the sound in Twi represented orthographically as *hw* before [i], [e], and [ɛ], though in fact it is not used in the Twi text transcribed in *Principles* (p. 46): [hɥ] is used instead. Approval of the symbol was withdrawn in 1976 (*Journal of the International Phonetic Association* 6 (p. 3)) in favor of equivalent digraphs such as [ʃʷ], [çʷ], and [hɥ].

Curly-Tail Esh

IPA Usage: Formerly recommended for a palatalized voiceless palato-alveolar median fricative. Equivalent to [ʃʲ]. Approval withdrawn in 1989. The symbol was rarely used. *Source:* Esh, modified with clockwise curly tail.

LOWER-CASE T

Voiceless alveolar or dental plosive.

AMERICAN USAGE

Same as IPA.

COMMENTS

Plain [t] would be used, ceteris paribus, for a pulmonic egressive alveolar stop. The transcription [t'] would indicate a glottalic egressive (ejective) alveolar stop. A dental stop distinct from an alveolar one would be transcribed [t̪]; the IPA has never recognized a need for distinct letters for alveolar and dental stops, although the two do contrast phonologically in many Dravidian and Australian languages.

SOURCE

Roman alphabet, lower case.

Barred T

Used in Meillet and Cohen 1952 (see, e.g., page xiii) for a voiceless dental fricative, i.e., the fricative analog of [t̪]. This follows the pattern seen in Crossed D, Barred D, etc.: a letter denoting a stop consonant is often given a lateral cross (on the upright) or bar (through the middle) to create a symbol for a homorganic fricative.

Front-Hook T

Used by Daniel Jones in early transcriptions to indicate a voiceless retroflex plosive, in particular for Sinhalese. According to Jones, the IPA symbol [ʈ] was introduced in 1927 (see Jones and Laver 1983 (p. 202, note 36)), replacing this character and the traditional [t]. An arbitrary modification of ⟨t⟩.

Left-Hook T

IPA Usage: Formerly represented a palatalized voiceless alveolar (or dental) plosive. The current IPA transcription would be [tʲ]. The sound occurs in Russian [pjatʲ] 'five'. *Source:* Roman alphabet lower-case *t* with the left-facing hook diacritic that the IPA formerly used for symbols denoting palatalized consonants.

RIGHT-TAIL T

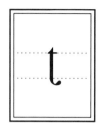

IPA USAGE

Voiceless retroflex (i.e., apico-postalveolar) plosive.

AMERICAN USAGE

Not normally used; [ʈ] is used instead.

COMMENTS

As in the sound represented by Hindi ⟨ट⟩.

The retroflexion diacritic used by the IPA in [ʂ] and [ʐ̩] is echoed by the rightward-swept elongation of the rightmost vertical stroke of a character in the IPA's special symbols for other retroflex consonants: [ɳ], [ɭ], [ɖ], and [ɽ]. In the interest of terminological consistency, we recognize in this family resemblance an IPA retroflexion indicator which we call "right tail."

SOURCE

Roman alphabet lower-case *t,* modified by the incorporation of the IPA diacritic for retroflexion.

Hooktop T

IPA Usage: Approved during the period 1989–93 for a voiceless glottalic ingressive (i.e., implosive) alveolar or dental stop; approval was withdrawn in 1993. *Comments:* Implosives tend, for aerodynamic reasons, to be voiced, but as pointed out in many works on phonetics (Pike 1947 (p. 40); Smalley 1963 (p. 381); Ladefoged 1971 (p. 25); and Catford 1988 (p. 27)), voiceless implosives are easy enough to produce. They are occasionally, but only very rarely, encountered in languages. Henton, Ladefoged, and Maddieson (1992, 81; data reproduced from Ladefoged et al. 1976) cite Owerri Igbo as a language with a bilabial alveolar implosive, though they do not use this symbol for it (they use the superscript left-facing pointer [ˁ], citing [ítˁa] 'to chew' as contrasting with [íthà], [ída], and [ídɦà], all of which occur in the language with other meanings). Pinkerton (1986) cites Tactic Pocomchi as having a voiceless alveolar implosive, but again she uses [tˁ] to represent it, as does Maddieson (1984, 106, 217). Hooktop T appears never to have been used in the published literature during its brief period of official recognition. The most obvious transcription for a voiceless alveolar implosive under currently approved IPA transcription principles would be [ƭ̥]. *Source:* By obvious visual analogy with [ɓ] and [ɗ], the symbols originally established by the IPA for voiced implosives. The hooktop modification is typographically rather unsatisfactory on ⟨t⟩, looking as it does like a crossed Stretched C, which is not mnemonically helpful.

Turned T

IPA Usage: Formerly used for a voiceless dental click (i.e., a voiceless velaric ingressive dental stop). Approval withdrawn in 1989. *Other uses:* Used in some very early work by Dorsey on Ponca (a Siouan language) to represent unaspirated [t] so that the symbol ⟨t⟩ could be reserved for the aspirated equivalent [tʰ] (see Boas and Swanton 1911 (p. 881)). *Comments:* Dental clicks occur linguistically in Khoisan languages of Africa, and in Southern Bantu languages that have borrowed them from Khoisan languages; for example, the letter *c* in the Zulu orthography represents a dental click. In English the sound occurs paralinguistically as a noise expressing disapproval that is often rendered "tut, tut" or "tsk, tsk" by novelists. Turned T was proposed for this value quite early in the history of the IPA; Beach (1938, 289) uses it, and *Principles* sanctions it (p. 14). But in 1989 the IPA withdrew it and adopted the system of transcription for clicks that had long been in use among South African linguists (and many Americans too), adding the symbols [ǀ], [ǂ], [ǁ], and [!] to its alphabet. The current IPA transcription for a dental click is [ǀ] (sometimes written [k͡ǀ], where the [k] component indicates voicelessness; see Ladefoged and Traill 1984). *Source:* Roman alphabet lower-case *t*, turned (rotated 180°).

Curly-Tail Turned T

Beach (1938, 289) suggests this symbol to represent a nasal dental click (i.e., a velaric ingressive dental stop articulated with lowered velum). The IPA transcription for such a sound, following the usage of recent sources such as Ladefoged and Traill 1984, would be [ŋǀ] or [ŋ͡ǀ].

T-S Ligature

IPA Usage: Formerly sanctioned as one transcription for a voiceless alveolar affricate (as in the initial consonant of German *Zeit* [tsaɪt] 'time'), but no longer used. The T-Esh Ligature symbol was somewhat more widely used (see entry for relevant comments). *Source:* Roman alphabet; a ligature of ⟨t⟩ and ⟨s⟩, representing the stop and release portions of the affricate.

T-Esh Ligature

IPA Usage: Formerly sanctioned as one transcription for a voiceless palato-alveolar affricate, but no longer used. *Comments:* In *Principles* (pp. 14–15) it is stated that "if a language contains affricates as well as such sequences as t+s, t+ʃ, the affricates may be denoted by ligature forms"; but at least two other suggestions are made there (use of the linking marks to indicate that adjacent stop and fricative symbols denote an affricate, and use of a hyphen to separate a stop + fricative sequence that is *not* an affricate). The ligatures were never widely used, and approval was finally withdrawn. Under current IPA policies, use of this symbol would be merely a typographical idiosyncrasy; [ʧ] would convey the same phonetic information as [tʃ]. *Source:* A ligature of ⟨t⟩ and ⟨ʃ⟩ (the palato-alveolar affricate has [t] as its stop component followed by a [ʃ] fricative release).

LOWER-CASE U

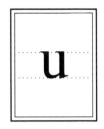

IPA USAGE

Cardinal Vowel No. 8: close back rounded.

AMERICAN USAGE

Same as IPA.

COMMENTS

As in French *ou* 'or'.

SOURCE

Roman alphabet, lower case.

Overdot U

Following the recommendations of Boas et al. (1916, 10) on the use of the overdot diacritic as an indicator for central vowels, used by Bloch and Trager (1942, 22) for a high central rounded vowel (IPA [ʉ]). Trager (1964, 16) suggests this and [ʉ] as alternatives.

Umlaut U

IPA Usage: According to *Principles* (p. 16), a high central rounded vowel, an alternative to [ʉ] recommended for use when the sound is clearly a member of a back vowel phoneme /u/. The current interpretation of the umlaut diacritic makes [ü] a central*ized* high back round vowel between [u] and [ʉ]. *American Usage:* According to the widely followed recommendation of Boas et al. (1916, 9) on the use of the umlaut with vowel symbols, [ü] represents a rounded high front vowel, i.e., a vowel with all of the properties of [u] but front instead of back. The IPA transcription would be [y]. Cf. Bloch and Trager 1942 (p. 22), Trager 1964 (p. 16), Pike 1947 (p. 5), Gleason 1955 (p. 8), and Smalley 1963 (p. 309). A case of almost total unanimity among American phoneticians on a usage that directly conflicts with the IPA. The IPA transcription for a high front rounded vowel is [y], which is occasionally found in American works and is acknowledged to be "in common use" by Bloch and Trager (1942, 21). *Comments:* The result of the change in the IPA's interpretation of the umlaut and its common use in a different sense in American practice is a rather confusing situation in which [ü] may denote a centralized back vowel (official IPA), a central vowel (*Principles*), or a front vowel (e.g., Bloch and Trager). *Source:* The character is used in German orthography to denote a close front rounded vowel.

BARRED U

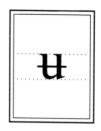

Close central rounded vowel, between Cardinal 1 and Cardinal 8.

AMERICAN USAGE

Same as IPA where used, as, e.g., by Pike (1947, 5).

A high central rounded vowel could be transcribed as [ú], using the overdot diacritic suggested by Boas et al. (1916, 10).

COMMENTS

The sound [ʉ] is heard in the Norwegian word *hus,* and in Scottish pronunciations of the English word *good.* (Note the novelist's device of writing the word as "guid" to indicate this vowel quality.)

Neither Smalley 1963 nor Halle and Clements 1983 give symbols for any central rounded vowels, and Gleason 1955 gives Barred U as denoting a high back unrounded vowel (IPA [ɯ]). The omission of central rounded vowels from the phonetic charts of so many phonologists may indicate not an oversight but rather a tacit phonological hypothesis that a three-way backness distinction in rounded vowels cannot exist in a language. This becomes explicit in Chomsky and Halle 1968 (p. 315), where it is suggested that the [y]/[ʉ] distinction in Swedish is not a function of the feature [back] but of the feature [covered], which relates to constriction of the pharynx and is independent of backness.

SOURCE

Roman alphabet lower-case *u,* modified with superimposed hyphen.

Half-Barred U

Proposed by Trager (1964, 16) for a high central rounded vowel, an alternative to the [ů] of Bloch and Trager 1942 (p. 22). A Trager suggestion that never caught on. The equivalent IPA transcription is [ʉ], but Trager has this for a high *front* rounded vowel.

Slashed U

Might be encountered as a typographical alternant of ⟨ʉ⟩; see, e.g., Chistovich et al. 1982 (p. 171).

> **Turned M**
> *Looks like a double-u ligature, but actually a turned* ⟨m⟩, *and listed as a variant of* ⟨m⟩; *see page 114.*

UPSILON

IPA USAGE

Near-close near-back unrounded vowel, between Cardinal 7 and Cardinal 8; the vowel in standard English pronunciations of the words *put* and *cook*.

AMERICAN USAGE

Same as IPA, though Small Capital U ([ᴜ]) is a common substitute (and some transcriptions have *book* and *boom* distinguished by [u] versus [u:]).

COMMENTS

The IPA originally sanctioned Closed Omega [ɷ] for this sound, approving Upsilon as an alternative only in a footnote (*Principles,* 8). But in 1989, approval of Closed Omega was withdrawn, leaving Upsilon as the official symbol by default. Since Upsilon is commonly used by Americans but Closed Omega never was, this brought IPA usage into closer alignment with the American tradition.

The letter is not an unmodified Greek *upsilon,* ⟨υ⟩. As with other Greek letters (e.g., *gamma* and *phi*), the original Greek letter shape has been modified to make it typographically harmonious with the other IPA letter shapes; but the Greek origin seems clear enough for our name to be appropriate.

Upsilon must be distinguished from the symbol we have called Script V: ⟨ʋ⟩. The latter represents a consonant (a labiodental approximant). Confusingly, the symbol we call Script V looks somewhat more like a Greek *upsilon* than IPA Upsilon does; and the version of Upsilon used in Smalley 1963 looks much more like Script V than like Upsilon. We regret not being able to terminologize better in this area, but we cannot see a clearly better alternative. (Some phoneticians refer to Upsilon by the name *Bucket,* but it looks more like an urn to us.)

The occurrence of this symbol in Tucker 1971 (p. 648) seems to have been set by the typesetter as a turned small capital *omega*. We take this to be a printer's substitution; the shapes are not the same.

SOURCE

Greek alphabet, lower case, with shape modified to be serifed and bilaterally symmetric.

Small Capital U

American Usage: Semi-high back rounded vowel, IPA [ʊ], between Cardinals 7 and 8. *Other uses:* Boas et al. (1916, 10) recommend that small capital letters be used for the voiceless versions of normally voiced sounds and hence [ʊ] could be found for a voiceless [u], IPA [u̥]. Its use for the semi-high back rounded vowel is far more common.

Overdot Small Capital U

Following the recommendation of Boas et al. (1916, 10) on the use of the overdot diacritic for central vowels, used by Bloch and Trager (1942, 22) for a lower-high central rounded vowel. Trager (1964, 16) suggests this symbol or ⟨ʉ⟩ as alternatives. The equivalent *Principles* transcription is [ü] or [ÿ].

Barred Small Capital U

Proposed by Trager (1964, 16) for a high front rounded vowel, as an alternative to the [Ü] of Bloch and Trager 1942 (p. 22). A Trager suggestion that never caught on. The equivalent IPA transcription is [y].

Turned Small Capital U

IPA Usage: Not used, but specifically mentioned in *Principles* (p. 19) as having been suggested for use as a "general symbol" for any vowel that has no current IPA symbol. For this reason, the symbol is included in the LaserIPA font marketed by Linguist's Software. *Other uses:* Used by Samarin (1967, 182) for a "mean-mid" back rounded vowel, in place of Trager's small capital *omega,* [Ω]. Used in Crothers 1978 (p. 137) for a higher-low back rounded vowel (IPA [ɔ̞]) instead of Bloch and Trager's [ɔ]. *Source:* Roman alphabet, small capital font, turned (rotated 180°).

Capital U

Boas et al. (1916, 10) recommend the use of small capitals to represent the voiceless versions of normally voiced sounds (either vowels or sonorants). Pike 1947 and Smalley 1963 both suggest the use of capital letters for voiceless vowels; thus the transcription [U] might be used for IPA [u̥]. Not frequently found.

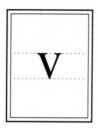

LOWER-CASE V

IPA USAGE

Voiced labiodental fricative.

AMERICAN USAGE

Same as IPA.

COMMENTS

The letter *v* represents [v] in English orthography but not in all roman-based orthographies; in Spanish, for example, it has both [b] and [β] as possible values.

The letter *v* is often used by phonologists to indicate an arbitrary vowel. Most often, the symbol used (as in "CV syllable structure" for consonant-vowel syllable structure) is capital *v*, which has no phonetic use, but a lower-case *v* might occasionally be found used in this way. (We have been told that early Iroquoianists used *v* to represent a neutral central low vowel, but have not been able to locate an instance of this in print.)

SOURCE

Roman alphabet, lower case.

Turned V

Typographically the same as a small capital version of Greek capital lambda, ⟨Λ⟩, *and also the same as a turned* ⟨v⟩, *but actually a vowel symbol with a similar use to the less common Small Capital A, hence listed as a crossbarless variant of* ⟨A⟩; *see page 18.*

SCRIPT V

IPA USAGE

Voiced labiodental approximant.

AMERICAN USAGE

Not generally used; but Gleason gives ⟨ʋ⟩ for IPA [β], a voiced bilabial fricative. Script V is used with its IPA value in Kurath 1939 (p. 140).

COMMENTS

The IPA interpretation represents the initial sound of Hindi *woo* 'he/she'.

Must be distinguished from [ʊ] (upsilon).

Used in the International African Institute's (1930) standard African alphabet for a voiced bilabial fricative, IPA [β], and hence in some phonetics texts (cf. Westermann and Ward 1933).

Used by Ladefoged (1968, 25) for a voiced bilabial approximant without strong lip rounding, as found in Bini, Esoko, and other Edo languages of West Africa.

SOURCE

Roman alphabet lower-case *v* as in some styles of handwriting.

LOWER-CASE W

Voiced rounded labial-velar approximant.

Used as a right superscript, it is the official IPA diacritic for labialized sounds. See the chart for IPA diacritics. The right superscript replaces the previous recommendations for forms of *w* written under a character.

AMERICAN USAGE

Same as IPA.

COMMENTS

The letter *w* does not represent [w] in all roman-based orthographies; in Welsh, for example, it represents [ʊ], and in German, Polish, and other languages, it represents [v].

J.R. Firth used ⟨w⟩ to represent [ʊ] in his "All-India" alphabet, which is employed in a number of works on Indian languages; see, e.g., Harley 1944 (p. xiii) and Bailey 1956 (p. xv).

Ladefoged uses [w˕] for a voiced rounded labiovelar fricative (1968, 25).

SOURCE

Roman alphabet, lower case.

Subscript W

IPA Usage: According to *Principles* (p. 17), used as a centered subscript to indicate labialization of a consonant; thus [t̫] is a voiceless alveolar stop with lip rounding. Approval was withdrawn in 1989 in favor of the more common use of a print *w* as a right superscript (e.g., [tʷ]). The IPA's choice of typographical shape suggested a subscript lower-case *omega* rather than *w,* but it seems sensible to call it a *w* nonetheless.

Overdot W

IPA Usage: According to IPA conventions (*Principles,* 17), this would represent a palatalized bilabial semivowel (glide); in other words, [ɥ]. *American Usage:* Not in general use. Following the recommendation of Boas et al. (1916, 10) for the use of the overdot as a diacritic for central vowels, Trager (1964, 16) uses [ẇ] for a central rounded semivowel. The *Principles*-type transcription corresponding to Trager's [ẇ] is [ɥ] or [ẅ].

Umlaut W

IPA Usage: Assuming the umlaut diacritic can be applied to semivowels (i.e., glides) as well as vowels, according to *Principles* (p. 16) a central rounded semivowel, i.e., a semivowel of [ʉ] quality. In 1976 the IPA altered the definition of the umlaut diacritic so that it marks a vowel as "centralized," not central (*Journal of the International Phonetic Association* 6 (p. 2)). Under this interpretation, [ẅ] would represent a centralized rounded semivowel. *American Usage:* Not generally used, but proposed by Trager (1964, 16), following the recommendations of Boas et al. (1916, 9) on the use of the umlaut diacritic, for a front rounded semivowel, IPA [ɥ]. Cf. Meillet and Cohen 1952 (p. xiii) for a use with this sense. *Comments:* The result of the change in the IPA's interpretation of the umlaut and its common use with a different sense in American practice is a rather confusing situation in which [ẅ] might denote a centralized back semivowel (official IPA), a central semivowel (*Principles*) or a front semivowel (e.g., Trager).

Slashed W

Used by Monzón and Seneff (1984, 456n) for a sound observed in certain Nahuatl dialects, described as "characterized by the parallel position of lips (as for [ƀ]) and a velar onglide—no friction has been noted." Perhaps, therefore, a voiced, unrounded, labiovelar approximant: a variety of [ɣ͡β] without friction, in IPA terms, and perhaps a variety of the sound for which Ladefoged suggested [ɯɥ], with added labial constriction.

Omega
Visually similar to a cursive w, *but actually the lower-case form of the Greek letter* omega; *see page 146.*

TURNED W

IPA USAGE

Voiceless rounded labial-velar approximant or fricative (i.e., devoiced [w]).

AMERICAN USAGE

Not used.

COMMENTS

Designed as a single-symbol representation of the sound written *wh* in those English dialects which distinguish *which* from *witch.*

SOURCE

Roman alphabet lower-case *w,* turned (rotated 180°). The character is distinct from Small Capital M.

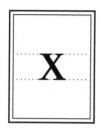

LOWER-CASE X

IPA USAGE

Voiceless velar median fricative.

AMERICAN USAGE

Same as IPA.

OTHER USES

Since ⟨x⟩ represents [ç] in many New World varieties of Spanish (note the pronunciation [meçiko] for *Mexico*) and represents [ʃ] in Portuguese, it commonly denotes a palatal or palato-alveolar voiceless fricative in Central and South American transcriptions. It also represents a palatal or "alveolopalatal" fricative (IPA [ç] or [ɕ]) in the Pinyin transliteration of Mandarin Chinese.

COMMENTS

The values that *x* has in English orthography, namely [z] initially and [ks] or [gz] elsewhere, have no connection to any recognized use of ⟨x⟩ in phonetic transcription and should be ignored.

This symbol must be carefully distinguished from [χ], Greek *chi,* which denotes a uvular fricative rather than a velar one.

Smalley (1963) does not recognize uvular obstruents per se, calling them "backed velars," and uses [x̠] for a voiceless "backed velar" fricative.

SOURCE

Cyrillic alphabet. While ⟨x⟩ has various values in roman-based Western European orthographies, in the Eastern European languages written with the Greek-derived Cyrillic alphabet (e.g., in Russian and Bulgarian), the letter with this shape denotes a voiceless velar fricative.

Subscript-Circumflex X

Given by Smalley (1963, 455) for a voiceless palatal central fricative, i.e., IPA [ç], corresponding to the [x̬] of Pike (1947, 7) and Gleason (1955, 7).

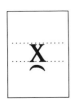

Subscript-Arch X

Used by Pike (1947, 7) and Gleason (1955, 7) for a voiceless palatal central fricative, i.e., IPA [ç], corresponding to the [x̬] of Smalley (1963, 455).

Capital X

Not standard, but may sometimes be found to indicate a voiceless uvular fricative, IPA [χ] (see, e.g., Hyman 1975, 241). Recommended for that use in Eskimo-Aleut languages by Thalbitzer et al. 1952.

IPA USAGE

Voiceless uvular median fricative.

AMERICAN USAGE

Same as IPA, if used, but alternatives such as [x̣] are also found.

Following the terminology of Boas et al. (1916, 4), Pike and Smalley do not recognize uvular obstruents as such, calling them "back[ed] velars," and using [x̣] for a voiceless "backed velar" fricative.

COMMENTS

Heard in some pronunciations of the French words *lettre* and *liberté*, where a uvular *r* is devoiced.

SOURCE

Greek *chi*. It represents a back fricative in Greek (but a velar one, not a uvular one).

LOWER-CASE Y

IPA USAGE

Cardinal Vowel No. 9: close front rounded. The secondary cardinal vowel corresponding to Cardinal 1.

AMERICAN USAGE

Voiced unrounded palatal median approximant (IPA [j]).

As a right superscript, indicates palatalization, as recommended by Herzog et al. (1934, 630), or (with an alveolar consonant symbol) palato-alveolar articulation; thus Pike's (1947) [lʸ] denotes a palato-alveolar lateral approximant; the IPA transcription would be [lʲ].

OTHER USES

Slavicists use ⟨y⟩ to represent a high central or back unrounded vowel, IPA [ɨ] or [ɯ], as in the standard romanization for Russian.

J. R. Firth used ⟨y⟩ for both [ɪ] and [j] in his "All-India" alphabet, which is used in a number of works on Indian languages; see, e.g., Harley 1944 (pp. xii–xvi) and Bailey et al. 1956 (pp. xv–xvi). The ambiguity here is not pernicious, since [ɪ] and [j] are in complementary distribution in the languages in question.

COMMENTS

The usage of the transcription [y] is perhaps the single most salient example of a problematic divergence between American and European transcription practices. It is unfortunate that the IPA's recommendation has not influenced the American community, which uses ⟨y⟩ for [j] when transcribing English and for [ɨ] when transliterating Slavic languages, making ⟨y⟩ ambiguous in three ways. As things stand, the literature contains many traps set for the unwary. For example, "[y]" on page 315 of Chomsky and Halle 1968 denotes IPA [y], but the "[y]" on page 316, the very next page, denotes IPA [j].

It is crucial to be aware of the background of the writer when interpreting an unexplained occurrence of "[y]." Yet mere geographical provenance cannot be relied upon simplistically; for example, Kurath (1939, 123), writing in the United States, uses ⟨y⟩ with its IPA meaning.

Matters become even more complex if one takes orthographic usages of *y* into consideration: it represents [j], [i], or [ɪ] in English orthography, [ə] or [ɪ] in Welsh orthography, [ɨ] in Polish orthography, and so on—though it does generally represent a high front rounded vowel in German.

The coexistence of the IPA and other uses of ⟨y⟩ (and hence ⟨j⟩) is recognized within the IPA community to be an ongoing problem. *Principles* notes that the "World Orthography" described in the International African Institute's (1930) *Practical Orthography of African Languages* and widely used for African languages differs from the IPA *only* in that "*j* and *y* are taken to have their English consonantal values." Despite a general recognition by the council of the IPA that the situation regarding [j] and [y] is undesirably confused, and considerable support for moving to the American interpretation of [y], resolution of the problem was deferred in 1976 (*Journal of the International Phonetic Association* 6 (pp. 2–3)) with the council split on whether to retain [j] as a palatal approximant or to use [y] instead.

SOURCE

Roman alphabet, lower case. IPA usage follows Old English and some other Germanic languages, but is at odds with English and many other orthographies.

Umlaut Y

IPA Usage: According to *Principles* (p. 16), a close central rounded vowel, i.e., equivalent to [ʉ], though the revised interpretation of the umlaut diacritic would make [ÿ] represent a central*ized* (i.e., somewhat retracted) front rounded vowel. *American Usage:* Not in general use, but proposed by Trager (1964, 16) (following the recommendations of Boas et al. (1916, 9) on the use of the umlaut diacritic) for a back unrounded semivowel, as an alternative to IPA [ɰ].   *Comments:* The result of the IPA's interpretation of the umlaut diacritic and its common use with a different sense in American practice is a rather confusing situation in which *y* with an umlaut diacritic could be interpreted as denoting a centralized close front vowel (official IPA), a close central rounded vowel (*Principles*), or a back unrounded semivowel (Trager).

 Turned H
Somewhat similar in shape to ⟨y⟩, but actually a turned version of ⟨h⟩, listed with the variants of ⟨h⟩; see page 79.

TURNED Y

Voiced palatal lateral approximant.

Same as IPA.

As represented by *gl* in Italian and *ll* in Castilian Spanish.

Roman alphabet lower-case *y,* turned (rotated 180°). Visually sugges-tive of a laterally reversed Greek *lambda.* Also suggestive of *y*—mis-leadingly, perhaps, since a palatal lateral approximant sounds a lot like the palatal median approximant [j], and *y* represents [j] in some or-thographies, but not in the IPA system.

 Lambda
Typographically similar to Turned Y, but actually the Greek letter lambda, *listed with the variants and relatives of* ⟨l⟩; *see page 110.*

SMALL CAPITAL Y

IPA USAGE

Semi-close front rounded vowel, i.e., rounded counterpart of [ɪ].

AMERICAN USAGE

Not generally used. Bloch and Trager (1942, 22) and sources following them use [ᴜ̈] for rounded [ɪ].

OTHER USES

Boas et al. (1916, 10) recommend that small capital letters be used for the voiceless versions of normally voiced sounds; since American [y] is a voiced unrounded palatal median approximant, Small Capital Y would represent a voiceless unrounded palatal median approximant.

COMMENTS

The vowel sound in German *fünf* and *Glück*.

SOURCE

Roman alphabet, small capital font; [ʏ] is to [y] as [ɪ] is to [i].

LOWER-CASE Z

IPA USAGE

Voiced alveolar or dental median fricative.

AMERICAN USAGE

Same as IPA.

COMMENTS

An obvious choice to represent [z] for speakers of English, but not necessarily for speakers of other languages with roman-based orthographies; z stands for [ts] in German, [θ] in Castilian Spanish, and [s] in Basque, Catalan, and New World Spanish.

Note that some diacritics indicate a more radical change of denotation: [ž] is the American transcription for a voiced alveopalatal fricative, IPA [ʒ], [ź] is used in the Polish orthography and some comparative studies for a voiced laminal palatal fricative, IPA [ʑ] (*Principles,* 12).

A capital z has been used by some Indo-Europeanists to represent "a laryngeal not retained in Hittite" (see Hamp 1965a (p. 123, note 3)), but we have not regarded this as meriting a separate entry for capital z.

SOURCE

Roman alphabet, lower case.

Comma-Tail Z

Found in grammars of Old High German representing the reflex of Proto-Germanic non-initial *t* after the Second Consonant Shift (see, e.g., Ellis 1953 (p. 21); Wright 1910 (p. 54); Prokosch 1939 (p. 81)). It is not clear what its phonetic value was, but it is generally agreed that it was some sort of dental fricative, and that it had collapsed with [s] by the end of the Middle High German period. See Brauner 1967 (pp. 12, 85). The symbol is quite specific to work on Old High German, and should not be regarded as a phonetic symbol for general use. Prokosch (1939, 81) has it as ⟨ʓ⟩, hence our name for it.

Wedge Z

American Usage: Generally used in place of the IPA [ʒ] for a voiced palato-alveolar median laminal fricative. *Comments:* The recommendations of Herzog et al. (1934, 631) on the use of the wedge diacritic in characters for palato-alveolar consonants required the substitution of [ž] for the earlier Americanist use of [j]. The recommendation has been almost universally followed. Herzog et al. recommended Yogh for a voiced alveolar affricate. Brugmann (1904, 1) uses ⟨ž⟩ with the value IPA [ʒ]. *Source:* Roman alphabet lower-case *z*, with wedge diacritic, as used in the Czech orthography. The diacritic is called the *haček* ('little hook') in Czech and called "wedge" by many American linguists.

CURLY-TAIL Z

IPA USAGE

Voiced "alveolo-palatal" median laminal fricative. Articulated further forward than [ʝ] (true palatal) but not as far forward as [ʒ] (palato-alveolar), and articulated laminally (with the flat blade of the tongue) rather than apically (with the tip of the tongue, as in [z̢], retroflex).

AMERICAN USAGE

Listed by Halle and Clements (1983, 29) as a voiced palatal median fricative, i.e., IPA [ʝ]. Usually not used by American phoneticians.

COMMENTS

Illustrated, according to *Principles* (p. 12), by the sound represented as ⟨ź⟩ in Polish *źle*.

The IPA's distinction between "alveolo-palatal" place of articulation (closer to palatal) and palato-alveolar (closer to alveolar) has not gained wide currency. The term *palato-alveolar* is standard, but the term *alveolo-palatal* is not, and in fact is rarely encountered. The term *alveopalatal* used by Gleason, Pike, and Smalley corresponds to the IPA's *palato-alveolar.*

SOURCE

Roman alphabet lower-case *z* (used for a voiced alveolar fricative) modified with the same curly tail used in ⟨ç⟩ (IPA voiceless "alveolo-palatal" median fricative).

RIGHT-TAIL Z

IPA USAGE

Voiced retroflex (i.e., apico-postalveolar) median fricative.

AMERICAN USAGE

Not used. [ʐ] would be used instead.

COMMENTS

The retroflexion diacritic used by the IPA in [ʂ] and [ʐ] is echoed by the rightward-swept elongation of the rightmost vertical stroke of a character in the IPA's special symbols for other retroflex consonants: [ɳ], [ɭ], [ɖ], and [ɽ]. In the interest of terminological consistency, we recognize in this family resemblance an IPA retroflexion indicator which we call "right tail."

SOURCE

Roman alphabet lower-case z, with the IPA's right-tail diacritic for retroflex consonants.

Crossed Two

IPA Usage: Recommended in *Principles* (p. 15) for a voiced alveolar affricate with laminal fricative release. Equivalent to [dz]. Given in case a single letter is needed for the voiced alveolar affricate where it patterns as a single segment. IPA approval was withdrawn in 1976 in favor of digraphs and ligatures (*Journal of the International Phonetic Association* 6 (p. 3)). An arbitrary invention, vaguely reminiscent of *z* in shape.   *American Usage:* Not used. For similar purposes, Herzog et al. (1934, 631) recommended ⟨ʒ⟩ for IPA [dz].

Turned Two

IPA Usage: Proposed in *Principles* (p. 19) for the voiceless pharyngeal fricative but not officially approved. The character is the numeral 2 turned (rotated 180°). An IPA invention suggestive of the Arabic character ⟨ح⟩ (*ḥa*).   *American Usage:* Not used.

YOGH

IPA USAGE

Voiced palato-alveolar median laminal fricative.

AMERICAN USAGE

Generally not used ([ž] being used instead). Recommended by Herzog et al. (1934, 631) to represent [dz] when it occurs as a single affricate consonant, but this usage is now not common.

OTHER USES

Some Slavicists use ⟨ʒ⟩ for IPA [dz]; this is the origin of the Herzog et al. recommendation, and it may be exhibited elsewhere in linguistic works; thus, for example, the reference to "[ǯ] and [ʒ]" in Kiparsky 1968 (p. 183) means IPA [ʤ] and [dz], respectively. Note also Hoijer 1945 (p. 12), where [ʒ] is used for the "voiceless, lenis, and unaspirated" alveolar affricate of Navaho, IPA [d̥z̥].

SOURCE

This Old Irish form of *g* was used in Old English orthography to represent, at various times, a voiced velar stop, a voiced velar fricative, and a palatal approximant. It survived into Middle English with the latter two values in the form ⟨ʒ⟩ and called "yogh." It is sometimes found set as ⟨ʒ⟩ (cf. Jones 1972). The letter was used in Scotland later than in England and English typesetters perceived a similarity between the ⟨ʒ⟩ form and a form of *z* and substituted the latter. This led, according to Jespersen (1949, 22), to the current spelling pronunciation of Scottish names like *Mackenzie*. The character occurs in this form with this value in Isaac Pitman's 1845 phonotypic alphabet (cf. Pitman and St. John 1969 (p. 82)).

Wedge Yogh

American Usage: The recommendations of Herzog et al. (1934, 631) which formalized the use of the wedge diacritic in American transcription used this character for a voiced palato-alveolar affricate consonant, IPA [ʤ]. It is used thus by Hockett (1955). The regular analogic pattern of the Herzog et al. recommendations was interrupted by the replacement of [ǯ] by [ǰ], presumably for considerations of typographical ease. Cf. Hoijer (1945, 8), who uses a transcription which is otherwise consistent with previous recommendations except in the use of ⟨ǰ⟩ for ⟨ǯ⟩. Cf. also Bloomfield (1933, 129), who uses ⟨ǰ⟩ for IPA [ʤ]. *Other uses:* Some Slavicists use ⟨ǯ⟩ for IPA [ʤ]; this is the origin of the Herzog et al. recommendation, and it may be exhibited elsewhere in linguistic works; thus, for example, the reference to "[ǯ] and [ʒ]" by Kiparsky (1968, 183) means IPA [ʤ] and [dz] respectively. *Source:* The character is Yogh with the wedge diacritic called *haček* ('little hook') or "wedge" used for certain palato-alveolar consonants in the Czech orthography.

Bent-Tail Yogh

IPA Usage: Recommended (*Principles*, 14) for a labialized variety of [ʒ] or [ʝ], i.e., voiced palato-alveolar or palatal fricative with lip rounding. Equivalent to [ʒʷ] or [ʝʷ]. Recommended for the sound represented orthographically as ⟨w⟩ before [i], [e], and [ɛ] in Twi (though the character is not used in the Twi sample (p. 46)). Approval was withdrawn in 1976 (*Journal of the International Phonetic Association* 6 (p. 3)) in favor of the equivalent digraph. *Comments:* Rarely if ever used, even during the period of its being sanctioned by the IPA. The occurrence in Pike 1943 (p. 75) in a quotation from Kenyon (1950) is spurious; it is a typesetter's error in quoting Kenyon's use of reversed *epsilon* with the rhotacization hook.

Curly-Tail Yogh

IPA Usage: Formerly represented a palatalized voiced palato-alveolar median fricative. Equivalent to [ʒʲ]. Approval withdrawn in 1989 after the Kiel convention. *Comments:* This symbol was very rarely used even when it was recognized. *Source:* Yogh, modified with clockwise curly tail.

Reversed Yogh

Used by Firth (1948) to represent the *'ain* (⟨ɛ⟩) of Arabic (IPA [ʕ], voiced pharyngeal fricative), apparently following an established tradition. Perhaps intended to be Turned Three, unofficially suggested by the IPA (*Principles,* 19). Firth also uses ⟨ʕ⟩ for Arabic *hamza* ⟨ʾ⟩ (see Firth 1948 (pp. 142, 147–49)). Clearly, visual similarity between Arabic ⟨ɛ⟩ and the laterally reversed *yogh* is the motivation for this use of the symbol.

Turned Three

IPA Usage: Proposed (*Principles,* 19) but not officially approved for the voiced pharyngeal fricative (standard IPA [ʕ]). *Comments:* The character in *Principles* is clearly a turned (rotated 180°) *three* in its rounded form, i.e., ⟨3⟩, which is visually suggestive of the Arabic character for the sound, ⟨ع⟩ (*'ain*). A reversed curved *yogh* would typographically look very much like a turned ⟨3⟩. Cf. Meillet and Cohen 1952 (p. xiii). The character used by Firth (1948, 142) for IPA [ʕ] (see below) is typographically ambiguous between a reversed *yogh* and a laterally reversed *three* with a flat top, i.e., ⟨Ɜ⟩.

GLOTTAL STOP

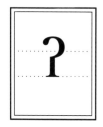

IPA USAGE

Glottal plosive.

AMERICAN USAGE

Same as IPA.

Used as a superscript diacritic with symbols for voiceless stops to form symbols for ejective or glottalized consonants, either over the symbols or as a right superscript. Used over vowels by Smalley (1963, 389ff) to represent laryngealization.

COMMENTS

Sometimes the question mark, ⟨?⟩, is used as a typographical substitute. Note also that differing fonts may have different-looking symbols for the glottal stop. For example:

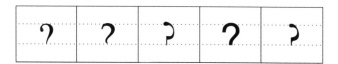

The ⟨ʟ⟩ listed for the glottal plosive at the beginning of the second edition of Gimson 1970 (p. ix) is a typesetter's error. The first (1962) and third (1980) editions are correct.

SOURCE

Question mark with dot removed and (in some fonts) leg lengthened. The shape may have been suggested by the Greek "smooth breathing" symbol ⟨'⟩ (called *spiritus lenis* in Latin), which indicates a frictionless vowel onset (as opposed to [h]).

Question Mark

Occasionally found as a more easily typed and typeset version of ⟨ʔ⟩, denoting a glottal stop.

Seven

Used in practical orthographies for Mayan languages to represent the glottal stop, IPA ʔ. See Kaufman 1976 (p. 25). It is useful in that it is vaguely suggestive of the glottal stop symbol in shape and is available on an unmodified typewriter, but distinct from punctuation marks.

BARRED GLOTTAL STOP

IPA USAGE

Epiglottal plosive.

COMMENTS

Epiglottal plosives are a variety of stop consonant involving a stop closure made by movement of the epiglottis backward till it touches the rear pharyngeal wall (Laufer and Condax 1981). According to Laufer (1991), epiglottal plosives occur in the "careful, deliberate, and slow speech" of some speakers of Hebrew and Arabic as an allophone of the voiced epiglottal fricative phoneme (described as a pharyngeal or "emphatic" fricative in the literature predating the discovery of the pharyngeal/epiglottal articulatory distinction). The 1989 revision of the IPA had this symbol as the transcription for a voiced epiglottal plosive. Laufer (1991) argued that it was a phonetic impossibility for such a plosive to be voiced, as the air chamber below the closure and above the larynx was too small to permit voicing to persist. Laufer recommended that the symbol be listed in the IPA chart under "Other symbols" without a voicing specification, and this suggestion was accepted (IPA 1993).

Inverted Glottal Stop

IPA Usage: Formerly used for a voiceless alveolar lateral click (i.e., a voiceless velaric ingressive alveolar laterally released stop). Approval withdrawn in 1989. *Comments:* Alveolar lateral clicks occur linguistically in Khoisan languages of Africa, and in Southern Bantu languages that have borrowed them from Khoisan languages; for example, the letter *x* in the Zulu orthography represents this sound. In English the sound occurs paralinguistically as a noise used for starting up a horse. The symbol was proposed quite early in the history of the IPA; Beach (1938, 289) uses it, and *Principles* sanctions it (p. 14). But in 1989 the IPA withdrew it and adopted the system of transcription for clicks that had long been in use among South African linguists (and many Americans too), adding the symbols [ǀ], [ǂ], [ǁ], and [ǃ] to its alphabet. The current IPA transcription for a dental click is [ǁ] (sometimes written [k͡ǁ], where the [k] component indicates voicelessness; see Ladefoged and Traill 1984). *Source:* Invention, possibly by Beach. Vertically inverted (not turned) glottal stop symbol. The symbol might be seen as a ⟨5⟩ without its top lateral stroke, but the version seen in Ladefoged 1971 (p. 23) is clearly an inverted glottal stop, and the name we have chosen reflects that interpretation.

Crossed Inverted Glottal Stop

IPA Usage: Recommended (*Principles,* 15) for a voiceless alveolar affricate with median fricative release in case a single letter is needed for the voiceless alveolar affricate where it patterns as a single segment; for example, the Georgian plain [ts] and ejective [ts'] can be transcribed [ʖ] and [ʖ']. IPA approval was withdrawn in 1976 in favor of the equivalent digraphs and ligatures (*Journal of the International Phonetic Association* 6, 3).   *Source:* An IPA invention. Perhaps a visual compromise between ⟨t⟩ (at the top) and ⟨s⟩ (at the bottom).

Curly-Tail Inverted Glottal Stop

Beach (1938, 289) suggests this symbol to represent a nasal alveolar lateral click (i.e., a velaric ingressive alveolar laterally released stop articulated with lowered velum). The IPA transcription for such a sound, following the usage of recent sources such as Ladefoged and Traill 1984, would be [ŋǁ] or [ŋ͡ǁ].

REVERSED GLOTTAL STOP

IPA USAGE

Voiced pharyngeal fricative.

Used as a right superscript, it is the official IPA diacritic for pharyngealized sounds. See the chart for IPA diacritics.

AMERICAN USAGE

Same as IPA, if used.

COMMENTS

The Arabic sound traditionally known as *'ain,* written ⟨ع⟩ in the Arabic orthography.

There is a confusing usage of this symbol in Firth 1948. Firth uses ⟨ʔ⟩ for the glottal stop in English dialects (see pages 132, 144–45) but uses ⟨ʕ⟩ for the glottal stop in Arabic (the *hamza,* ⟨ʼ⟩ in the Arabic orthography; see pages 138–40). For IPA [ʕ], the Arabic *'ain,* he uses ⟨ɛ⟩ (see pages 142, 147–49). Firth is clearly vacillating between distinct transcription systems: the standard IPA and a variant used for Semitic dialects. (Note the visual similarities: ⟨ʕ⟩, ⟨ʼ⟩, and ⟨ɛ⟩, ⟨ɛ⟩.)

Nine

Smalley's suggestion (1963, 444) for a voiced pharyngealized vowel glide, i.e., the Arabic *'ain* sound, IPA [ʕ], is to use 9 with a subscript tilde to indicate pharyngealization. According to Smalley, this symbol is "arbitrary" but "does have the advantage that the English word *nine* sounds something like the Arabic word *ayin* for anyone who happens to remember it"!

BARRED REVERSED GLOTTAL STOP

Voiced epiglottal fricative.

COMMENTS

Epiglottal fricatives are made by moving the epiglottis backward till it forms a narrow stricture with the rear pharyngeal wall. Such sounds were described as pharyngeal or "emphatic" fricatives in the literature predating the discovery of the pharyngeal/epiglottal articulatory distinction. This discovery was made in the 1980s (see, e.g., Laufer and Condax 1981), and the IPA did not provide symbols for epiglottal sounds until the 1989 Kiel revision.

EXCLAMATION POINT

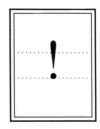

Velaric ingressive stop (i.e., click) with alveolar or postalveolar place of articulation.

AMERICAN USAGE

When used, usually same as IPA.

OTHER USES

Suggested by Boas et al. (1916, 14), as a diacritic to mark a preceding stop consonant as fortis ("exploded"). It is used throughout the *Handbook of American Indian Languages* (Boas 1911) and other grammars of the period.

Used by some Africanists to mark the "downstep" tone, the distinctive lowering of the tonal register within which other tones take their values. This use is attributed to Daniel Jones by Arnott (1964, 37).

COMMENTS

The click sound denoted by [!] is similar to the pop of a cork being drawn from a bottle. It occurs as a consonant in most Khoisan languages and in some Southern Bantu languages. It is represented by *q* in the Zulu orthography.

In the South African tradition stemming from 19th-century work on the Khoisan languages, often used also by American researchers who have worked on them, [!] represents a click with an articulation often referred to as palatal. However, Ladefoged and Traill (1984, 2), departing from most previous work on languages with clicks, describe [!] as an *alveolar* click, disagreeing with earlier writers about what should be considered the primary place of articulation. Caution is necessary, therefore, when this symbol is encountered.

SOURCE

Due to 19th-century orthographic proposals by German philologists, particularly J. G. Krönlein. Cf. Beach 1938 (p. 289).

PIPE

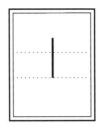

Velaric ingressive stop with dental place of articulation (i.e., dental click). Given in the chart for IPA suprasegmental symbols as an indicator of a minor (foot) group. In this use it could descend below the line of writing.

AMERICAN USAGE

Same as IPA.

OTHER USES

Trager and Smith (1951, 45ff) propose an entirely distinct use of Pipe as a representation of "level juncture," indicating the division (juncture) between phrases across which the pitch remains relatively steady, as for example between the items in a list.

COMMENTS

The click transcribed [ǀ] is similar to the sound used in making the English paralinguistic disapproving noise commonly written by novelists as "tut tut" or sometimes "tsk tsk." It occurs as a consonant in most Khoisan languages and in some Southern Bantu languages. It is represented by *c* in Southern Bantu orthographies. The symbol is associated with the South African tradition stemming from 19th-century work on the Khoisan languages; it is used in such standard works as Westphal 1971.

Of the sound denoted, Ladefoged and Traill (1984, 18) comment: "If it were not for the confusion that would be caused, in view of previous descriptions of clicks, we could more properly call this click denti-alveolar, since the contact area at the time of release definitely includes both the upper teeth and the whole of the alveolar ridge."

Slash is sometimes used instead of Pipe, yielding the transcription '[/]'. Since the pipe symbol has sometimes been used by phonologists in an extra-representational way, typically to enclose underlying phonological representations (see, e.g., Gruber 1973 (p. 427, note 1), for a motley assortment of pipes and slashes in different uses), the possibility of a representation of the form '||||' arises. This should presumably be avoided, perhaps by using '|/|' instead.

SOURCE

The plain vertical bar we call "Pipe" here is occasionally referred to as the "Sheffer stroke" in logic, and is also used in algebra to give set definitions like '$\{x|F(x)\}$'. Trager (1964) calls it "single bar," but it seemed desirable not to confuse this vertical-stroke character with the short horizontal stroke referred to in names like *Barred I*. The name *Pipe* originates in the community of users of the UNIX computer operating system.

Slash

An alternative to Pipe. In the South African tradition stemming from 19th-century work on the Khoisan languages, often used also by American researchers who have worked on them, represents a velaric ingressive stop (i.e., a click) with dental articulation. It is very common to use Pipe and Slash interchangeably; cf. Ladefoged and Traill 1984, where Slash appears in the text but Pipe is used in the legend to the diagrams. Slashes are used by phonologists in a metatranscriptional way to enclose phonemic or other phonological representations, thus: /kæt/ 'cat'. The expression '///' for a dental click phoneme should presumably be avoided in favor of '/|/'. *Source:* Due to 19th-century orthographic proposals by German philologists, particularly J. G. Krönlein (see Beach 1938, 289).

DOUBLE-BARRED PIPE

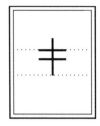

IPA USAGE

Velaric ingressive stop (i.e., click) with palatoalveolar place of articulation.

AMERICAN USAGE

When used, same as IPA.

COMMENTS

Beach asserts that this sound "has been wrongly termed 'palatal' by most writers on Hottentot, including Tindall, Krönlein and Schultze" (1938, 77). But Ladefoged and Traill (1984, 18), after a careful instrumental reinvestigation of this and other clicks, "disagree with Beach in his rejection of the term palatal" for this sound, in effect agreeing with the earlier descriptions (and disagreeing with much other work of this century, e.g., Doke 1926a (p. 146)). They regard the palate as the primary place of articulation, and state that "there is no doubt that [≠] should be described as a palatal sound." Caution is necessary, therefore, when this symbol or the term *palatal click* are encountered in future work, for most modern sources before Ladefoged and Traill agree with Beach.

Slash is sometimes substituted for Pipe, as it is in the above quotation from Ladefoged and Traill, giving the transcription "[≠]", Double-Barred Slash.

SOURCE

Invented during the 19th century, probably by J. G. Krönlein (see Beach 1938 (p. 288ff). Modified to Double-Barred Esh by Beach (1938, 77f).

Double-Barred Slash

An alternative to Double-Barred Pipe. It is very clear that the two symbols are regarded by some writers as interchangeable; for example, Beach (1938, 77) refers to the "upright transversal" of ⟨≠⟩, as if it contained a vertical bar rather than an oblique stroke. Invented during the 19th century, probably by J. G. Krönlein (see Beach 1938 (p. 288ff)). Basically identical with the "not equal to" sign in mathematics.

DOUBLE PIPE

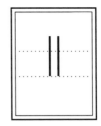

Velaric ingressive stop (i.e., click) with alveolar place of articulation and lateral release. Given in the chart for IPA suprasegmental symbols as an indicator of a major (intonational) group. In this use it could descend below the line of writing.

AMERICAN USAGE

When used, same as IPA.

OTHER USES

Trager and Smith (1951, 45ff) propose an entirely distinct use of Double Pipe as a representation of "terminal rise," one of their four juncture phonemes, which is realized by the rising intonation contour typical of English polar (*yes*/*no*) questions.

COMMENTS

The lateral click is "sometimes used in Western Europe to urge on horses" (Catford 1977 (p. 72)). It occurs as a consonant in most Khoisan languages and in some Southern Bantu languages, e.g., Zulu (Doke 1926b), and is represented as *x* in the Zulu orthography.

The slash (solidus or oblique stroke) is sometimes found instead of the pipe, giving the transcription '[//]'.

SOURCE

Trager (1964, 25) calls this symbol "double bar," but we have dubbed it Double Pipe (the name *pipe* is current among users of the UNIX computer operating system for the vertical bar symbol) in order to avoid ambiguity about what *bar* means in such names as Barred I or Doubled-Barred Pipe.

Double Slash

A typographical alternative to the official IPA symbol Double Pipe, representing a lateral click (velaric ingressive stop). Found in such sources as Cole 1966. The letter *x* is used for the same sound in Southern Bantu orthographies, so the spelling *Xhosa* is used for the language name that some transcriptions would represent as [//hosa]. Introduced into the phonetic transcription of Khoisan languages during the 19th century, probably by J. G. Krönlein (see Beach 1938 (pp. 288ff)).

Triple Slash

Used by Cole (1966, 469) for a retroflex click (i.e., velaric ingressive retroflex stop). The literature on retroflex clicks is complicated and contradictory, but it is clear that genuinely retroflex clicks are extremely rare, and that early work sometimes used the term *retroflex* where it was not justifiable (see Doke 1926b (p. 128), for an acknowledgment of this). Westerman and Ward (1933, 101) persist in the error, however, using a slash with underdot to represent the alleged retroflex click of Nama (cf. Beach 1938 and Ladefoged and Traill 1984 for closer examination of Nama, and see the entry for [!] above). The IPA definition of ʗ in *Principles* (p. 14) has the error yet again, describing the Zulu *q* click as "retroflex" despite Doke's statement (1926b, 128) that this is an error of earlier work (including his own dissertation), the Zulu *q* being "palato-alveolar." The 1979 IPA chart corrects the description by positioning [ʗ] as post-alveolar but not retroflex.

Doke (1926a, 148) explicitly describes a retroflex click contrasting with a post-alveolar or palatal click in ʗhũ:, a Northern Bushman language, which is apparently what Cole is alluding to ("reported for one language, !khū, of the Northern group"; 1966, 469), but Doke represents them with ad hoc symbols of his own devising (see 1926a (p. 144) for a chart), not with Triple Slash, which may be idiosyncratic to Cole.

Number Sign

Not a phonetic symbol (except perhaps for Trager); typically found indicating the (grammatically defined) boundaries of a word in phonological representations. Used along with Plus Sign to mark morphological boundaries of various sorts, typically the boundary between words. (Cf. Chomsky and Halle 1968 (pp. 12–13).) In Trager and Smith (1951, 45ff) analysis of English intonation, used to mark the "terminal fall juncture" phoneme, the falling intonation contour typical of English declarative sentences. The symbol has a variety of names, including *crosshatch, double cross, hash mark, number sign,* and *pound sign.*

Ampersand

The phonemic transcription proposed for Marshallese in Bender 1968 uses the ampersand as the symbol for a vowel with at least three phonetic representations, IPA [ɪ], [ɨ], and [ʊ]. Bender says, "The ampersand is chosen over *u* or *o* to represent this 'fourth' vowel in order to avoid any connotations of inherent rounding" (p. 32, note 7). He calls /&/ the "fourth" vowel in the four-vowel system because he sees some indications of its having a derivative or perhaps diphthongal phonological status. Because data citations in Bender's article are italicized, it is the italic form of the ampersand, looking rather different from the usual unitalicized form shown above, that actually appears in print in all but one or two phonological formulae. Bender remarks (p. 33, note 13) that *ie* or *ei* would be good choices for representing the vowel phoneme in a practical orthography, but this course is not followed in Bender 1969, where Ampersand (this time in an open-top style from a typewriter font) is again used without remark. Ampersand is also used in the orthography for Inuktitut (Canadian Eskimo) adopted by the Inuit Cultural Institute and used in books such as Spalding 1979, where it represents a voiceless lateral fricative, IPA [ɬ]. This is an orthographic rather than a phonetic use of the symbol, but may be encountered in some linguistic works on Eskimo languages. The ampersand originates as a manuscript abbreviation for the Latin word *et* 'and', later conventionalized in print and used for English *and.*

Asterisk

IPA Usage: Suggested (*Principles,* 17) as a prefix to indicate a word that is a proper name. This recommendation seems to be rarely followed. *American Usage:* No standard use as a phonetic symbol. *Other uses:* Ladefoged (1993, 169) suggests the use of the asterisk and an accompanying explanation for any sound that otherwise has no agreed symbol (and made the same proposal in earlier editions); but this seems idiosyncratic.

Historical linguists use ⟨*⟩ to prefix reconstructed forms—representations of sound properties that do not derive from observation but are rather deduced through historical and comparative reasoning. August Schleicher first used the asterisk in this way.

The most common use of the asterisk among linguists, including phonologists, is as a prefix for ungrammatical or nonexistent forms, sentences, or expressions. This use largely supplants all others in current linguistic practice and is at least as old as Sweet 1898 (p. 3).

CHAO TONE LETTERS

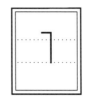

IPA USAGE

Iconic representations of tones. The symbols shown for illustration on this page represent tones that are, respectively, high, mid, low, rising, high rising, and fall-rise. Other such letters may be devised by analogy. See the chart for IPA suprasegmental symbols.

COMMENTS

Though proposed by a distinguished linguist and sinologist over six decades ago, these letters were not adopted as official by the IPA until 1989, when a decision was made not to decide between two different representations of tone, but to accept both of them. Chao's symbols are clearly iconic: the small stroke attached to the vertical bar is drawn to reflect an idealized picture of the movement of fundamental frequency heard when a syllable with that tone is pronounced: high for a high tone, sloping upward for a rising tone, and so on.

SOURCE

The invention of Yuen-Ren Chao, who published his proposal in Chao 1933.

IPA DIACRITICAL TONE MARKS

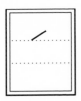

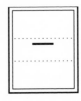

IPA USAGE

Iconic representations of tones. The symbols shown for illustration on this page represent tones that are, respectively, high, mid, low, rising, falling, and fall-rise. Other such marks are also permitted; for example, extra-high tone may be indicated by [̋]. See the chart for IPA suprasegmental symbols.

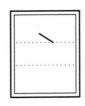

COMMENTS

In 1989 the IPA decided not to decide between two different representations of tone, but to accept both. Those shown here are (partially iconic uses of) marks shaped like various accents that have often been used for tone marking, especially by linguists working on African languages. To some extent, the accent marks reflect an idealized picture of the movement of fundamental frequency heard when a syllable with that tone is pronounced. However, the mapping from picture to accent mark is not entirely straightforward; the acute accent [́] is used for a high tone (the position of the right-hand end is what is iconic for high), [̌] is used for rising (the direction of the right-hand half of the symbol represents the rise), and so on.

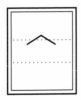

SOURCE

See the *Journal of the International Phonetic Association* 19 ((1989), 75–77), for a discussion of the uses and motivation of these symbols.

Macron

IPA Usage: The current IPA interpretation is for mid tone. As a superscript to a vowel symbol, recommended (*Principles,* 18) as a transcription for a high level tone. The suggestion in *Principles* that tone markings be iconic reserved the macron or hyphen as a representation for a level tone, with the pitch to be represented by vertical positioning on the line. Therefore [-ba] would represent a syllable on a mid level tone, [⁻ba] or [bā] a high level tone, and [ba] or [ba̲] a low level tone. This iconic use of line position was never common, and is no longer approved (see IPA Diacritical Tone Marks). *American Usage:* Used to mark length or tenseness of a vowel, as in Chomsky and Halle 1968 (p. 51). Also occasionally used in other ways; for example, Mohanan and Mohanan (1984, 598) write [s̄] and [r̄] for palatalized [s] and [r]. Boas et al. (1916, 13) recommend the macron as a diacritic to distinguish a strongly trilled *r* sound from its nontrilled counterpart. The recommendation is not generally followed, but it is perhaps the source of the similar use of the tilde by Pike and Smalley. *Other uses:* Very commonly used for marking vowel length in teaching grammars and in English dictionary pronunciation guides.

Minus Sign

IPA Usage: When not used simply as a hyphen in the ordinary way in broadly transcribed texts, *Principles* (p. 17) suggests its use for a retracted variety of a vowel or consonant; thus [a−] would denote a vowel somewhat retracted (further back) from Cardinal 4. *Principles* allowed it to be written [a⊣] if [a−] might be misconstrued as [a] fol-

lowed by a hyphen. The 1989 revision makes the retraction diacritic
a subscript, Underbar. *American Usage:* Reserved by Boas et al.
(1916, 8) as a nonphonetic character to be used in indicating the morphological analysis of words in texts.

Underbar

IPA Usage: Indicates retraction, e.g., alveolar place of articulation in
a language (e.g., Tamil) that also has dentals. Thus [t̠] is specifically
alveolar, leaving [t] to represent the dental stop. This is the current
official IPA interpretation. See the chart for IPA diacritics. Under a
vowel symbol or before a symbol, recommended (*Principles,* 18) as a
transcription for a low level tone. The IPA suggestion that tone markings be iconic reserves the macron or hyphen as a representation for a
level tone, with the pitch to be represented by vertical positioning on
the line. Therefore [-ba] would represent a syllable on a mid level tone,
[‾ba] or [bā] a high level tone, and [ba] or [ba̠] a low level tone. This
iconic use of line position is rare in practice. *American Usage:* Unfortunately, sometimes used as a substitute for [̪] to indicate dental
place of articulation as opposed to alveolar. Thus Mohanan and Mohanan (1984) use [t] for alveolar and [t̠] for dental in the voiceless stops,
the direct converse of the IPA usage. *Other uses:* Pike's *Phonemics*
(1947) uses underbar to indicate voicelessness; thus Pike's [m̠] is IPA
[m̥]. Used as a diacritic in transliterations of Arabic symbols for emphatic (velarized) consonants (cf. Al-Ani 1970 (p. 29)). The underdot
is also a common diacritic for such transliterations (cf. Beeston 1958
(p. 11)). *Comments:* Clearly, caution is in order when the underbar
is encountered. It is unfortunate as a diacritic for other reasons as well,
notably that a typesetter will normally set an underlined manuscript
character in italic font unless a specific marginal note is attached.

Plus Sign

IPA Usage: Indicates an advanced (further front) variety of a vowel or consonant; thus [ɑ+] is a vowel a little further forward than Cardinal 5, and [k+] is a [k] articulated somewhat closer to the palatal area. The official IPA diacritic is written as a subscript. Cf. *Principles* (p. 16). *American Usage:* Not generally used as a phonetic character. Boas et al. (1916, 7) recommend its use as an indicator of grammatically insignificant, rhetorical lengthening when transcribing (spoken) texts. *Other uses:* Widely used, along with the number sign ⟨#⟩ and occasionally the equals sign ⟨=⟩ (cf. Aronoff 1976), as an indicator of a morphological boundary. See, e.g., Chomsky and Halle 1968 (pp. 12–13) where it is used as a formative boundary. Used by Trager and Smith (1951, 38) to mark an "internal open juncture" phoneme that they posit in their analysis of English. The "plus juncture" is the distinguishing element between the pronunciation of English *nitrate* (Trager and Smith's /náytrèyt/) and *night rate* (Trager and Smith's /náyt+rèyt/), which are otherwise identical segmentally and suprasegmentally. It is intended to represent a break in the normal articulatory transition between the two consonants across the word boundary in the compound.

Subscript Plus

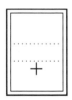

IPA Usage: Indicates an advanced (further front) variety of a vowel or consonant. See the chart for IPA diacritics. *Other uses:* Used by Smalley (1963, 420) and Samarin (1967, 183) as a diacritic for "breathy" vowels. The IPA diacritic for breathy voice is Subscript Umlaut.

Superscript Cross

IPA Usage: Indicates mid-centralization (i.e., an articulation tending toward that of the sound [ə] of vowels. *Comments:* This diacritic apparently does the work that would formerly have been done by means of a right superscript Schwa under the policy enunciated in *Principles* (p. 17): "Small index letters may be used to indicate shades of sound." The transcription [ě] is apparently supposed to mean the same as [eᵊ]. *Source:* An ad hoc invention added to the IPA's alphabet in 1989. Possibly intended to be iconic, the crossed strokes suggesting the center of the two-dimensional vocal tract elevation, where the sound represented by [ə] is abstractly located.

Superscript Equals

Used by Wells (1982, xvii) as a diacritic for unaspirated consonants, but not officially sanctioned by the IPA.

Subscript Bridge

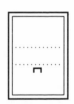

IPA Usage: Under a symbol normally denoting an alveolar consonant, indicates dental place of articulation. Thus [n], [t], and [d] are alveolar, and [n̪], [t̪], and [d̪] represent dentals with the same manners of articulation.   *American Usage:* Same as IPA, if used, but various substitutes are found. Pike (1947, 7) and Gleason (1955, 7), following Boas et al. (1916, 10), write [t̪] for a voiceless dental stop (IPA [t̪]); Smalley (1963, 454) writes [t̪]; Mohanan and Mohanan (1984, 598), in a recent study of a language with both dental and alveolar consonants, write [t̪].

Subscript Turned Bridge

IPA Usage: Used beneath dental/alveolar symbols to indicate apical (tongue-tip) rather than laminal (tongue-blade) articulation of lingual consonants.   *Comments:* Clearly, the availability of this diacritic means that apico-labial consonants could have been represented by [p̺], [b̺], [m̺], etc. Thus the addition of the seagull diacritic to the IPA's alphabet was apparently unnecessary.   *Source:* A turned version of the long-established Subscript Bridge diacritic for dentality, introduced into the IPA symbol inventory in 1989.

Subscript Box

IPA Usage: Used beneath dental/alveolar symbols to indicate laminal (tongue-blade) rather than apical (tongue-tip) articulation. For example, the variety of American English rhotacization that produced with the tongue tip down and the blade raised (see Ladefoged 1993 (p. 84)) might be narrowly transcribed with [ɚ̻].   *Source:* Added to the IPA's alphabet after the 1989 Kiel convention.

Raising Sign

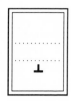

IPA Usage: Raising or closing sign: [e˔] indicates a vowel a little higher (closer) than Cardinal 2. Can also be written as a subscript, e.g., [e̝]. The connection between higher and closer gives the use of [w˔] for a voiced labial-velar central fricative in Ladefoged 1968 (p. xviii). Cf. *Principles* (p. 16).

Lowering Sign

IPA Usage: Indicates lower or more open articulation. For example, [e̞] indicates a vowel a little lower (more open) than Cardinal 2. Sometimes known as the "tiny T" diacritic in IPA circles. The connection between lower and more open gives the use of [ɣ˕] for a voiced velar central approximant in Ladefoged 1968 (p. xviii), where the diacritic is set beside the Gamma rather than beneath it. Cf. *Principles* (p. 16).

Advancement Sign

IPA Usage: Under current (1993) IPA principles, indicates an articulation with advanced tongue root. *Comments:* Originally (in *Principles*) this symbol was a diacritic to indicate advanced (fronted) articulation of any sort (for example, under [k] it would indicate a somewhat fronted articulation, between [k] and [c]). *Source:* An IPA invention, basically iconic in origin (note that the crossbar points to the left, which is toward the front given the usual orientation of vowel charts and mid-sagittal cut diagrams).

Retraction Sign

IPA Usage: Under current (1993) IPA principles, indicates an articulation with retracted tongue root. *Comments:* Originally (in *Principles*) this symbol was a diacritic to indicate retracted articulation of any sort (for example, under [k] it would indicate a somewhat backed articulation, between [k] and [q]). *Source:* An IPA invention, basically iconic in origin (note that the crossbar points to the right, which is toward the back given the usual orientation of vowel charts and mid-sagittal cut diagrams).

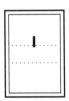

Vertical Stroke (Superior)

IPA Usage: Placed as a separate character, indicates primary stress on the following syllable. *Billow* might be transcribed [ˈbɪloʊ], and *below* as [bɪˈloʊ]. *American Usage:* Not entirely standard, but often same as IPA. Boas et al. 1916 recommends the vertical stroke over a vowel symbol as an indicator of mid tone where it is necessary to mark it. *Other uses:* Used by Winston (1960) (cf. Welmers 1973 (p. 85)) in his transcription of Igbo to mark "downstep," the distinctive lowering of the tonal register within which other tones take their values.

Typographically the character is a vertical stroke of even width. The single quote symbol in most typewriter fonts, which is tapered at the bottom or teardrop shaped, is often used indifferently for this character and for Apostrophe, Reversed Apostrophe, and Left Quote.

Vertical Stroke (Inferior)

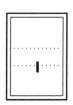

IPA Usage: Placed as a separate character, indicates a secondary, less prominent stress on the following syllable. *Photographic* might be transcribed [ˌfoʊtəˈgræfɪk].

Syllabicity Mark

IPA Usage: Indicates that the symbol it is written under represents a syllabic sound. Thus, the word *little* is usually transcribed [lɪtl̩]. *American Usage:* Same as IPA, if used. *Comments:* Not used under symbols for vowels (they are always syllabic) or oral stops, but typically under symbols for liquids or nasals, and occasionally also fricatives. The inverse of ⟨ˌ⟩ is ⟨˘⟩, which is used to indicate the *non-*syllabicity of a vowel.

Corner

IPA Usage: Following a stop consonant symbol, approved (*Journal of the International Phonetic Association* 6 (p. 2)) as the official diacritic to represent lack of audible release. Positioned before a syllable, suggested (*Principles,* 18) as a possibility for use in narrow tone transcription for raised or lowered rising tones. *American Usage:* After a stop consonant symbol, used to indicate that the stop is unreleased. Cf. Trager 1964 (p. 26).

Up Arrow

IPA Usage: Indicates upstep in tone transcription. See the chart for IPA suprasegmental symbols. *Other uses:* Catford (1988, 29) uses Up Arrow to indicate egressive airstream on consonant transcriptions that would normally be associated with ingressive airstream; thus he writes [ɟ↑] for a voiceless velaric egressive dental stop. The up arrow is iconic for egressive airstream if one conceptualizes the airstream as typically going straight up the pharynx on its way to the oral and nasal apertures.

Down Arrow

IPA Usage: Indicates downstep on the preceding phonological phrase in a tone language. See the chart for IPA suprasegmental symbols. *Other uses:* Used by Catford (1988, 27) to indicate ingressive airstream in consonants that would normally be associated with egressive airstream; thus he writes [k'↓] for a voiceless glottalic ingressive velar stop (voiceless glottalic stops are typically egressive, i.e., ejective). *Comments:* Down Arrow is rather clearly iconic in its use to indicate downstep, a characteristic lowering of pitch as the phonological word or phrase proceeds. It could be seen as iconic in Catford's use too if the ingressive airstream is visualized as going down the throat instead of straight up on its way out of the lungs.

Northeast Arrow

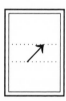

IPA Usage: Marks a global rise in intonation. (Clearly iconic.) See the chart for IPA suprasegmental symbols.

Southeast Arrow

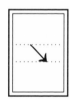

IPA Usage: Marks a global fall in intonation. (Clearly iconic.) See the chart for IPA suprasegmental symbols.

Left Pointer

Often found as an indication of fronting of vowel or consonant articulations; see, e.g., Kurath 1939 (p. 129), Pike 1947 (p. 7), Smalley 1963 (p. 371), and Trager 1964 (pp. 25–26). Thus Trager writes [k<] for a fronted [k] (IPA [kʲ]), [u<] for an advanced [u] (IPA [u-]), and so on. The intent is for the diacritic to be iconic: given the familiar convention of diagramming the production of sounds on a mid-sagittal cut outline facing to the left (so that the front is at the left as with the standard layout of the vowel and consonant charts), Left Pointer points in the direction of advancement. A distinct use differs confusingly from the foregoing one: Left Pointer has sometimes been used to indicate implosive (glottalic ingressive) airstream, especially for voiceless implosives and other implosives with no approved IPA symbolization. Thus Maddieson 1984, Pinkerton 1986, Henton, Ladefoged, and Maddieson 1992, and other works use [p<] to represent a voiceless bilabial implosive, [t<] to represent a voiceless alveolar implosive, and so on. The intent is doubtless for this use of the diacritic to be iconic too, but here the orientation of the iconic interpretation does *not* match the orientation of vowel and consonant charts: the arrow points back against the direction of writing, but (to the extent that air does flow into the mouth during the articulation of implosives, which is often not very great) this is the opposite of the direction that the inward airflow would be indicated on a standard mid-sagittal cut diagram. (Even more confusingly, *Right* Pointer has also been used for ingressive airflow; see the entry for Subscript Right Pointer. And to add to the confusion, Catford 1988 (pp. 27–29) uses a different iconic scheme, writing [↓] after a consonant transcription to indicate ingressive airstream and [↑] to indicate egressive airstream.)

Right Pointer

Often found (generally following, or as a right superscript to, an alphabetic symbol) as an indication of backing of vowel or consonant articulations; see, e.g., Kurath 1939 (p. 129), Pike 1947 (p. 7), Smalley 1963 (p. 371), and Trager 1964 (pp. 25–26). The intent is for the diacritic to be iconic: given the familiar convention of diagramming the production of sounds on a mid-sagittal cut outline facing to the left (so that the front is at the left as with the standard layout of the vowel and consonant charts), Right Pointer points in the direction of retraction.

Subscript Right Pointer

Fuller (1990), describing certain pulmonic ingressive sounds attested in the Tfuea dialect of the Austronesian language Tsou (spoken on Mt. Ali in southern Taiwan), uses this diacritic below consonant symbols to represent them as having pulmonic ingressive airstream mechanism. There are only two such sounds in the language: a labiodental fricative and a glottal fricative, both voiceless, and both occurring only word-initially before a consonant, usually a glottal stop. For example, he cites [f̰ʔuhu], glossed 'back'. Traill (1991) uses the same convention in narrow transcription of certain "delayed aspirated" clicks in the Khoisan language !Xóõ which have pulmonically initiated ingressive nasal flow during the articulation of a velaric ingressive voiceless nasal stop. The direction of the pointer can be regarded as iconic, since it points in the direction of airflow assuming the usual orientation of a mid-sagittal cut diagram, i.e., facing left. Regrettably, Left Pointer [ˁ] has also been used for *in*gressive airflow (though it is not IPA-approved or otherwise standard), and under the interpretation just cited this would be anti-iconic. However, in practical terms there will be little opportunity for confusion to arise over this point, simply because speech sounds with any kind of pulmonic ingressive airflow are rare to the point of nonexistence. The pulmonic ingressivity of the Tsou fricatives cited by Fuller has been reinvestigated by Ladefoged and Zeitoun (1993), who find that it must be at best an idiosyncrasy of Fuller's informant: no one else who used ingressive fricatives could be found in the informant's village—neither his mother nor his father used them, for example. And as for the inward pulmonic airflow discovered by Traill in !Xóõ, that airflow is not the primary airstream in the segments in question. Apart from these two cases, the only use of pulmonic ingressive airstream initiation ever reported in the literature would appear to be a lateral sound in Damin, a ritual language of the Lardil people of Mornington Island, Australia, which seems to have been deliberately and consciously designed by its developers to be phonetically elaborate (see Catford 1977 (p. 65), citing a personal communication from Kenneth Hale of MIT). Hockett (1955, 26) states that Maidu (an Amerindian language of California) has not only pulmonic ingressive stops but whole syllables with pulmonic ingressive airflow even on the vowel, but this is not correct. Maidu has ordinary implosives with glottalic ingressive airstream, and no ingressive vowels. Hockett labored under a disadvantage in that he was writing before the appearance of the first reliable report on Maidu (Shipley 1956). Smalley 1963 (p. 379), repeats Hockett's claim without any such excuse.

 ## Superscript Left Arrow

Used by Smalley (1963, 427) and Samarin (1967, 183) as a diacritic for click (velaric ingressive stop) consonant symbols. Hence [p$^{\leftarrow}$] would be the transcription of a voiceless bilabial unaspirated click.

Overdot

IPA Usage: According to *Principles* (p. 17), it may be added to a character to denote palatalization. Thus [ż] = [ʐ], [ṡ] = [ʂ], etc. The IPA withdrew approval in 1976 (*Journal of the International Phonetic Association* 6 (p. 3)). *American Usage:* Not standard, but may be used as recommended by the IPA. According to the diacritic principles set forth by Boas et al. (1916, 10) the overdot is used over front and back vowel symbols to create symbols for central vowels. Following this recommendation, Bloch and Trager (1942, 16) and Trager (1964, 22) use [o] to represent a back vowel, [ȯ] a central vowel, and [ö] a front vowel; [e] to represent a front vowel, [ė] a central vowel, and [ë] a back vowel. *Other uses:* Also found as the variant of Underdot used with letters which have descenders (e.g., [ġ] in Trager 1964 (p. 22)). *Source:* The convention of writing an overdot on a consonant that is phonetically palatalized is found in many works on Old English, e.g., Sweet's *Anglo-Saxon Primer* (1882). The Americanist usage is considered a logical extension of the convention for the use of the umlaut diacritic for reversal of backness.

Raised Period

IPA Usage: Strictly speaking, not used (but may be found as a typographical substitution for the half-length mark ⟨ˑ⟩). *American Usage:* Used after a symbol to indicate that the preceding segment is distinctively long. According to the recommendations of Boas et al. (1916, 7), the raised period (⟨˙⟩) is the recommended length mark to be used after a symbol to indicate that the sound is long. The colon was designated as marking excessive length, longer than that represented by ⟨ˈ⟩. For languages which make a contrast between only two degrees of length, the colon is generally used as the length mark. Where both indicators occur, the colon represents greater length.

Period

IPA Usage: Represents a syllable break. *American Usage:* Often used in the same way as the IPA's current official use.

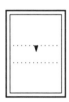

Half-Length Mark

IPA Usage: Indicates that "the sound represented by the preceding letter is half-long" (*Principles,* 17). In a narrow transcription of English, the IPA (*Principles,* 20) transcribes *he blew* as [hiˑˌbluː]. See the chart for IPA suprasegmental symbols. *American Usage:* Same as IPA, if used, but a raised period would generally be used instead.

Underdot

IPA Usage: Indicates a closer (i.e., higher) variety of a vowel; thus IPA [ẹ] represents a slightly higher front vowel than IPA [e], as does the alternative notation [e⊥] or [ẹ]. This use has been extended (*Jour-*

nal of the International Phonetic Association 6 (p. 2)) to disambiguate the voiced fricative symbols ⟨β⟩, ⟨ð⟩, ⟨z⟩, ⟨ɹ⟩, and ⟨ʁ⟩, which had been officially ambiguous between a fricative and a frictionless approximant. With the underdot, one of these symbols unambiguously denotes the fricative value. Also extended to [w]. Hence [ẉ] would denote a voiced labiovelar fricative. The corresponding indicator of the approximant value is the subscript half-ring. Thus, the *r*-sounds in English *dread* and *red* may be distinguished as [ɹ̣] and [ɹ̯] respectively. *American Usage:* Generally, used as a retraction sign for consonants. Thus [x̣] may be found for a backed velar or uvular fricative, [r̃] for a uvular trilled *r*-sound, and so on. Cf. Boas et al. 1916 (p. 10). Retroflex consonants are considered to be retracted alveolars, making the use of the underdot consistent with the Indic and Dravidian use described below. The overdot is sometimes written above letters with descenders (cf. [ġ] in Trager 1964 (p. 22)). (The underdot occurs in the American transcription [ḥ] for a voiceless pharyngeal fricative, IPA [ħ], without its retraction sense.) *Other uses:* Following a tradition established by Sanskritists and commonly used in transliteration of Indic and Dravidian languages, the underdot under a symbol for an alveolar sound indicates retroflex articulation; thus [ṭ] = IPA [ʈ], etc. Used in Brugmann 1904 (p. 1) as a diacritic for retroflex consonants, and also with *e* and *o* as a diacritic for close vowels. Meillet and Cohen (1952, xiv) use it with the latter sense. Used in some works on African languages to indicate various varieties of vowels. For example [ụ] may be found for unrounded IPA [ɯ], [ị] may be used for a narrow (retracted tongue-root) variety of high front vowel, and so on (cf. Tucker 1971, Welmers 1973). Also used by Arabists for the "emphatic" consonants, i.e., to denote velarization or pharyngealization (cf. Beeston 1968 (p. 11)). *Comments:* The underdot has had too many diverse uses to be used without a note of explanation, and it should be avoided where possible for this reason. The most widely recognized use is probably to represent retroflexion.

Umlaut

IPA Usage: A diacritic used over vowels to indicate centralization. That is, retraction for a front vowel or advancement for a back vowel. *Principles* (p. 16) recommends its use on a front or back vowel symbol to make a symbol for a central vowel of the same height and rounding as the base vowel: [ï] is an alternative to [ɨ]; [ü] is an alternative to [ʉ]. The diacritic was recommended to indicate that the vowel in question was a member of a back or front vowel phoneme. In 1975, the secretary of the IPA pointed out that "it is widely believed—at least among phoneticians in Britain—that the vowel diacritic [¨] means 'centralized': so that [ë] is between front and central, [ü] between central and back," disagreeing with *Principles*. (He cited Gimson 1970 (p. 38) as an example of this interpretation.) In 1976 the IPA altered the definition of the diacritic [¨] so that it marks a vowel as "centralized," not central (*Journal of the International Phonetic Association* 6 (p. 2)). According to this interpretation, [ü] would represent a vowel between [u] and [ʉ]. This is the current official IPA interpretation of this diacritic. *American Usage:* Most commonly employed as indicator of reversal of backness of vowels. Suggested in the recommendations of Boas et al. (1916, 9) as a means of extending cardinal vowel signs to create signs for additional vowels. A vowel sign with the umlaut denotes a vowel with the same properties as the base vowel sign with the opposite value for backness. Hence [ï] is a vowel with the same properties as [i] but back instead of front, i.e., IPA [ɯ]; and [ü] is high rounded and front, i.e., IPA [y], and so on. *Comments:* The diacritic of two dots over a vowel symbol is referred to either as the "umlaut" or "dieresis," depending upon the function that it serves. In the orthographies for some European languages (e.g., German) it is used to mark the vowels IPA [y] and [ø] (cf. German *über* 'over', *ölen* 'to oil') which were originally introduced via a vowel-fronting sound change called *umlaut*. Functioning as an indicator of dieresis, it is used over the second of two consecutive vowel symbols to indicate that the vowels are to be interpreted as being in separate syllables rather than as a diphthong or else to block the interpretation of the two vowel symbols as a digraph (e.g., English *coöperate, coördinate*). The name *umlaut* has been chosen here because it is generally used to modify vowel symbol denotations in a manner similar to (but much broader than) its use in German orthography.

Subscript Umlaut

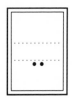

IPA Usage: Indicates "breathy voice" or "murmur." Thus [b̤] is a murmured (nearly voiced) stop, [b̤ʱ] is a murmured stop with breathy off-glide. The IPA (*Journal of the International Phonetic Association* 6 (p. 2)) has adopted this proposal. *American Usage:* Same as IPA, if used. *Other uses:* Used in Meillet and Cohen 1952 (p. xiv) for a diacritic for retroflex consonants.

Colon

IPA Usage: Strictly speaking, not used (but often found as a typographical substitute for the length mark, [ː]). *American Usage:* Marks length of the preceding segment; thus [t:] = [t͡t], [e:] = [e͡e]. According to the recommendations of Boas et al. (1916, 7), the raised period (⟨˙⟩) is the recommended length mark to be used after a symbol to indicate that the sound is long. The colon was designated as marking excessive length, longer than that represented by ⟨˙⟩. For languages which make a contrast between only two degrees of length, either the colon or the raised period may be used as the length mark. Where both occur, the colon represents greater length. *Comments:* As a punctuation mark, the colon represents something of a pause, so it is a not unnatural choice for indicating increased length.

Length Mark

IPA Usage: Indicates that "the sound represented by the preceding letter is long." Thus [tː] = [t͡t]; [eː] = [e͡e]. See the chart for IPA suprasegmental symbols. *American Usage:* Same as IPA, if used. The colon ⟨ː⟩ is generally substituted as a more readily available typographical alternative.

Apostrophe

IPA Usage: Used to derive symbols for ejective (glottalic egressive) consonants like [p'], [t'], and [s']. *American Usage:* Same as IPA, but also recommended by Boas et al. (1916, 14) to represent glottal stop (IPA [ʔ]). Its use was extended as a diacritic for glottalized or ejective consonants, either following the symbol (e.g., [p']) or over the symbol (e.g., ⟨p̓⟩). When used as a diacritic for vowels, it represents laryngealization ("creaky voice"). *Other uses:* Standardly used by Slavicists to indicate palatalization of a preceding consonant. *Comments:* Apostrophe is a raised comma, not the vertical stroke generally found in typewriter fonts. It should be distinct from the (laterally) Reversed Apostrophe and the Left Quote.

Reversed Apostrophe

IPA Usage: Recommended in *Principles* for weak aspiration after voiceless stops. No longer approved. *Journal of the International Phonetic Association* (6, 2) records the approval of a superscript *h* (ʰ) as an alternative to avoid confusion with Apostrophe for glottalization. Could be used to distinguish weakly aspirated stops like [p'] in English from strongly aspirated stops like [pʰ] in Hindi.   *American Usage:* Not in general use, but the use recommended by Boas et al. (1916, 14) is the same as the IPA's: weak aspiration after voiceless stops.   *Other uses:* Might be found as a substitute for Left Quote as the transliteration of the Arabic character *'ain,* ⟨ε⟩, which represents a voiced pharyngeal fricative (IPA [ʕ]).   *Comments:* The "rough breathing" of Ancient Greek represented an /h/ onset to a vowel or voiceless onset to an /r/, and looks very similar. This may have influenced the IPA's choice.

Left Quote

American Usage: Used by Trager and Smith (1951, 11) as a diacritic for aspiration, rather than Reversed Apostrophe (the latter having the approval of Boas et al. (1916) and the IPA, but being less available typographically).   *Other uses:* Prokosch (1939, 50) uses Left Quote in a similar way. Left Quote is also commonly used to transliterate Arabic *'ain,* ⟨ε⟩, (IPA [ʕ], the voiced pharyngeal fricative; see, e.g., Beeston 1968 (p. 11)), though Reversed Apostrophe may also be found. Another use of this symbol is as an orthographic representation of the glottal stop (IPA [ʔ]) in Hawaiian, though Apostrophe is commonly substituted.   *Comments:* There is considerable vacillation between Apostrophe, Reversed Apostrophe, and Left Quote in several of their uses. The latter two have broadly similar shapes and can easily be confused. A certain amount of caution is advisable when interpreting phonetic texts containing either of them. *Source:* Standard punctuation mark in many fonts, probably picked for its similarity to the Greek "rough breathing" mark.

Comma

IPA Usage: A punctuation symbol in the usual sense; no phonetic value. *American Usage:* No phonetic value. *Other uses:* Slavicists sometimes use the comma to indicate palatalization of the preceding consonant (much like the IPA's diacritic hook as seen in ⟨t̡⟩); thus Russian [brat̡] 'to take' might be written ⟨brat,⟩.

Reversed Comma

IPA Usage: Not in general use or included in the IPA chart, but specifically mentioned in the "Further improvements" section of *Principles* (p. 19) as having been suggested "as a sign to denote that a stop has no plosion." *Comments:* Presumably the idea was to use [t˒] to transcribe a final unexploded [t]. In current IPA, this would be [t˺]. Though never actually included in the IPA chart, this symbol did get included in the LaserIPA font from Linguist's Software, and in the WordPerfect phonetic font included with WordPerfect for Windows 6.0. *Source:* Standard punctuation mark, laterally reversed.

Over-Ring

IPA Usage: May be used over letters with descenders as an alternative to Under-ring to indicate devoicing. Thus *Principles* (p. 16) gives [b̥] and [d̥], but [g̊] rather than [g]. *American Usage:* No standard use. *Other uses:* Abercrombie (1957, 150) and Ladefoged (1982, 51) use a right superscript over-ring to indicate lack of release, e.g., [p°] for unreleased [p]. When the IPA approved the use of the corner symbol ⟨ ⌐⟩ as the accepted diacritic for unreleased stops (*Journal of the International Phonetic Association* 6 (p. 2)), the right superscript ring received nearly as many votes. Right superscript over-ring is also used to indicate labialization, e.g., in transcriptions for Caucasian languages (Hewitt 1979 is an example). Also used with the IPA sense by Prokosch (1939, 50). *Source:* The orthographies of the Scandinavian languages use ⟨å⟩ to represent a low back rounded vowel, as in Swedish *skål* 'bowl', suggesting a source for its occasional use as a right superscript to indicate labialization. The over-ring of ⟨ů⟩ in the Czech orthography is called the *kroužek* ('little circle') in Czech. In the various orthographies that employ the over-ring, it has usually originated in a digraph in which an *o* was written above an accompanying vowel.

Under-Ring

IPA Usage: Official IPA devoicing diacritic. IPA [r̥] is a voiceless trilled *r* (as in certain Scottish dialects in word-final position); [b̥] is a weak (lenis) voiceless bilabial stop (with the slack articulation of a voiced stop but lacking the voicing); [i̥] is a voiceless high front unrounded vowel; and so on. *American Usage:* Generally same as IPA. The under-ring was used as a marker of devoicing in early Americanist work (cf. Boas 1911 (p. 13ff)). The recommendations of Boas et al. (1916, 15) substituted the convention for small capital letters for this use and recommended its use as a marker of syllabic consonants. This recommendation was not widely followed and the mark of syllabicity is a short vertical stroke beneath the symbol. *Other uses:* Used by some Indo-Europeanists (e.g., Brugmann (1904, 1) and Meillet and Cohen (1952, xiv)) as a marker of syllabicity for consonants. Prokosch (1939, 50) uses it in its IPA sense.

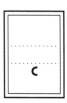

Subscript Left Half-Ring

IPA Usage: The official IPA diacritic to mark decreased rounding. See the chart for IPA diacritics. Recommended (*Principles,* 16) to mark open varieties of vowels; thus [ẹ] is an alternative to [e⊤] or [ę]. The IPA (*Journal of the International Phonetic Association* 6 (p. 2)) has extended the use of this diacritic to disambiguate the voiced fricative symbols ⟨β⟩, ⟨ð⟩, ⟨z⟩, ⟨ɹ⟩, and ⟨ʁ⟩, which had been officially ambiguous between a fricative and a frictionless approximant. With the subscript left half-ring the symbol unambiguously represents the approximant value. The corresponding indicator of the fricative value is Underdot. Thus, the *r*-sounds in English *dread* and *red* may be distinguished as [ɹ̪] and [ɹ] respectively. *American Usage:* Found in at least one source (Gleason 1955 (p. 69)) marking sounds that start voiceless and become voiced. *Comments:* The diacritic is rarely encountered. Some attempts at Polish Hook may look like this when the diacritic is not tied properly to the character body.

Right Half-Ring

Used to indicate pulmonic ingressive airstream in the discussion of pulmonic ingressive articulations in Laver 1994, section 6.1.2 (pp. 168–170). For a discussion of such sounds, see the entries for Left Pointer and Subscript Right Pointer.

Subscript Right Half-Ring

IPA Usage: Indicates "more rounded." See the chart for IPA diacritics. *American Usage:* Found in Gleason 1955 (p. 69) marking sounds that start voiced and become voiceless. *Comments:* The diacritic is rarely found. Some typographical attempts at a cedilla or a left hook look like this when not tied properly to the character body.

Tilde

IPA Usage: Nasalization marker for vowels, or occasionally for consonants; thus [ɑ̃] is a nasalized [ɑ] as in French *en* 'in', [ɣ̃] is a voiced velar fricative articulated with lowered velum, etc. *American Usage:* Various uses. Pike (1947) and Smalley (1963) use it in a number of ways: over ⟨n⟩ for a palatal or palato-alveolar nasal; over other consonants to represent trills ([r̃] alveolar trill; [ɾ̃] uvular trill; [p̃] voiceless bilabial trill; [ɓ] voiced bilabial trill); and also over other consonants and vowels to indicate nasalization.

Mid Tilde

IPA Usage: Indicates velarization or pharyngealization. (Since these do not contrast in attested languages, there is no ambiguity in practice.) Thus [ɫ] is the velarized "dark" *l*-sound heard in postvocalic position in English; [ḍ] can be used for the Arabic "emphatic" *d*-sound; and so on. *American Usage:* Sometimes same as IPA, but some departures are found. For example, [ɫ] may be found for a voiceless alveolar lateral fricative, IPA [ɬ]; and [ƛ] is used for a voiceless alveolar lateral affricate, the tilde being used in place of the crossing bar recommended by Herzog et al. (1934, 631). Halle and Clements (1983, 29) give the superimposed tilde for a "velarized or uvularized" consonant. Most sources do not refer to any such possibility as uvularization (Chomsky and Halle 1968 (p. 307), has the word in a chart but no discussion in the text). Possibly Halle and Clements mean to refer to pharyngealization.

Subscript Tilde

IPA Usage: Diacritic to indicate creaky voice (laryngealization). It is used by Ladefoged (1982, 302) and was accepted by the IPA in 1989. *American Usage:* Not standard. Recommended by Smalley (1963, 441) to indicate pharyngealization.

Subscript Seagull

IPA Usage: Used beneath alveolar consonant symbols to represent linguo-labials. *Comments:* A linguo-labial (or apico-labial) voiceless stop was reported for "Bororo" by Hockett (1955, 99), who used the transcription [t̼], i.e., [t] with Subscript Arch. (Hockett cites a personal communication from Floyd Lounsbury, but no published source. Peter Ladefoged reports to us that the language involved may have been Umotina, which is in the Bororo family, but he was not able to get any further information from Lounsbury.) Linguo-labials were not recorded or described for a general phonetic audience until Maddieson (1987) documented them, in phonological contrast with both bilabial and lingual (alveolar) consonants, in several of the languages of Vanuatu, for example Big Nambas (locally called V'enen Taut). The transcription Maddieson uses involves the subscript bridge diacritic under a bilabial symbol, and the merits of other possible transcriptions are discussed. Using a diacritic for these extremely rare sounds removes the necessity of introducing a series of new letters for different linguo-labial consonants such as the ones recommended for clinical phonetic use by PRDS (1983); see Ball 1987 for an accessible summary. The idea of Subscript Seagull is that a voiceless linguo-labial should be transcribed [t̼]. But since the 1989 revision of the IPA introduced another diacritic, [̺], for indicating that a sound has apical articulation, it is hard to see why the seagull is necessary: linguo-labials could be transcribed [p̺], [b̺], [m̺], etc. *Source:* Suggested by Caroline Henton, and added to the IPA's alphabet in 1989 after the Kiel convention. Apparently iconic, suggesting a pair of lips.

Acute Accent

IPA Usage: The current IPA interpretation is high tone. See the chart for IPA suprasegmental symbols. Recommended (*Principles,* 18) as a transcription for a high rising tone. The IPA suggestion that tone marking be iconic reserved the acute accent for rising tones, with pitch represented by vertical positioning on the line. Therefore [ˊba] (or [bá]) could represent a syllable on a high rising tone, [ˏba] (or [ba̩]) on a low rising tone. The iconic use of line position is rare in practice. *American Usage:* Generally used either as a tone marker (high tone) or indicator of stress (strongest stress). The recommendations of Boas et al. (1916, 7–8) use the acute accent placed over the vowel sign as an indicator of high tone and as a marker of primary stress when used after the vowel sign. (In languages without tone, the stress may be marked over the vowel.) The Trager and Smith (1951, 37ff) analysis of English stress posits four suprasegmental stress phonemes, marked by ⟨ˊ⟩ (primary), ⟨ˆ⟩ (secondary), ⟨ˋ⟩ (tertiary), and ⟨ˇ⟩ (weak). The principal contrast in single words is among primary, tertiary, and weak. Trager and Smith's "secondary stress" generally arises as the demotion of the primary stress of a word in a compound. Hence stressed as separate words they give *élĕvàtŏr* and *ópĕràtŏr,* but stressed as a compound, *élĕvàtŏr ôpĕràtŏr.* The most widely used interpretation of these accents as indicators of stress is: acute, strongest; grave, weaker; breve, weakest. *Comments:* By extension of the IPA's iconic principles for tone marking, acute accent represents a high (level) tone in register tone languages (e.g., most African tone languages) in contrast to the grave accent for low tone. (Cf. *Practical Orthography of African Languages* (International African Institute 1930)).

Used as an indicator of palatalization (e.g., Brugmann 1904 (p. 1)). When written as a right superscript it can be referred to as a prime. It may also be written over a character which has no ascender (e.g., ń, ś, ź in the Polish orthography).

Grave Accent

IPA Usage: The current IPA interpretation is low tone. See the chart for IPA suprasegmental symbols. Recommended (*Principles,* 18) as a transcription for a high falling tone. The IPA suggestion that tone marking be iconic reserved the grave accent for falling tones, with pitch represented by vertical positioning on the line. Therefore [`ba] (or [bà]) could represent a syllable on a high falling tone, [ˌba] (or [ba̖]) on a low falling tone. The iconic use of line position is rare in practice. *American Usage:* May vary, but generally used either as a tone marker (low tone) or indicator of stress (nonprimary stress). The recommendations of Boas et al. (1916, 7–8) use the grave accent placed over the vowel sign as an indicator of low tone and as a marker of secondary stress when used after the vowel sign. (In languages without tone, the stress may be marked over the vowel.) The Trager and Smith (1951, 37ff) analysis of English stress posits four suprasegmental stress phonemes, marked ⟨´⟩ (primary), ⟨ˆ⟩ (secondary), ⟨`⟩ (tertiary), and ⟨˘⟩ (weak). The principal contrast in single words is among primary, tertiary, and weak. Trager and Smith's "secondary stress" generally arises as the demotion of the primary stress of a word in a compound. Hence stressed as separate words they give *élĕvàtŏr* and *ópĕràtŏr,* but stressed as a compound, *élĕvàtŏr ôpĕràtŏr.* The most widely used interpretation of these accents as indicators of stress is: acute, strongest; grave, weaker; breve, weakest. *Other uses:* By extension of the IPA's iconic principles for tone marking, grave accent represents a low (level) tone in register tone languages (e.g., most African tone languages) in contrast to the acute accent for high tone. (Cf. *Practical Orthography of African Languages* (International African Institute, 1930)).

Circumflex

IPA Usage: The current IPA interpretation is falling tone. See the chart for IPA suprasegmental symbols. Recommended (*Principles,* 18) as a transcription for a rising-falling tone. The IPA suggestion that tone markings be iconic reserves the circumflex for a tone which is a combination of the tones represented by ⟨´⟩ and ⟨ˋ⟩ (in that order). The recommended interpretation of these diacritics as rising and falling tone respectively gives the interpretation of the circumflex as rising-falling. Where the acute and grave accents are interpreted as high and low tones respectively, the circumflex would represent a falling tone. The iconic value as a pointer up apparently explains its use in the IPA examples of Yoruba (*Principles,* 45) and Sotho (*Principles,* 49) as a marker of register-rising upstep. *American Usage:* As a tone marking it signifies either rising-falling tone (same as IPA) or falling tone. The Trager and Smith (1951, 37ff) analysis of English stress posits four suprasegmental stress phonemes, marked ⟨´⟩ (primary), ⟨ˆ⟩ (secondary), ⟨ˋ⟩ (tertiary), and ⟨˘⟩ (weak). The principal contrast in single words is among primary, tertiary, and weak. Trager and Smith's "secondary stress" generally arises as the demotion of the primary stress of a word in a compound. Hence stressed as separate words they give *élĕvàtŏr* and *ópĕràtŏr,* but stressed as a compound, *élĕvàtŏr ôpĕràtŏr.* *Comments:* The most widely used interpretation of these accents as indicators of stress is: acute, strongest; grave, weaker; breve, weakest. When used as a tone symbol, it probably represents the concatenation of whatever tones the acute and grave accents (respectively) represent. This composition of grave and acute accents to form complex tone symbols is generalized in Goldsmith 1976 (p. 43) where a vowel is marked [ã], the result of combining a high tone (´) with a rising tone on [ǎ]. *Source:* Diacritic used over vowels in the orthography of French (e.g., *bête,* 'beast'), but not to mark tone. The circumflex marks vowels which in earlier stages of the language preceded an [s] which has now been lost.

Subscript Circumflex

Used by Smalley (1983, 454) as a fronting diacritic instead of the ⟨ ̯⟩ (Subscript Arch) recommended by Boas et al. (1916, 10). Thus [t̞] is Smalley's transcription of a voiceless dental stop, [x̞] represents a voiceless palatal fricative (IPA [ç]), and so on.

Wedge

IPA Usage: The current IPA interpretation is rising tone. See the chart for IPA suprasegmental symbols. Recommended (*Principles,* 18) as a transcription for a falling-rising tone. The IPA suggestion that tone markings be iconic reserves the wedge for a tone which is a combination of the tones represented by ⟨ˋ⟩ and ⟨ˊ⟩ (in that order). The recommended interpretation of these diacritics as falling and rising tone respectively gives the interpretation for the wedge as falling-rising. Where the acute and grave are interpreted as high and low tones respectively, the wedge would represent a rising tone. The iconic value as a pointer down apparently explains its use in the IPA examples of Igbo, Tswana, and Sotho (*Principles,* 45–49) as a marker of register-lowering downstep. (Welmers (1973, 85) attributes the Igbo example to Ida C. Ward and suggests that it is the earliest valid analysis of a "downstep" tone system.) *American Usage:* Sometimes same as IPA, as a tone symbol. Its principal use is on symbols for alveolar or palatal consonants to represent palato-alveolar fricatives or affricates; thus [š] = IPA [ʃ], [ž] = IPA [ʒ], [č] = IPA [tʃ], [ǰ] = IPA [dʒ]. This use of the wedge is borrowed from Slavic orthography and explicitly recommended in Herzog et al. 1934 (p. 631). Also used above ⟨r⟩ to indicate certain specific articulation types, e.g., flapped (Smalley 1963

(pp. 456–57)) or fricative (Maddieson 1984 (p. 240)). *Other uses:*
When used as a tone symbol, it probably represents the concatenation
of whatever tones the grave and acute accents (respectively) represent.
This composition of grave and acute accents to form complex tone
symbols is generalized in Goldsmith 1976 (p. 43) where a vowel is
marked [ä], the result of combining a high tone (´) with a rising tone
on [ǎ]. *Source:* Used in the Czech orthography, where it is called
the *haček* ('little hook'), roughly as in the American usage. As a tone
mark, it is of course primarily iconic.

Subscript Wedge

IPA Usage: Official IPA diacritic to indicate that the symbol represents a voiced sound. For example, [s̬] might be used to denote [z] in a
language with no [s] ~ [z] contrast but where the *s*-sound was to some
extent voiced when between vowels. According to the IPA's conventions for indicating tone, [a̬] could be used for a vowel [a] with a low
falling-rising tone, though the iconic use of line position is rare in
practice. *American Usage:* Not standardly used.

Polish Hook

IPA Usage: Not used. Not to be confused with the right hook recommended (*Principles,* 14) for *r*-colored vowels. *American Usage:*
Boas et al. (1916, 8) recommend the use of a centered subscript
rightward hook under vowel or consonant symbols as a nasalization
diacritic. Sometimes used instead of the IPA's tilde diacritic, as by
Smalley (1963, 333). Distinct from the IPA diacritic ⟨ˌ⟩. *Other uses:*

Used to mark nasalized vowels in Polish orthography (letters ę and ą). Used by Brugmann (1904, 1) as a nasalization diacritic for vowels. Used by Meillet and Cohen (1952, xiv) as a diacritic for open vowels, a use similar to the one in historical Germanic studies, which uses it with *e* and *o* as a diacritic for mutated vowels. (Cf. the entries for Polish-Hook E and Polish-Hook O.)

Cedilla

IPA Usage: Not used as an independent diacritic. *American Usage:* Not used as an independent diacritic. *Other uses:* Used by Brugmann (1904, 1) as an "open vowel" diacritic in contrast to the underdot: [o̧] is open *o,* [ọ] is close *o;* [ȩ] is open *e,* [ẹ] is close *e.* Note the use of the rightward Polish hook (e.g., [ę] as a diacritic for mutated vowels in Germanic, cf. Prokosch 1939 (p. 110)). Brugmann uses the Polish hook as a nasalization diacritic. *Source:* The cedilla is a diacritic mark on the letter *c* in French orthography.

Left Hook

IPA Usage: Diacritic modification formerly used for constructing symbols for palatalized consonants. The official symbolization for palatalization is now a right superscript *j.* An IPA invention; visually reminiscent of ⟨j⟩, which denotes a palatal approximant in the IPA system. *American Usage:* Used to some extent as the IPA uses it, though other ways of showing palatalization are often found (e.g., superscript *y* or *j). Comments:* The hook is attached to any convenient lower-right part of the basic consonant symbol. The distinctive feature is its leftward turn (by contrast to the rightward turn of the retroflexion diacritic). For example, Catford (1977, 192) gives the following symbols for Russian palatalized sounds:

Plain	p	b	m	f	v	t	d	n	l	r	s	z
Palatalized	p̡	b̡	m̡	f̡	v̡	t̡	d̡	n̡	l̡	ɼ	ˌs	z̡

(We correct Catford's ⟨ş⟩ to the IPA's ⟨ˌs⟩. We also change ⟨m̡⟩ to ⟨m̡⟩, as we suspect a typographical error; ⟨ɱ⟩ has another meaning.)

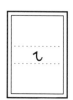

Rhoticity Sign

IPA Usage: The diacritic for rhoticity (i.e., *r*-coloration) under the IPA principles as of 1993. Used on the right hand side of a symbol to indicate an articulation involving [ɹ]-like tongue position (and acoustically, a marked lowering of the third formant). Typically it will be used with a vowel symbol, often the symbol for a central vowel such as Schwa [ə] or Reversed Epsilon [ɜ]. The combinations formed by Schwa and Reversed Epsilon with either Right Hook or some version of the Rhoticity Sign were separately recognized characters at earlier periods in the IPA (see the entries for Right-Hook Schwa and Right-Hook Reversed Epsilon), but the 1993 revision no longer recognizes them as letters. Instead, they can be composed by means of the Rhoticity Sign. *Source:* An IPA invention going back to Daniel Jones. The history is reviewed in the entry for the earlier form of the diacritic, namely Right Hook (see next entry).

Right Hook

IPA Usage: Diacritic modification recommended in *Principles* (p. 14) for constructing symbols for vowels with rhotacization (*r*-coloration). Approval for the general use of this diacritic with vowels was withdrawn in 1976 (*Journal of the International Phonetic Association* 6 (p. 3)) in favor of a digraph such as [aɹ] or [aʴ]. The two symbols [ɚ] and [ɝ] were deemed useful enough to be retained. The IPA's decision to withdraw recognition from this diacritic was prompted by an opinion of the secretary of the IPA, who said of the symbols for rhotacized vowels: "I think no one but Jones ever really liked these symbols, and even he was not enthusiastic" (*Journal of the International Phonetic Association* 5 (p. 57)). But cf. Albright 1958 (p. 61). *American Usage:* Not used. This rightward hook used by the IPA for indicating rhotacization should not be confused with the centered "Polish hook"; for example, [ą] is used in Polish orthography and Americanist (e.g., Smalley's) transcription for nasalized vowels. *Comments:* The similarity to the retroflexion diacritic used by the IPA in [ʂ] and [ʐ] is probably not accidental. This diacritic for retroflexion seems to be latent in certain special symbols for retroflex consonants in the form of a rightward-swept elongation of the rightmost vertical stroke in [ɳ], [ʈ], [ɖ], [ɭ], and [ɽ]. In the interests of terminological consistency, we recognize in this family resemblance an IPA retroflexion indicator, which we call "right tail."

Breve

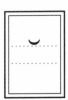

IPA Usage: Given in the IPA chart of suprasegmental symbols as a diacritic for "extra-short." Used to mark "the weaker element of a diphthong"; thus [ĭu] is like [ju], but [iŭ] is like [iw]. Also used in representing prenasalized stops such as [m̆b], [n̆d], etc. Also suggested (*Principles,* 18) as a possibility for use in narrow tone transcriptions, though no particular interpretation is suggested. In the 1993 IPA system, designated for representing "extra-short" vowels. *American Usage:* Sometimes same as IPA; also used to identify specifically unstressed vowels. Recommended by Boas et al. (1916, 7) for use following a symbol to indicate segments which are excessively short. Rare in such use. *Other uses:* Used to mark short vowels in Classical Latin (in contrast to the macron) as a pedagogical aid. This use gives rise to its occurrence to mark short or lax vowels in the pronunciation guides of some English dictionaries.

Round Cap

American Usage: Not used except as a variant of the subscript arch diacritic ⟨ ͜ ⟩, indicating advancement, with letters which have descenders. Cf. ⟨ĝ⟩ in Trager 1964 (p. 23). *Other uses:* Used by Brugmann (1904) as a diacritic for palatal stops: [n̂] is the palatal nasal (p. 1). He uses (p. 52) [k̂] and [ĝ] as "palatal" stops and [q] and [g] as true velars, reserving ⟨k⟩ and ⟨g⟩ for cases of uncertainty. (Cf. Prokosch 1939 (p. 42).)

Subscript Arch

IPA Usage: IPA Diacritic for nonsyllabic sonorants. Suggested (*Principles,* 18) as a possibility for use in narrow tone transcriptions (but with no value suggested). *American Usage:* Used by some writers (e.g., Pike (1947, 7) and Gleason (1955, 7)), following Boas et al. (1916, 10), to indicate fronted articulation of a consonant; thus [ŋ̟] may mean a palatal nasal (IPA [ɲ]) and [n̟] may mean a dental nasal (IPA [n̪]). *Other uses:* Used by Brugmann (1904, 1), Wright (1910, 50), and others under a base vowel symbol to denote a semivowel corresponding to the vowel. In their inventory of sounds for Indo-European they provide [u̯] as an alternative to [w], and [i̯] as an alternative to [j]. Used in this sense by Trager and Smith (1951, 11).

Top Ligature

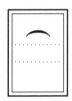

IPA Usage: Synchronic articulation sign: [ŋ͡m] is a labiovelar nasal; [ə͡ɹ] could represent an *r*-colored schwa (same as [ɚ]); [a͡ɪ] represents a diphthong composed of [a] and [ɪ]; and so on. *American Usage:* Same as IPA, if used. *Comments:* The bottom ligature is used for the same purpose with characters which do not have descenders. The "close-up" notation a͡z as an editor's mark in proof correction indicates that the two characters should be brought together. Trager and Smith (1951, 37) call it the "tie line."

Bottom Ligature

IPA Usage: Given in the chart for IPA suprasegmental symbols as a linking diacritic for absence of a break. Also occurs as a synchronic articulation sign: [b͜d] would indicate a simultaneously bilabial and alveolar stop; [ə͜ɹ] could represent an *r*-colored schwa (same as [ɚ]); [a͜ɪ] represents a diphthong composed of [a] and [ɪ]; and so on.

American Usage: Same as IPA, if used. *Comments:* The top ligature is used for the same purpose with characters which have descenders. The "close-up" notation $\widehat{a\,z}$ as an editor's mark in proof correction indicates that the two characters should be brought together. Trager and Smith (1951, 37) call it the "tie line."

GLOSSARY

This glossary is not a complete dictionary of phonetic terminology, but it gives basic definitions for the technical terms used in this book, and explains equivalences between terms used in quotations from authors that we cite.

Advanced. Articulated with a tongue position closer to the front of the mouth (relative to some given position).

Affricate. Consonant composed of an initial stop phase followed by a release phase taking the form of a homorganic fricative.

Alveolar. Relating to the alveolar ridge, the bony ridge behind the upper teeth.

Alveolo-palatal. Relating to the region just behind the palato-alveolar, but further forward than the palatal. (This term is now not much used.)

Alveopalatal. Relating to the region between the alveolar ridge and the (hard) palate. (A term used in many American texts, e.g., Smalley 1963, Gleason 1955, covering both the palato-alveolar and alveolo-palatal regions of the IPA system.)

Apical. Relating to the apex (tip) of the tongue.

Approximant. Frictionless continuant. For Ladefoged, who coined the term (1964), a consonantal sound articulated in a manner involving an opening in the oral tract not radical enough to produce audible friction; thus, IPA [j], [w], [l], etc. Catford 1977 (pp. 119–22) refines this, defining approximants as having non-turbulent airflow when voiced but turbulent airflow when voiceless.

Articulator. A delimited part of the vocal tract that plays a specific role in the production of a speech sound; thus, articulators include the lips, teeth, tongue-tip, hard palate, uvula, etc.

Arytenoid cartilages. A pair of cartilages on top of the larynx, attached to the back of the vocal cords and capable of separating them (as in the production of voiceless sounds) and partially or completely bringing them together.

Aspirated. Immediately followed by a brief delay in onset of normal voicing state. Used of pulmonic stop consonants, particularly voiceless ones, e.g., English [pʰ] in [pʰɛt] 'pet'.

Back. (Of vowels) Articulated with the highest point of the tongue at the back of the mouth, i.e., below the soft palate.

Bilabial. Relating to articulation involving the two lips.

Breathy voice. Murmur; articulation with heavy airflow through the slightly open glottis and some vibration of the vocal cords, but not as much as in full voicing.

Cacuminal. An older synonym for retroflex.

Cardinal. (Of vowels) Relating to the system of cardinal vowels devised by Daniel Jones for representing vowel quality in terms of a grid of absolute values. Cardinal 1 is defined as the highest and most front vowel physiologically producible; Cardinal 5 is defined as the lowest and most back vowel physiologically producible; Cardinals 1, 2, 3, and 4 are front unrounded vowels whose openness evenly increases toward the maximum possible, and Cardinals 5, 6, 7, and 8 are back vowels whose closeness and rounding evenly increases toward the maximum possible. A second series, Cardinals 9 through 16, is then defined as having identical tongue positions but opposite rounding. (Cf. the charts on pp. 293–94.)

Central. (Of consonants) Non-lateral, i.e., articulated in a manner that involves airflow predominantly down the center line of the oral cavity (from uvula to middle front teeth) rather than around the sides of the tongue; (of vowels) involving a tongue position with its highest point neither in the front third nor in the back third of the oral cavity, i.e., roughly below the junction of the hard and soft palates. Note that for consonants the center referenced is between left and right cheeks, but for vowels the center is between front and back of the oral cavity. *Median* is an unambiguous and thus preferable term for the former.

Centralized. (Of vowels) Articulated with the highest tongue position somewhat closer to the center (between front and back) than is normal for the vowel type in question; that is, for a front vowel, somewhat retracted, and for a back vowel, somewhat advanced. (A central vowel, clearly, cannot be centralized.)

Cerebral. An older synonym for retroflex.

Click. Stop consonant formed with a velaric ingressive airstream, i.e., with inflowing release of air triggered by release of a stop closure in the forward part of the oral tract, using suction developed by downward movement of the tongue body while maintaining a dorso-velar closure.

Close. (Of vowels) High; with tongue position close to the roof of the mouth; the opposite of open.

Coarticulated. Articulated in a manner simultaneously involving two (or more) distinct areas of the vocal tract. This may mean two or more articulatory gestures of a similar sort at different locations (e.g., dorso-velar stop closure together with bilabial closure in a labial-velar stop such as [kp]) or superimposition of a less radical articulatory gesture on a more radical one (as with labialization of a velar stop such as [kʷ]).

Coronal. Articulated by raising the tongue blade out of its neutral or rest position.

Creaky voice. Laryngealization; articulation with the back end of the vocal cords held together by the arytenoid cartilages so that only the other end can vibrate.

Dental. Relating to the upper front teeth.

Diphthong. Sequence of two perceptibly different vowel sounds (or a vowel sound and a glide) in the same syllable.

Dorsal. Relating to the dorsum, the back third of the tongue.

Egressive. (Of airstreams) Going outward.

Ejective. Glottalic egressive consonant.

Emphatic. A term traditionally used to describe the pharyngealized series of consonants in Arabic.

Epiglottal. Pertaining to the epiglottis (a cartilaginous appendage that is attached to the hyoid bone, the root of the tongue, and the arytenoid cartilages, and marginally movable through retraction of the tongue root).

Flap. Consonant articulated in a manner that involves one articulator being retracted and then striking another in passing during the trajectory of its return to its rest position.

Flat. (Articulatory) Not grooved. (Not the same as the acoustic sense of this term, which refers to the property of displaying a general downward shifting of formant structure.)

Fortis.   Articulated in a manner involving more energetic tensing of the articulatory musculature; opposite of lenis.

Fricative.   Consonantal sound articulated in a manner involving approximation of articulators to narrow a part of the oral tract radically enough to produce audible friction.

Front.   (Of vowels) Articulated with the highest point of the tongue in the front region of the mouth, i.e., below the hard palate.

Glide.   Nonvocalic central approximant; semivowel.

Glottal.   Relating to the glottis or to the vocal cords.

Glottalic.   Relating to a mode of creating oral airflow in the pharynx by raising or lowering the larynx with glottis closed. (Lowering the larynx can create implosive stops; raising the larynx can create ejectives.)

Glottis.   The space between the vocal cords through which air passes during production of pulmonic egressive sounds.

Grooved.   Articulated with a slight concavity of the upper surface of the tongue in proximity to the alveolar or palato-alveolar region, forming a groove through which air passes with strong friction.

Guttural.   According to Prokosch (1939, 42): "This somewhat inept term is generally used in comparative grammars to designate consonants that are articulated either against the hard or the soft palate, and it may well serve as a collective term of expedience." The term has been revived from obsolescence in recent years by phonologists who define it as covering articulations involving either the glottis or the tongue root.

Half-close.   (Of vowels) Articulated with a tongue height between mid and close.

Half-open.   (Of vowels) Articulated with a tongue height between mid and open.

High.   (Of vowels) Articulated with a tongue height that involves raising the body of the tongue above its neutral position to (or near) the maximal extent possible; (fully) close.

Higher-mid.   (Of vowels) Articulated with a tongue height slightly higher than the mid position; at or around the height of Cardinal 2.

Higher-low.   (Of vowels) Articulated with a tongue height slightly higher than the maximally low position; between the height of Cardinal 3 and Cardinal 4.

Homorganic. Having the same place of articulation (as some given adjacent segment, for example).

Implosive. Stop consonant formed with a glottalic ingressive air-stream, that is, with inflowing release of air using suction developed by downward movement of the larynx while another complete obstruction is maintained further forward in the oral tract.

Ingressive. (Of airstreams) Moving inward.

Interdental. Relating to the gap between the upper and lower front teeth.

Labial. Involving use of or contact with the lips.

Labialized. Articulated in a manner that secondarily involves the rounding of the lips.

Labiodental. Articulated by bringing the lower lip into contact with the upper teeth.

Labial-velar. Relating to an articulation involving both the lips (either rounded or closed) and the dorsal part of the tongue raised toward the velum. (Sometimes *labiovelar* is found with this meaning.)

Laminal. Relating to the blade of the tongue (the middle third), as opposed to the tip or the back.

Laryngal, Laryngeal. Relating to the larynx.

Laryngealized. Articulated with creaky voice, i.e., with the back end of the vocal cords held together by the arytenoid cartilages so that only the other end can vibrate.

Lateral. Articulated in a manner that involves oral airflow predominantly around a central obstruction across the sides of the tongue rather than down the center line of the oral cavity.

Lax. The opposite of tense.

Lenis. Articulated in a manner involving laxer operation of the articulatory musculature; opposite of fortis.

Liquid. A term used for the general category comprising the lateral sonorants and (most varieties of) *r*-sounds.

Low. (Of vowels) Articulated in a manner that involves lowering the tongue below its neutral position to (or near) the maximal extent possible; (fully) open.

Lower-high. (Of vowels) Articulated with the highest point of the tongue slightly lower than the maximally high position; between the height of Cardinal 1 and Cardinal 2.

Lower-mid. (Of vowels) Articulated with the highest point of the tongue slightly lower than the mid position; at or around the height of Cardinal 3.

Mean-mid. (Of vowels) Articulated with the highest point of the tongue at the mean (average) of the mid-region; between the higher-mid (Cardinal 2) and lower-mid (Cardinal 3) positions. A term used in Bloch and Trager 1943.

Median. (Of consonants) Central, i.e., articulated in a manner that involves airflow predominantly down the center line of the oral cavity (from uvula to middle front teeth) rather than around the sides of the tongue. The word *central* refers ambiguously to a non-lateral consonant or to a vowel between front and back, hence *median* is preferable for the former.

Mid. (Of vowels) Articulated with the highest point of the tongue at its neutral position, half way between fully open (low) and fully close (high); between the heights of Cardinal 2 and Cardinal 3.

Murmur. Breathy voice.

Nasal. Stop consonant articulated with a lowered velum, produced by airflow through the nasal cavity rather than the oral cavity. (As an adjective, it is synonymous with *nasalized*.)

Nasalized. Articulated with the velum lowered so that airflow is permitted through the nasal cavity as well as through the oral cavity.

Obstruent. Non-resonant consonant, i.e., specifically a stop, fricative, or affricate.

Open. (Of vowels) Low; with the jaw relatively open and the highest part of the tongue far from the roof of the mouth.

Oral. Articulated with the velum raised so that airflow is permitted solely through the oral cavity, not the nasal cavity.

Palatal. Relating to the hard palate or roof of the oral cavity.

Palatalized. Articulated in a manner that involves a secondary articulatory gesture of raising the blade of the tongue toward the hard palate.

Palate. The roof of the mouth. The hard palate is the bony central region of the roof of the mouth; the soft palate or velum is the soft flap of tissue between it and the uvula.

Palato-alveolar. Relating to the region just behind the alveolar ridge. (The IPA draws a distinction between the palato-alveolar region, roughly where the English consonant in *shy* is articulated, and the alveolo-palatal region, which is slightly further back, but still not palatal; see *Principles,* p. 10.)

Peripheral. (Of vowels) Involving a tongue position with its highest point in either the front or the back of the oral cavity; not central.

Pharyngal, Pharyngeal. Relating to or involving the pharynx.

Pharyngealized. Articulated in a manner which secondarily involves constriction of the pharynx by retraction of the root of the tongue.

Phonation. The generation of acoustic energy at the larynx in speech production.

Plosive. Pulmonic egressive stop consonant.

Postvelar. Relating to the region immediately behind the velum; as a position of articulation for consonants, effectively equivalent to *uvular.*

Pulmonic. Relating to a mode of creating airflow in the vocal tract by the use of the respiratory muscles.

Radical. Pertaining to the root (Latin *radix*) of the tongue.

Raised. Articulated with a higher tongue position.

Resonant. Consonant articulated in a manner in which either the oral or the nasal passage is relatively free of obstruction. In other words, a non-obstruent. Covers the glides, nasals, laterals, and (most varieties of) *r*-sounds.

Retracted. Articulated with a tongue position closer to the back of the mouth (relative to some given position).

Retroflex. Articulated in a manner involving retraction of the apex of the tongue so that its lower surface is brought into proximity to the hard palate.

Retroflexed. Rhotacized.

Rhotacized. *R*-colored; produced with a secondary articulatory gesture involving tongue positioning similar to that employed for *r*-sounds (especially the retroflex glide *r*-sound).

Rounded. Articulated in a manner that involves rounding of the lips.

Secondary articulation. Modifying articulatory gesture, usually involving less radical constriction of the vocal tract than another simultaneous one; thus, e.g., labialization of a velar stop as in [kʷ].

Semivowel. Nonvocalic central approximant; glide.

Shibilant. A term occasionally found for a fricative corresponding to a "hushing" sound, e.g., IPA [ʃ] (more technically, a grooved laminal fricative). Not a standard term.

Sibilant. An older term for a fricative corresponding to a "hissing sound," e.g., [s]; more technically, a grooved apical fricative.

Soft palate. The older and less technical term for the velum (revived in recent phonology as the name of the articulator node that dominates the feature [±nasal] in the feature-geometry tree).

Sonant. An older term for a voiced sound. Obsolete.

Sonorant. Consonant articulated in a manner in which either the oral or the nasal passage is relatively free of obstruction. In other words, a non-obstruent. Covers the glides, nasals, laterals, and (most varieties of) *r*-sounds.

Spirant. An older term for a fricative. Almost obsolete.

Spirantization. A change from a stop articulation to a spirant (fricative) one by sound change or by phonological rule.

Spread. (Of vowels) The opposite of rounded; another term for unrounded.

Stop. Consonant articulated in a manner involving a complete blockage of airflow somewhere in the oral tract.

Strangulated. A term found in Boas et al. 1916, apparently meaning "articulated with constriction of the pharynx." Not accepted phonetic terminology.

Stricture. Constriction of the air flow by narrowing some part of the speech tract in the production of a consonant.

Surd. An older term for voiceless sound. Obsolete.

Tap. Consonant formed in a manner that involves a mobile active articulator (typically the apex of the tongue) tapping once very rapidly on a passive articulator (e.g., the alveolar ridge).

Tense. A problematic term phonetically; it is claimed by some that there is an identifiable class of tense speech sounds characterized by an articulation involving relatively more forceful and extreme motions of the articulators, but there is considerable controversy in the experimental literature about such phonetic correlates. In phonology, the feature has played an important role in Chomsky and Halle's (1968) classification of the English vowels, the long vowels and diphthongs being called tense and the short vowels lax.

Trill. Consonant articulated in a manner that involves a mobile active articulator fluttering in a turbulent air stream and striking another articulator rapidly and repeatedly—for example, the apex of the tongue fluttering against the alveolar ridge, or the uvula vibrating against the root of the tongue.

Upper. (Of vowels) Articulated with the highest point of the tongue between the mid position and the high position; at or around the height of Cardinal 2.

Uvula. The small appendage of soft tissue hanging down at the back of the mouth, at the lower end of the velum.

Uvular. Relating to the uvula.

Velar. Relating to the velum.

Velaric. Relating to a mode of creating oral airflow by movement of a closure formed by the dorsal region of the tongue against the velum.

Velarized. Articulated in a manner which secondarily involves raising the tongue toward the velum.

Velum. The movable fold of tissue at the back of the roof of the mouth, commonly known as the soft palate.

Voiced. Articulated in a manner involving free vibration of the vocal cords under influence of pulmonic airflow through the larynx and glottis.

Voiceless. Articulated in a manner not involving free vibration of the vocal cords under influence of pulmonic airflow through the larynx and glottis.

REFERENCES

Abercrombie, David. 1967. *Elements of General Phonetics.* Edinburgh: Edinburgh University Press.

Al-Ani, Salman H. 1970. *Arabic Phonology.* The Hague: Mouton.

Albright, Robert William. 1958. The International Phonetic Alphabet: Its backgrounds and development. *International Journal of American Linguistics* 24. Indiana University Research Center in Anthropology, Folklore and Linguistics, Publication no. 7. Bloomington, Ind.

Arnott, D. W. 1964. Downstep in the Tiv Verbal System. *African Language Studies* 5:34–51.

Aronoff, Mark. 1976. *Word Formation in Generative Grammar.* Cambridge: MIT Press.

Ashton, E. O. 1944. *Swahili Grammar.* 2d ed. London: Longmans, Green & Co. 1947.

Bailey, T. Grahame. 1956. *Teach Yourself Urdu.* Edited and revised by J. R. Firth and A. H. Harley. London: The English Universities Press.

Baldi, Philip. 1983. *An Introduction to the Indo-European Languages.* Carbondale, Ill.: Southern Illinois University Press.

Ball, Martin J. 1987. Linguo-labials revisited: The PRDS solution. *Journal of the International Phonetic Association* 17:115–17.

Beach, D. M. 1938. *The Phonetics of the Hottentot Language.* Cambridge: Heffer.

Beeston, A. F. L. 1968. *Written Arabic.* Cambridge: Cambridge University Press.

Bender, Byron W. 1968. Marshallese phonology. *Oceanic Linguistics* 7:16–35.

———. 1969. *Spoken Marshallese.* Honolulu: University of Hawaii Press.

Berry, Jack, and Joseph H. Greenberg, eds. 1971. *Linguistics in Sub-Saharan Africa.* Current Trends in Linguistics 7. The Hague: Mouton.

Bleek, D. F. 1926. Note on Bushman orthography. *Bantu Studies* 2 (1923–1926): 71–74.

Bloch, Bernard, and George L. Trager. 1942. *Outline of Linguistic Analysis.* Baltimore: Linguistic Society of America.

Bloomfield, Leonard. 1933. *Language.* New York: Holt, Rinehart and Winston.

Boas, Franz. 1911. *Handbook of American Indian Languages,* part 1. Smithsonian Institution Bureau of American Ethnology, Bulletin no. 40. Washington, D.C.: Government Printing Office.

Boas, Franz, P. E. Goddard, Edward Sapir, and A. L. Kroeber. 1916. *Phonetic Transcription of American Indian Languages: Report of Committee of American Anthropological Association.* Smithsonian Institution, Publication no. 2415. Also in Smithsonian Miscellaneous Collections 66 (1917), publication no. 2478, item no. 6. Washington, D.C.: Smithsonian Institution.

Boas, Franz, and John R. Swanton. 1911. Siouan: Dakota (Teton and Santee dialects) with remarks on the Ponca and Winnebago. In Boas 1911, 875–965.

Brauner, Wilhelm. 1967. *Althochdeutsche Grammatik.* Edited by Walther Mitzka. Tübingen: Max Niemeyer. Reader. New York: Henry Holt and Co.

Bright, James W. 1935. *Bright's Anglo-Saxon Reader.* 1959 reprint. Revised and enlarged by James R. Hulbert. New York: Henry Holt and Co.

Brugmann, Karl. 1904. *Kurze Vergleichende Grammatik der Indogermanischen Sprachen.* Strassburg: Karl J. Trübner.

Bush, Clara, et al. 1973. On specifying a system for transcribing consonants in child language: A working paper with examples from American English and Mexican Spanish. Unpublished paper, Child Language Project, Stanford University.

Caffee, N. M. 1940. Southern 'l' plus a consonant. *American Speech* 15:259–61.

Campbell, Lyle. 1973. On glottalic consonants. *International Journal of American Linguistics* 39:44–46.

Carmody, Francis J. 1945. *Is* in Modern Scottish Gaelic. *Word* 1: 162–87.

Cartier, Francis A., and Martin T. Todaro. 1971. *The Phonetic Alphabet.* 3d ed. Dubuque, Iowa: Wm. C. Brown.

Catford, J. C. 1977. *Fundamental Problems in Phonetics.* Bloomington, Ind.: Indiana University Press.

———. 1988. *A Practical Introduction to Phonetics.* Oxford: Clarendon Press.

———. 1990. A proposal concerning central vowels. *Journal of the International Phonetic Association* 20:26–28.

Chao, Yuen-Ren. 1933. A system of tone letters. *Le Maître Phonétique* 30:24–27.

———. 1934. The non-uniqueness of phonemic solutions of phonetic systems. *Bulletin of the Institute of History and Philology, Academia Sinica,* vol. 4, part 4: 363–97. Page references to the reprint in Joos 1966, 38–54.

Chicago Manual of Style. 1993. 14th ed. Chicago: University of Chicago Press.

Chistovich, L. A., et al. 1982. Temporal processing of peripheral auditory patterns of speech. In *The Representation of Speech in the Peripheral Auditory System,* ed. Rolf Carlson and Björn Granström, 165–80. New York: Elsevier Biomedical Press.

Chomsky, Noam. 1964. Current issues in linguistic theory. In Fodor and Katz 1964, 50–118.

Chomsky, Noam, and Morris Halle. 1968. *The Sound Pattern of English.* New York: Harper and Row.

Cole, Desmond T. 1966. Bushman languages. *Encyclopedia Britannica,* vol. 4, 468–70.

Cowan, William. 1979. Review of *The* Mots Loups *of Father Mathevet,* by Gordon M. Day. *International Journal of American Linguistics* 45:88–94.

Crothers, John. 1978. Typology and universals of vowel systems. In *Universals of Human Language.* Volume 2: *Phonology,* ed. Joseph H. Greenberg, 93–152. Stanford, Calif.: Stanford University Press.

Damourette, Jacques, and Eduoard Pichon. 1911–27. *Essai de Grammaire de la Langue Française* (7 volumes). Paris: Collection des Linguistes Contemporains.

Danesi, Marcel. 1982. The description of Spanish /b, d, g/ revisited. *Hispania* 65:252–58.

Dinnsen, Daniel A. 1974. Constraints on global rules in phonology. *Language* 50:29–51.

Doke, Clement M. 1926a. An outline of the phonetics of the language of the Ƙhũ: Bushmen of North-West Kalahari. *Bantu Studies* 2 (1923–26): 129–65.

———. 1926b. *The Phonetics of the Zulu Language*. Bantu Studies Supplement. Johannesburg: University of the Witwatersrand Press. Repr. Nendeln/Lichtenstein: Kraus, 1969.

Ellis, Jeffrey. 1953. *An Elementary Old High German Grammar, Descriptive and Comparative*. Oxford: Clarendon Press.

Fairbanks, Gordon H., and Bal Govind Misra. 1966. *Spoken and Written Hindi*. Ithaca, N.Y.: Cornell University Press.

Firth, J. R. 1948. Sounds and prosodies. *Transactions of the Philological Society*, 127–52. Reprinted in Firth 1957, 121–38, and in Jones and Laver 1973, 47–65; photoreproduced from the original source in Palmer 1970, 1–26. Page references to the original.

———. 1957. *Papers in Linguistics 1934–1951*. London: Oxford University Press.

Fodor, Jerry A., and Jerrold J. Katz, eds. 1964. *The Structure of Language: Readings in the Philosophy of Language*. Englewood Cliffs, N.J.: Prentice-Hall.

Fontanals, Joaquín Rafel. 1976. Areas léxicas en una encrucijada lingüística. *Revista de filología española* 5 (1974–75): 231–75.

Fortescue, Michael. 1984. *West Greenlandic*. London: Croom Helm.

Fuller, Michael. 1990. Pulmonic ingressive fricatives in Tsou. *Journal of the International Phonetic Association* 20:9–14.

Gimson, A. C. 1962. *An Introduction to the Pronunciation of English*. 1st ed. London: Edward Arnold. 2d ed., 1970. 3d ed., 1980.

Gleason, Henry Allan. 1955. *Workbook in Descriptive Linguistics*. New York: Holt, Rinehart and Winston.

Goddard, Ives, and Kathleen Bragdon. 1988. *Native Writings in Massachusett*. Memoirs of the American Philosophical Society, 185 (2 volumes). Philadelphia: American Philosophical Society.

Goldsmith, John. 1976. An overview of autosegmental phonology. *Linguistic Analysis* 2:23–68.

Greenberg, Joseph H. 1970. Some generalizations concerning glottalic consonants, especially implosives. *International Journal of American Linguistics* 36:123–45.

———, ed. 1978. *Universals of Human Language*. Volume 2: *Phonology*. Stanford, Calif.: Stanford University Press.

Gruber, Jeffrey S. 1973. ǂHòã kinship terms. *Linguistic Inquiry* 4:427–49.

Grunwell, Pam, et al. 1980. The phonetic representation of disordered speech. *British Journal of Disorders of Communication* 15:215–20.

Guthrie, Malcolm. 1948. *The Classification of the Bantu Languages*. London: Oxford University Press.

Halle, Morris, and G. N. Clements. 1983. *Problem Book in Phonology*. Cambridge: MIT Press.

Halle, Morris, and K. P. Mohanan. 1985. The segmental phonology of modern English. *Linguistic Inquiry* 16:57–116.

Hamp, Eric P. 1951. Morphophonemes of the Keltic mutations. *Language* 27:230–47.

———. 1965a. Evidence in Albanian. In Winter 1965, 123–41.

———. 1965b. Evidence in Keltic. In Winter 1965, 224–35.

Hamp, Eric P., Fred W. Householder, and Robert Austerlitz, eds. 1966. *Readings in Linguistics II*. Chicago: University of Chicago Press.

Harley, A. H. 1944. *Colloquial Hindustani*. London: Kegan Paul, Trench, Trubner and Co. Ltd.

Heffner, R.-M. S. 1950. *General Phonetics*. Madison: University of Wisconsin Press.

Henton, Caroline. 1990. One vowel's life (and death?) across languages: the moribundity and prestige of /ʌ/. *Journal of Phonetics* 18:203–27.

Henton, Caroline, Peter Ladefoged, and Ian Maddieson. 1992. Stops in the world's languages. *Phonetica* 49:65–101.

Herzog, George, Stanley S. Newman, Edward Sapir, Mary Haas, Morris Swadesh, and Charles F. Voegelin. 1934. Some orthographic recommendations. *American Anthropologist*, n.s., 36:629–31.

Hewitt, B. G., in collaboration with Z. K. Khiba. 1979. *Abkhaz. Lingua Descriptive Studies* 2. Amsterdam: North-Holland.

Hockett, Charles F. 1955. *A Manual of Phonology*. IJAL Memoir 11. *International Journal of American Linguistics* 21, no. 4, part 1. Chicago: University of Chicago Press.

Hoffmann, C. F. 1963. *A Grammar of the Margi Language.* Oxford: Oxford University Press.

Hoijer, Harry. 1945. *Navaho Phonology.* University of New Mexico Publications in Anthropology, no. 1. Albuquerque, N.M.: University of New Mexico Press.

Hughes, Arthur, and Peter Trudgill. 1979. *English Accents and Dialects.* London: Edward Arnold.

Hunt, Geoffrey. 1992. Central vowels in the 1989 IPA. *Journal of the International Phonetic Association* 22:63–64.

Hyman, Larry. 1975. *Phonology: Theory and Analysis.* New York: Holt, Rinehart and Winston.

Ingram, David. 1976. *Phonological Disability in Children.* London: Edward Arnold.

International African Institute. 1930. *Practical Orthography of African Languages.* International African Institute, Memorandum no. 1. Oxford: Oxford University Press.

International Phonetic Association. 1949 (repr. 1967). *The Principles of the International Phonetic Association.* London: Dept. of Phonetics, University College (now Dept. of Phonetics and Linguistics, University College London).

———. 1989. Report on the 1989 Kiel Convention. *Journal of the International Phonetic Association* 19:67–80.

———. 1993. Council actions on revisions of the IPA. *Journal of the International Phonetic Association* 23:32–34.

Ikekeonwu, Clara I. 1991. Igbo. *Journal of the International Phonetic Association* 21:99–101.

Jespersen, Otto. 1949. *A Modern English Grammar on Historical Principles.* Part 1, *Sounds and Spellings.* Copenhagen: Einar Munksgaard; London: George Allen and Unwin.

———. 1962. *Growth and Structure of the English Language.* 9th ed. Oxford: Basil Blackwell.

JIPA: Journal of the International Phonetic Association (formerly *Le Maître Phonétique*). London: International Phonetic Association.

Jones, Charles. 1972. *An Introduction to Middle English.* New York: Holt, Rinehart and Winston.

Jones, Daniel. 1918. *An Outline of English Phonetics.* 1st ed. Cambridge: W. Heffer and Sons.

———. 1956. *The Pronunciation of English.* 4th ed. Cambridge: Cambridge University Press.

———. 1957. *The History and Meaning of the Term 'Phoneme'.* First published as a supplement to *Le Maître Phonétique,* and issued as a pamphlet by the International Phonetic Association (University College London). Reprinted as an appendix to Daniel Jones, *The Phoneme,* 3d ed. (Cambridge: Heffer, 1967), 253–69. Reprinted in Jones and Laver 1973, 187–204.

———. 1962. *An Outline of English Phonetics.* 9th ed. Cambridge: W. Heffer and Sons.

Jones, W. E., and J. Laver, eds. 1973. *Phonetics in Linguistics: A Book of Readings.* London: Longman.

Jones, William. 1911. Algonquian (Fox). (Revised by Truman Michelson.) In Boas 1911, 735–873.

Joos, Martin, ed. 1966. *Readings in Linguistics I.* 4th ed. Chicago: University of Chicago Press.

Kaufman, Terrence. 1976. *Proyecto de alfabetos y ortografías para escribir las lenguas mayances.* Antigua, Guatemala: Proyecto Lingüístico Francisco Marroquín.

Kenyon, John Samuel. 1950. *American Pronunciation.* 10th ed. Ann Arbor, Mich.: George Wahr.

Kiparsky, Paul. 1968. Linguistic universals and linguistic change. In *Universals in Linguistic Theory,* ed. Emmon Bach and Robert T. Harms, 170–202. New York: Holt, Rinehart and Winston.

Kurath, Hans. 1939. *Handbook of the Linguistic Geography of New England.* Providence, R.I.: Brown University.

Kurath, Hans, and Raven McDavid, Jr. 1961. *The Pronunciation of English in the Atlantic States.* Studies in American English, 3. Ann Arbor, Mich.: University of Michigan Press.

Ladefoged, Peter. 1968. *A Phonetic Study of West African Languages.* 2d ed. Chicago: University of Chicago Press.

———. 1971. *Preliminaries to Linguistic Phonetics.* Chicago: University of Chicago Press.

———. 1982. *A Course in Phonetics.* 2d ed. New York: Harcourt Brace Jovanovich.

Ladefoged, Peter, and Ian Maddieson. 1996. *The Sounds of the World's Languages.* Oxford: Basil Blackwell.

285

Ladefoged, Peter, and Peter Roach. 1986. Revising the International Phonetic Alphabet: A plan. *Journal of the International Phonetic Association* 16:22–29.

Ladefoged, Peter, and Anthony Traill. 1984. Linguistic phonetic description of clicks. *Language* 60:1–20.

Ladefoged, Peter, Kay Williamson, B. Elugbe, and Sister Ann Angela Owulaka. 1976. The stops of Owerri Igbo. *Studies in African Linguistics,* Supplement 6: 147–63.

Ladefoged, Peter, and Elizabeth Zeitoun. 1993. Pulmonic ingressive phones do not occur in Tsou. *Journal of the International Phonetic Association* 23:13–15.

Laufer, Asher. 1991. Does the 'voiced epiglottal plosive' exist? *Journal of the International Phonetic Association* 21:44–45.

Laufer, Asher, and Iovanna D. Condax. 1981. The function of the epiglottis in speech. *Language and Speech* 24:39–62.

Laver, John. 1994. *Principles of Phonetics.* Cambridge: Cambridge University Press.

Lepsius, Richard. 1863. *Standard Alphabet for Reducing Unwritten Languages and Foreign Graphic Systems to a Uniform Orthography in European Letters.* Edited by J. Alan Kemp. Amsterdam Studies in the Theory and History of Science, 5. Amsterdam: John Benjamins, 1981.

McCloskey, James. 1979. *Transformational Syntax and Model-Theoretic Semantics.* Dordrecht: D. Reidel.

Maddieson, Ian. 1984. *Patterns of Sounds.* Cambridge: Cambridge University Press.

Maddieson, Ian. 1987. Revision of the IPA: Linguo-labials as a test case. *Journal of the International Phonetic Association* 17:26–30.

Meillet, A., and Marcel Cohen. 1952. *Les Langues du Monde.* Paris: C.N.R.S.

Mohanan, K. P., and Tara Mohanan. 1984. Lexical phonology of the consonant system in Malayalam. *Linguistic Inquiry* 15:575–602.

Monzón, Cristina, and Andrew Roth Seneff. 1984. Notes on the Nahuatl phonological change $k^w \rightarrow b$. *International Journal of American Linguistics* 50:456–62.

Moore, Samuel, and Thomas A. Knott. 1955. *The Elements of Old English.* 10th ed. Revised by James R. Hulbert. Ann Arbor, Mich.: George Wahr.

Palmer, F. R., ed. 1970. *Prosodic Analysis.* London: Oxford University Press.

Paulian, Christiane. 1975. *Le kukuya, langage teke du Congo: phonologie, classes nominales.* (Bibliothèque de la SELAF, 49–50.) Paris: Société d'études linguistiques et anthropologiques de France.

Pike, Eunice V. 1963. *Dictation Exercises in Phonetics.* Santa Ana, Calif.: Summer Institute of Linguistics.

Pike, Kenneth L. 1943. *Phonetics.* Ann Arbor, Mich.: University of Michigan Press.

––––––. 1947. *Phonemics: A Technique for Reducing Languages to Writing.* Ann Arbor, Mich.: University of Michigan Press.

Pinkerton, Sandra. 1986. Quichean (Mayan) glottalized and nonglottalized stops: A phonetic study with implications for phonological universals. In J. J. Ohala and J. J. Jaeger, eds., *Experimental Phonology,* 125–39. Orlando, Fla.: Academic Press.

Pitman, James, and John St. John. 1969. *Alphabets and Reading.* New York: Pitman Publishing.

Polomé, Edgar. 1965. The laryngeal theory so far. In Winter 1965, 9–78.

Postal, Paul M. 1964. Limitations of phrase structure grammars. In Fodor and Katz 1964, 137–51.

PRDS Group. 1983. *Final Report: The Phonetic Representation of Disordered Speech.* London: The King's Fund.

Prokosch, E. 1939. *A Comparative Germanic Grammar.* Philadelphia: Linguistic Society of America, University of Pennsylvania.

Quilis, Antonio, and María Vaquero. 1974. Realizaciones de /c/ en el área metropolitana de San Juan de Puerto Rico. *Revista de filología española* 56 (1973): 1–52.

Quirk, Randolph, and C. L. Wrenn. 1957. *An Old English Grammar.* London: Methuen; New York: Holt, Rinehart and Winston.

Robertson, John S. A reconstruction and evolutionary statement of the Mayan numerals from twenty to four hundred. *International Journal of American Linguistics* 52:227–41.

Samarin, William J. 1967. *Field Linguistics.* New York: Holt, Rinehart and Winston.

Sánchez A., Micaela, and Olga Castro G. 1977. *Una Gramatica Pedagogica del Waunana (Primera Parte).* Panama: Instituto Lingüistico de Verano and Instituto Nacional de Cultura.

Sapir, Edward. 1925. Sound patterns in language. *Language* 1:37–51.

Shipley, William F. 1956. The phonemes of Northeastern Maidu. *International Journal of American Linguistics* 22:233–37.

Smalley, William A. 1963. *Manual of Articulatory Phonetics.* Rev. ed. Tarrytown, N.Y.: Practical Anthropology.

Spalding, Alex. 1979. *Learning to Speak Inuktitut.* London, Ontario: Centre for Research and Teaching of Canadian Native Languages, University of Western Ontario. Republished as *Inuktitut: A Grammar of North Baffin Dialects* (Winnipeg, Manitoba: Wuerz Publishing, 1992).

Spier, Leslie. 1946. *Comparative Vocabularies and Parallel Texts in Two Yuman Languages of Arizona.* University of New Mexico Publications in Anthropology, 2. Albuquerque, N.M.: University of New Mexico Press.

Suarez, Jorge A. 1983. *The Mesoamerican Indian Languages.* Cambridge: Cambridge University Press.

Sweet, Henry. 1877. *A Handbook of Phonetics.* Oxford: Henry Frowde.

———. 1882. *Sweet's Anglo-Saxon Primer.* Revised by Norman Davis. Oxford: Clarendon Press.

———. 1891. *A New English Grammar, Logical and Historical. Part 1, Introduction, Phonology, and Accidence.* Oxford: Clarendon Press.

———. 1898. *A New English Grammar, Logical and Historical. Part 2, Syntax.* Oxford: Clarendon Press.

Thalbitzer, William. 1911. Eskimo. In Boas 1911, 967–1069.

Thalbitzer, W., L. L. Hammerich, Erik Holtved, and Knut Bergsland. 1952. Eskimo-Aleut phonetic notation. *International Journal of American Linguistics* 18:112–13.

Trager, George L. 1964. *Phonetics: Glossary and Tables.* 2d ed., rev. *Studies in Linguistics: Occasional Papers* 6. Buffalo, N.Y.: George L. Trager.

Trager, George L., and Henry Lee Smith, Jr. 1951. *An Outline of English Structure. Studies in Linguistics: Occasional Papers* 3. Norman, Okla.: Battenburg Press. Page references to 6th printing, American Council of Learned Societies, Washington, D.C., 1965.

Traill, Anthony. 1991. Pulmonic control, nasal venting, and aspiration in Khoisan languages. *Journal of the International Phonetic Association* 21:13–18.

Trubetzkoy, N. S. 1932. Das mordwinische phonologische System verglichen mit dem Russischen. *Charisteria V. Mathesio oblata,* 21–24. Prague: Cercle Linguistique de Prague. Page references to the reprint in Hamp et al. 1966, 38–41.

———. 1969. *Principles of phonology.* Translated by Christiane A. M. Baltaxe. Berkeley, Calif.: University of California Press.

Tucker, A. N. 1971. Orthographic systems and conventions in Sub-Saharan Africa. In Berry and Greenberg 1971, 618–53.

Wells, J. C. 1982. *Accents of English I.* Cambridge: Cambridge University Press.

Welmers, William E. 1973. *African Language Structures.* Berkeley, Calif.: University of California Press.

Westerman, D., and Ida C. Ward. 1933. *Practical Phonetics for Students of African Languages.* London: Oxford University Press.

Westphal, E. O. J. 1971. The click languages of Southern and Eastern Africa. In Berry and Greenberg 1971, 367–420.

Whitney, William D. 1889. *Sanskrit Grammar.* 2d ed. Cambridge: Harvard University Press.

Winston, F. D. D. 1960. The 'mid-tone' in Efik. *African Language Studies* 1:185–92.

Winter, Werner, ed. 1965. *Evidence for Laryngeals.* The Hague: Mouton.

Wright, Joseph. 1910. *Grammar of the Gothic Language.* Oxford: Clarendon Press.

Yuan Jia Hua. 1960. *Hanyu Fangyan Gaiyao. [Chinese Dialect Outline.]* Beijing: Wenzi Gaige Chubanshe.

SYMBOL CHARTS

The Cardinal Vowels 1–8

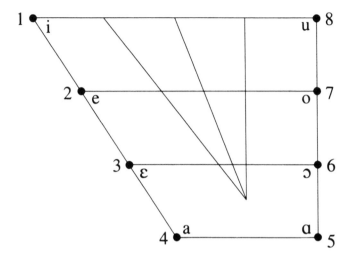

THE EIGHT ORIGINAL PRIMARY CARDINAL VOWELS

Cardinal 1 is defined to be the maximally close and front unrounded vowel articulation which can be produced. Cardinal 5 is defined to be the maximally open and back unrounded vowel articulation which can be produced.

The height of the front of the tongue decreases by even intervals between the cardinals on the line from 1 to 4; the height of the back of the tongue increases by even intervals between the cardinals on the line from 5 to 8. Lip rounding steadily increases from neutral to maximum from 5 to 8.

Acoustically, the first formant steadily increases in frequency from 1 to 4 and decreases from 5 to 8 (i.e., it is inversely correlated with vowel height). The second formant steadily decreases from 1 through 8. See Ladefoged 1982 (pp. 174ff).

The Cardinal Vowels 9–16

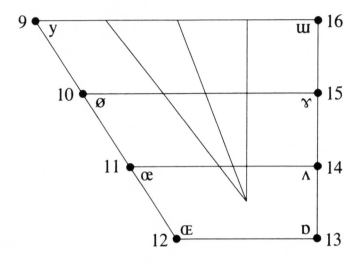

THE EIGHT SECONDARY CARDINAL VOWELS

These vowels have the same articulations as the corresponding primary cardinal vowels, but with reversed lip rounding: [y] is as strongly rounded as possible, and the rounding decreases in even intervals with each vowel along the line from 9 to 13. Cardinals 14 to 16 are unrounded vowels.

IPA Symbols for Unrounded Vowels

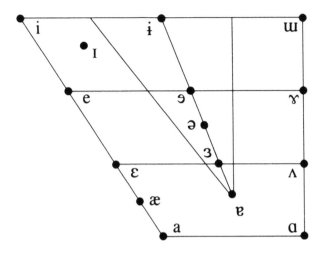

IPA symbols for unrounded vowels as of the 1993 revision. The names of the symbols are:

Front

i Lower-Case I
ɪ Small Capital I
e Lower-Case E
ɛ Epsilon
æ Ash
a Lower-Case A

Central

ɨ Barred I
ɘ Reversed E
ə Schwa
ɜ Reversed Epsilon
ɐ Turned A

Back

ɯ Turned M
ɤ Ram's Horns
ʌ Turned V
ɑ Script A

IPA Symbols for Rounded Vowels

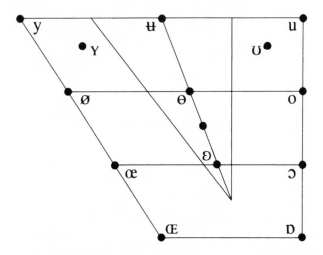

IPA Symbols for rounded vowels as of the 1993 revision. The names of the symbols are:

Front	*Central*	*Back*
y Lower-Case Y	ʉ Barred U	u Lower-Case U
ʏ Small Capital Y	ɵ Barred O	ʊ Upsilon
ø Slashed O	ɞ Closed Epsilon	o Lower-Case O
œ O-E Ligature		ɔ Open O
ɶ Small Capital O-E Ligature		ɒ Turned Script A

Note: Since the second edition of this book went to press, the IPA has changed its policy on the status of Closed Epsilon, announcing (see *Journal of the International Phonetic Association* 25, no. 1, p. 48; dated June 1995 but published in 1996) that it was approved unintentionally owing to a typographical error. The IPA had intended to approve Closed Reversed Epsilon (see p. 57), which should be substituted for Closed Epsilon in the chart above.

Bloch and Trager's Vowel Symbols

	Unrounded	Rounded	Unrounded	Rounded	Unrounded	Rounded
High	i	ü (y)	ɨ	u̇	ï (ɯ)	u
Lower-high	I	Ü	ɪ	U̇	Ï	U
Higher-mid	e	ö (ø)	ė	ȯ	ë (ɤ)	o
Mean-mid	E	Ӫ	Ė (=ə)	Ω̇	Ё	Ω
Lower-mid	ɛ	ɔ̈ (œ)	ɛ̇	ɔ̇	Ɛ̈ (ʌ)	ɔ
Higher-low	æ	ω̈	æ̇	ω̇	ǽ	ω
Low	a	ɒ̈	ȧ	ɒ̇	ä (ɑ)	ɒ
	Front		Central		Back	

The Bloch and Trager (1942, 22) vowel transcription system is based upon the primary cardinal vowels. The eight primary cardinal vowel symbols are used with their articulatory descriptions, giving four degrees of height (high, higher-mid, lower-mid, and low) and two degrees of backness (front and back). Between each of the four heights an intermediate value is posited, which gives lower-high, higher-low, and their idiosyncratic "mean-mid." Basic symbols are provided for these eight new vowels.

Note that all of the back vowels which have basic symbols are rounded and all of the front vowels with basic symbols are unrounded. Two diacritics are sufficient to extend these 14 basic vowel symbols to give the 42 symbols above. The umlaut is used to indicate reversal of backness, providing symbols for the secondary cardinal vowels, the front rounded vowels and the back unrounded vowels. (The IPA symbols for these are listed as synonyms.) The overdot diacritic indicates a central vowel. Used with basic symbols for front vowels, it provides symbols for unrounded central vowels; with basic symbols for back vowels, it provides symbols for rounded central vowels.

American Usage Vowel Symbols

		Front		Central		Back	
		Unround	Round	Unround	Round	Unround	Round
High	(Higher)	i	ü	ɨ	ʉ	ï	u
	Lower	I	Ü	ɪ	ʊ	ï	U
Mid	Higher	e	ö	ə		ë	o
	Lower	ɛ	ö̤	ʌ			ɔ
Low		æ		a/ɑ			

Lower-Low	a	ɑ	ɒ	

This chart is an attempt to generalize the usage of several American authors to represent the points of agreement and disagreement among them and to highlight differences between what we have called "American Usage" and the IPA.

American vowel charts frequently have only five heights; the low front cardinal vowel (4) is considered central. Smalley and Pike distinguish two heights of low vowels, but disagree on the properties of [b]. The independent lower-low rank (Smalley's term) is meant to indicate its optionality. The three symbols in that rank are not always distinguished, but when they are, they are ordered from front to back as indicated. When those symbols are treated as lower-low, Turned V may be considered (upper-) low.

The range of Turned V and Schwa is variable (cf. their entries for details). Open O is usually considered a low back rounded vowel, though some authors may agree with the cardinal description of it as lower-mid. Sometimes the distinction between higher- and lower-mid is maintained only in the front vowels, in which case the central and back vowels may simply be described as "mid." (Cf. Gleason 1955.)

Though some of the symbols for the secondary cardinals may be used in American transcription, we have chosen the compositional symbols using the umlaut diacritic to illustrate their denotations.

The Chomsky/Halle Vowel System

		[−back]		[+back]		
		[−round]	[+round]	[−round]	[+round]	
$\begin{bmatrix} +\text{high} \\ -\text{low} \end{bmatrix}$	[+tense]	i	ü	ɨ	u	*(high vowels)*
	[−tense]	I	Ü	ɪ	U	
$\begin{bmatrix} -\text{high} \\ -\text{low} \end{bmatrix}$	[+tense]	e	ö	Λ	o	*(mid vowels)*
	[−tense]	ɛ				
$\begin{bmatrix} -\text{high} \\ +\text{low} \end{bmatrix}$		æ	œ	a	ɔ	*(low vowels)*

Vowel symbols according to the tradition established by Chomsky and Halle (1968) and later work. Adapted from Halle and Mohanan (1985) with minor changes. (Front rounded symbols from Chomsky and Halle have been included. Halle and Mohanan's [ɨ̄] has been replaced by standard [ɨ].) Where separate symbols for tense and non-tense (i.e., lax) vowels are not shown, a macron (overbar) is used to indicate a tense vowel. The symbol [ə] is also used in transcription as a totally unstressed vowel of indeterminate feature composition (see entry for Schwa). Note that the distinctions represented reflect phonological rather than phonetic considerations.

American Usage Consonant Symbols

Pulmonic Obstruents

Plosives	Bilabial	Dental	Alveolar	Retroflex	Palatal	Velar	Uvular	Glottal
Voiceless	p	t̪	t	ṭ	ḵ	k	q	ʔ
Voiced	b	d̪	d	ḍ	g̠	g	ɢ	

Fricatives	Bilabial	Labio-dental	Inter-dental	Dental	Alve-olar	Retro-flex	Palato-alveolar	Palatal	Velar	Uvular	Pharyn-geal	Glottal
Voiceless	ɸ	f	θ	s̪	s	ṣ	š	x̌	x	x̣	ħ	h
Voiced	β	v	ð	z̪	z	ẓ	ž	γ̌	γ	γ̣	ʕ	ɦ

Affricates

	Alveolar	Palato-alveolar	Lateral
Voiceless	¢	č	ƛ
Voiced	dz	ǰ	λ

Affricates may be written as digraphs, but there are special characters which are used for some alveolar and palato-alveolar affricates when they function as single segments phonologically.

American Usage Consonant Symbols

Pulmonic Resonants

Nasals

	Bilabial	Labiodental	Alveolar	Retroflex	Palatal	Velar	Uvular
	m	ɱ	n	ṇ	ñ	ŋ	ɴ

Laterals

1	Voiced alveolar approximant
ɬ	Voiceless alveolar fricative
ḷ	Retroflex approximant

R-Sounds

Very little can be said to be standard in American usage for r-sounds except:

r	Apical
ɽ	Retroflex or Uvular

Glides

w	Labio-velar
y	Palatal

Non-Pulmonic Consonants

Implosives
(Glottalic Ingressive)

ɓ	Bilabial
ɗ	Alveolar
ɠ	Velar

Ejectives
(Glottalic Egressive)

p'	Bilabial
t'	Alveolar
k'	Velar

IPA Consonant Symbols
Consonants (Pulmonic)

	Bilabial	Labiodental	Dental	Alveolar	Postalveolar	Retroflex	Palatal	Velar	Uvular	Pharyngeal	Glottal
Plosive	p b			t d		ʈ ɖ	c ɟ	k ɡ	q ɢ		ʔ
Nasal	m	ɱ		n		ɳ	ɲ	ŋ	ɴ		
Trill	ʙ			r					ʀ		
Tap or Flap				ɾ		ɽ					
Fricative	ɸ β	f v	θ ð	s z	ʃ ʒ	ʂ ʐ	ç ʝ	x ɣ	χ ʁ	ħ ʕ	h ɦ
Lateral fricative				ɬ ɮ							
Approximant		ʋ		ɹ		ɻ	j	ɰ			
Lateral approximant				l		ɭ	ʎ	ʟ			

Where symbols appear in pairs, the one to the right represents a voiced consonant. Shaded areas denote articulations judged impossible.

IPA Consonant Symbols

Consonants (non-pulmonic)

Clicks

ʘ	*Bilabial*
ǀ	*Dental*
ǃ	*(Post)alveolar*
ǂ	*Palatoalveolar*
ǁ	*Alveolar lateral*

Voiced Implosives

ɓ	*Bilabial*
ɗ	*Dental/alveolar*
ʄ	*Palatal*
ɠ	*Velar*
ʛ	*Uvular*

Ejectives; ' as in:

p'	*Bilabial*
t'	*Dental/alveolar*
k'	*Velar*
s'	*Alveolar fricative*

Other Symbols

ʍ	*Voiceless labial-velar fricative*
w	*Voiced labial-velar approximant*
ɥ	*Voiced labial-palatal approximant*
ʜ	*Voiceless epiglottal fricative*
ʢ	*Voiced epiglottal fricative*
ʡ	*Epiglottal plosive*

ɕ	ʑ	*Alveolo-palatal fricatives*
ɺ		*Alveolar lateral flap*
ɧ		*Simultaneous ʃ and x*

Affricates and double articulations can be
represented by two symbols joined by a tie bar
if necessary.

k͡p	t͡s

IPA Suprasegmental Symbols

		ˌfounəˈtɪʃən
ˈ	Primary stress	
ˌ	Secondary stress	
ː	Long	eː
ˑ	Half-long	eˑ
˘	Extra short	ĕ
.	Syllable break	ɹi.ækt
		Minor (foot) group	
‖	Major (intonation) group	
‿	Linking (absence of a break)	

Tones and Word Accents

Level		Contour	
e̋ or ˥	Extra high	ě or ꜛ	Rising
é ˦	High	ê ꜖	Falling
ē ˧	Mid	e᷄ ꜗ	High Rising
è ˨	Low	e᷅ ꜘ	Low Rising
ȅ ˩	Extra low	e᷈ ꜖	Rising-falling etc.
↓	Downstep	↗	Global rise
↑	Upstep	↘	Global fall

IPA Diacritics

Diacritics may be placed above a symbol with a descender, e.g., ŋ̊

̥	Voiceless	n̥ d̥	̤	Breathy-voiced	b̤ a̤	̪	Dental	t̪ d̪
̬	Voiced	s̬ t̬	̰	Creaky-voiced	b̰ a̰	̺	Apical	t̺ d̺
ʰ	Aspirated	tʰ dʰ	̼	Linguolabial	t̼ d̼	̻	Laminal	t̻ d̻
̹	More rounded	ɔ̹	ʷ	Labialized	tʷ dʷ	̃	Nasalized	ẽ
̜	Less rounded	ɔ̜	ʲ	Palatalized	tʲ dʲ	ⁿ	Nasal release	dⁿ
̟	Advanced	u̟	ˠ	Velarized	tˠ dˠ	ˡ	Lateral release	dˡ
̠	Retracted	i̠	ˤ	Pharyngealized	tˤ dˤ	̚	No audible release	d̚
̈	Centralized	ë	̴	Velarized or Pharyngealized	ɫ			
̽	Mid-centralized	e̽	̝	Raised	e̝ (ɹ̝ = voiced alveolar fricative)			
̩	Syllabic	ɹ̩	̞	Lowered	e̞ (β̞ = voiced bilabial approximant)			
̯	Non-syllabic	e̯	̘	Advanced tongue root	e̘			
˞	Rhoticity	ɚ	̙	Retracted tongue root	e̙			

LANGUAGE INDEX

Some entries for names of language families (e.g., Germanic, Slavic, Indic) and areal designations (e.g., African languages, Amerindian languages, Australian languages) cite pages where the name or designation is implicit rather than literal.

SUBJECT INDEX

accent. *See* stress
acoustic properties of vowels, 293
advanced tongue root, 236, 306
advancement (fronting), 233, 236–37,
    241, 247, 260, 265–66, 306
affricate, 27, 29, 42, 91, 95–96, 110,
    151, 171, 179–80, 205, 208, 214,
    255, 260, 269
alveolar articulation, 34, 36, 39, 42,
    44, 80–81, 103–5, 109, 117–18,
    120, 125, 160–62, 165–66, 170,
    175, 177–79, 202, 205, 207,
    214–15, 219, 225–26, 232, 246,
    255, 260, 269, 301–4
alveolo-palatal articulation, 31, 33,
    157, 194, 204, 269, 304
alveopalatal articulation, 27–28, 33,
    91, 93, 118, 120, 202, 269
American Anthropologist, 122
apicality, 235, 256, 269, 306
apico-labial. *See* linguo-labial
    articulation
approximant (glide, semivowel),
    xxxiv, 79–81, 91–92, 103, 106,
    108, 116, 164–65, 169, 189–90,
    197, 200, 236, 246, 253, 266, 269,
    272, 275, 302–4
archiphonemes, 126
ASCII (American Standard Code for
    Information Interchange), xxvi
aspiration, 20, 151, 242, 250, 270,
    306

backing. *See* retraction
barred symbols (with bar across

body of symbol), 21, 28, 37, 61,
    86, 88, 93, 96–97, 104, 119, 134,
    145, 150, 151, 175, 183–84, 187,
    213, 218. *See also* double-barred
    symbols
bilabial articulation, 20, 23–26, 58,
    109, 111–13, 117, 132, 151–52,
    168, 189, 270, 301–4
breathy voice. *See* murmur

Cardinal Vowel system, 293–94
central vs. median, xxxiv, 270, 274
charts of symbols, xxx–xxxii,
    293–306
click (velaric ingressive stop), viii,
    xxi, xxxi, 34, 100–101, 132, 173,
    178–79, 214–15, 219–27, 271,
    304
close/open distinction, xxxiii–xxxiv,
    271, 274
compositionality, xxiv, xxvii
consonant symbol charts, 301–4
coronal (feature), 27, 132, 271
covered (feature), 183
creaky voice. *See* laryngealization
crossed symbols (with cross bar on
    vertical ascending or descending
    stroke), xxviii, 21, 36, 61, 74, 99,
    110, 205, 214
Cyrillic alphabet, 22, 194

dental articulation, xxxi–xxxii, 36,
    39, 72, 91, 119, 170, 175, 177–79,
    202, 221, 232, 234–35, 271,
    301–4, 306

devoicing, 252
diacritics chart, 306
dictionary pronunciation guides, 7,
    231, 265
digraphs and ligatures, xxvi, 10, 12,
    14, 17, 41–42, 46–47, 49, 56, 73,
    107, 113, 132, 140–41, 145, 159,
    179–80, 215, 264, 266
diphthongization, 45
disordered speech, xxi, 24, 117, 141,
    154, 256
dorsal articulation, 43, 271
double-barred symbols (with two
    bars across body of symbol), 173,
    223–25
downstep, 219, 237, 240, 260, 305

egressive airstream, 239, 241, 271
ejective, 15–16, 99, 151–52, 170,
    211, 214, 249, 271, 272, 302, 304
emphatic consonants. *See* pharyn-
    gealization; velarization
epiglottal articulation, 82, 213, 218,
    271, 304

faucal pharyngeals. *See* pharyngeal
    articulation
feature specifications, xxx
flap, 44, 160–61, 163, 166–67, 271,
    303–4
fonts and typography, xxii, xxiii,
    xxv, xxix, 63, 76, 101, 122, 135,
    137–38, 156, 173, 207, 210, 232,
    266–67
foot group, 221, 305
formants, xxxiii, 293
fortis (feature), 76, 219, 272
fricative, 21, 26, 31, 33, 37, 52, 61,
    67–69, 72, 91–92, 94, 98–99,
    104–5, 107, 116, 135, 151, 153,
    160, 162, 167, 169, 170–74, 180,
    188, 190, 193–96, 202–10, 216,
    218, 236, 238, 246, 250, 253,
    260–61, 272, 301, 303–4

frictional vowels, 89–90
fronting. *See* advancement

glides. *See* approximants
glottal articulation, 72–73, 75,
    211–12, 242, 250, 272, 301, 303
glottalization. *See* ejectives
Greek alphabet, xxv, xxviii, 8, 19,
    26, 43, 52, 54, 56–57, 67–68, 89,
    110, 119, 122, 129, 135, 138, 142,
    146, 155, 159, 173, 185–86, 194,
    196, 200, 210, 250–51

*Handbook of American Indian
    Languages,* xxiii, 14, 219
Hebrew traditional grammar, 49
Helvetica font, 63
hooktop modification (of letters),
    xxviii, 23, 32, 40, 62, 65, 75–76,
    97, 100, 152, 158, 178

ich-laut, 28, 31
iconicity, xxi, 229–31, 234, 237,
    240–42, 256–61
implosive (glottalic ingressive stop),
    23, 32, 39–40, 62, 65, 76, 93, 97,
    100, 132, 152, 158, 177, 241, 273,
    302, 304
implosive, voiceless, viii, 32, 100,
    132, 152–53, 158, 177, 241
ingressive airstream, 240–42, 273
interdental articulation, 36–37, 43,
    135, 155, 273
internal open juncture, 233
International African Institute, xix,
    58, 92, 189, 198, 257–58
*International Journal of American
    Linguistics* (*IJAL*), xxix, 15
International Phonetic Association,
    viii, xviii, xix, xxi–xxii, xxvii,
    xxix, xxxv, 49, 92
intonation, 225, 229–30, 240
intonational group, 225, 305
Inuit Cultural Institute, 228

inverted symbols (flipped top to bottom), xxviii, 11, 16, 147, 169, 214–15

Journal of the International Phonetic Association (JIPA), xxxii, xxxiii, 14, 17, 41, 46, 49, 92, 94, 108, 116, 120, 132, 140, 145–46, 149, 154, 162, 174, 192, 198, 206, 208, 215, 230, 239, 244–46, 248, 250, 253, 264
juncture, 221, 225, 233

Kiel (Germany), 1989 Convention of the International Phonetic Association at, ix, xxxiii, 71, 89, 97, 108, 162, 209, 218, 235, 256
kiss, transcription of, 132
'Kutscher R,' 24, 154

labialization, 129, 151, 153, 157, 174, 190–91, 208, 252, 273, 306
labial-velar (labiovelar) articulation, 132, 155, 190–93, 236, 266, 273, 302, 304
labiodental articulation, 20, 23, 26, 41, 58, 112, 119, 151, 159, 188–89, 242, 273, 301–3
laminality, 235
Language: Journal of the Linguistic Society of America, xxix
laryngealization (creaky voice), 211, 249, 255, 271, 273, 273, 306
laryngeals, 15, 48, 51, 83, 148, 202
lateral, 103–10, 166, 200, 214–15, 225–26, 255, 273, 302–3
lax (= nontense; feature), 15, 18, 51, 88, 130, 273
Le Maître Phonétique (later *Journal of the International Phonetic Association*), xxxii
lenis (feature), 76, 252, 273
level juncture, 221
ligature. *See* digraphs and ligatures

Linguistic Atlas of New England, 11, 55
linguo-dental articulation, 29, 31
linguo-labial (apico-labial) articulation, 24, 29, 31, 117, 141, 154, 235, 256, 306
logical conjunction symbol, 19

major group. *See* intonational group
median vs. central, xxxiv, 270, 274
mid-centralization, 234
minor group. *See* foot group
morphology, 232–33
morphophonemes, 15, 66, 126, 170
murmur (breathy voice), 75–76, 233, 248, 270, 274, 306

nasal, 111–13, 117–26, 215, 274, 302–3
nasalization, 5, 25, 35, 46, 126, 128, 145, 174, 179, 254–55, 261–62, 274, 306
new entries in second edition, xxxvi

open juncture, 233
open variety diacritic, 262
orthography, xix, xxi, 5, 7, 16, 22, 27–28, 30–31, 34, 43, 46–47, 85, 92, 104, 136, 139, 141–42, 155, 162, 170–71, 182, 188, 190, 194, 198, 202, 212, 219–20, 225, 247–48, 257, 261–62, 264

palatal articulation, 22, 27–28, 31–34, 60, 67, 79, 91, 93–98, 110, 118, 120–21, 157, 170, 174, 195, 197, 200, 202, 204, 219, 223, 226, 254, 265, 274, 301–4
palatalization, 28, 91, 112, 176, 191, 197, 209, 231, 244, 257, 262–63, 274, 306
palato-alveolar articulation, 27, 29, 31, 33, 78, 91, 95, 120, 170–71, 173–74, 180, 203–4, 207–9, 223, 254, 260, 274, 301

SYMBOL NAME INDEX